Unit	Grammar	Word Focus	Communication strategies	Interaction
9 **Favourite places** p56–61	*much / many, a lot of / lots of* p57 *have got, need / need to* p59	Home sweet home p58	Reacting to news p60	On the move p61
10 **Finding solutions** p62–67	Past simple *be* p63 *too* + adjective / *not* + adjective + *enough* p64	Something is not right p64	Telephoning p66	Customers' expectations p67
11 **Turning points** p68–73	Past simple 1 (regular verbs) p69 Past simple 2 (irregular and questions) p71	Talking about the past p69	Asking questions p72	Completing a CV p73
12 **Getting away** p74–79	Present continuous p75 Present continuous or present simple? p77	*have* + noun p75 Present trends p77	What do you call it? p78	Company presentation p79
Review 9–12 p80–81				
13 **Money matters** p82–87	*will* for predictions p83 First conditional p85	Money p83 *borrow* and *lend* p84	Responding p86	Investing money p87
14 **Teamwork** p88–93	Future plans: *going to* p89 *to* or *-ing*? p91	Working in a team p88 *play, go* or *do*? p90	Making it better p92	Cooperating and competing p93
15 **What an experience!** p94–99	Present perfect p94 *Have you ever …?* p96	Positive and negative responses p96	Checking information p98	Life experiences p99
16 **Take a break** p100–105	Future arrangements (present continuous) p101 *who* and *which* p103	Time expressions for the future p101 Film and music p102	Explaining needs p104	Planning a trip p105
Review 13–16 p106–107				

1

A Present simple *be*
B Personal information
C **Communication strategies** Requesting
D **Interaction** From start to finish

Arrivals

Present simple be

Speaking: Meeting new people

1 Greet the person next to you and say your name. You can say something about yourself, too.

> *Hello, I'm Rita. I'm from Russia.*
> *Hi! My name's Peter. I'm from Germany. I'm a hairdresser.*

Listening: Meeting at a fashion trade show

2 🔊 **1.1** Listen to some people at an international fashion trade show. Match the names with the jobs.

1 Paul Alexander is a —— bodyguard.
                            designer.

2 Pamela Elson is a journalist.
                            make-up artist.

3 Jackie Yang is a model.
                            photographer.

4 Victor Serrano is a reporter.

3 🔊 **1.2** Read the article below. Then listen to Matt and Paul. Find two differences between the text and the conversation.

Paul Alexander is a creative designer for a company called City Star. The company's headquarters are in Vancouver, Canada. Paul is Canadian, but he isn't from Vancouver. He and his wife Ana are originally from Ottawa. They aren't together at the fashion show this evening because Ana is at the Stanley Theatre. She's an actress.

> ⚠️ We use *a* before words beginning with a consonant sound (/b/, /p/, /g/, /k/, /d/, /t/, etc.):
>
> *Matt is **a** journalist.*
>
> Before words beginning with a vowel sound (æ/, /e/, /ɪ/, /ɒ/, etc.), we use *an*:
>
> *Kate is **an** events manager.*
>
> We do not use *a / an* before a plural noun:
>
> *They are shop assistants.*
>
> ~~*I'm manager*~~ is WRONG. Say: *I'm **a** manager.*

Lifestyle

English for work, soc...

Elementary Coursebook

Irene Barrall & John Rogers

PEARSON
Longman

Contents

Grammar: Present simple *be*

4 Look at the table below and complete the examples. Look at exercise 3 if you need help.

Present simple *be*: positive (+), negative (–), questions (?)
+ Hi, I'm (= am) *Matt Heyns*.   – I'm not (= am not) *a journalist.*

+ Hi, I'm (= am) *Matt Heyns*.

You're (= are) *Canadian.*

He/She [1]____ (= is) *from Toronto.*

We're (= are) *at a fashion trade show.*

They're (= are) *in the fashion business.*

– I'm not (= am not) *a journalist.*

You aren't (= are not) *late, don't worry.*

He/She [2]____ (= [3]____) *from Vancouver.*

We [4]____ (= are not) *at the theatre.*

They aren't (= [5]____) *together.*

? *Am I late? Are you from Spain? Is he/she a model? Are we late? Are they together?*

In speaking, we often use short forms ('m, 're, aren't, 's, isn't). We often use them in informal writing, too.

!   *Is this company French?*   ~~Yes, it's.~~ Yes, it is.
     Are those models Italian? ~~Yes, they're.~~ Yes, they are.
     Are you Turkish?   ~~Yes, I'm.~~ Yes, I am.

>> For more information on the verb *be* and short forms, see page 142.

5 Complete Pamela Elson's website profile with forms of the verb *to be*. Use short forms where possible.

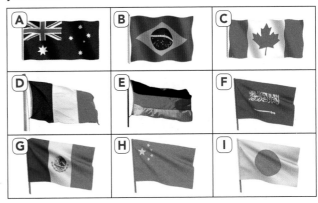

Hi! My name [1]_____ Pamela Elson. I [2]_____ Australian. I live in Sydney but I [3]_____ from Perth originally. As you know, I [4]_____ a supermodel.
   Dan, my husband, [5]_____ Australian, too. He [6]_____ a fashion hairdresser, so we [7]_____ often together at fashion shows and film festivals. International fashion shows in Singapore and China [8]_____ great, but shows in small Australian towns [9]_____ very interesting.
   My life [10]_____ very busy, so we [11]_____ at home very often. But I like to spend time with Dan. We [12]_____ both interested in sport, in different ways. I [13]_____ really interested in aerobics and surfing*. And Dan? Well, Dan [14]_____ always in front of the TV watching football … Oh yes, men [15]_____ all the same!

surfing: riding on big waves in the sea on a special board

Word focus: Countries

6 Work in pairs. Look at the flags. How many countries can you name?

A	B	C
D	E	F
G	H	I

7))) **1.3** Listen to a radio programme and number the eight countries in the order in which you hear them.

o	Oo	oO	Ooo	oOoo	ooO
Spain France	Russia China Turkey Poland Qatar	Japan Brazil	Canada Italy Germany Mexico	Australia	the USA

8))) **1.4** Check your answers. Then practise saying the words.

9 Work in pairs. Look at the list in exercise 7. Tell your partner what your three favourite countries are.

Speaking: Greetings and introductions

10 Practise this conversation with some other people in the group. Make sure you remember their names.

A: Hello. My name's _____. What's your name?
B: Hi. I'm _____.
A: Nice to meet you.
B: And you. I'm from _____. How about you?
A: Really! I'm from _____, (too).
   I'm a(n) _____. And you? What's your job?
B: I'm a(n) _____, (too).

11 Work in pairs. Make mini conversations about countries and nationalities. Student A: Turn to File 1, page 108. Student B: Turn to File 31, page 116.

TALKING POINT   •   Which fashion labels (e.g. Zara, Givenchy, Max Mara) are popular in your country? Where are they from?

     •   Is the label important for you when you buy clothes? Why?/Why not?

Reading: Arriving in the UK

1 Work in pairs. Before arriving in the UK, visitors from outside Europe have to fill in a card for UK Customs. Make a list of the personal information you think they need to give.

- *surname* (= *family name*)
- *first name*
- ....

2 Read the article and try to guess the correct answers 1–5.

Visitors to and from Britain

Every year, about [1]*10 / 30 / 50* million visitors come to Britain. About [2]*50 / 60 / 70* per cent of them are from France, Ireland, Germany, Spain, Italy and the USA.

Over [3]*20 / 40 / 60* per cent of all visitors to the UK come for a holiday or to visit friends and relatives, and [4]*15 / 25 / 35* per cent travel on business.

Visitors from outside Europe sometimes find it strange that they need to fill in a 'landing card' before entering the UK. But they just need to give basic personal details: family name, forenames*, sex, date and place of birth, occupation*, nationality, address in the UK, and a signature*.

And what about British tourists, by the way? Where do they go? The top destinations* for British tourists are usually … Spain, France, the USA, Ireland, Italy and [5]*Germany / Australia / India*!

forenames: first names

occupation: job

signature: your name when you write it in a special way at the end of a letter, on a cheque, etc.

destinations: places that people travel to

3))) **1.5** Listen and <u>underline</u> the correct answers 1–5 in the article.

4 Are these statements true (T) or false (F)? Correct the ones that are wrong.

1 About half of all visitors to Britain are from the USA.

2 Tourists from non-European countries fill in a special form before entering the UK.

3 You need to write your home address on the landing card.

4 Japan, Brazil and Russia are not in the top five destinations for British tourists.

Listening: Numbers and letters

5 Tick (✓) the numbers that you remember. Do not write the numbers! Then add to the list other numbers that you remember.

- my passport number
- my credit card number
- my office / college telephone number
- my best friend's age
- my _____ number
- my _____ number
- my _____

6))) **1.6** Listen to how you say these phone numbers and email addresses. Then listen again and practise saying each number or address after you hear it.

Phone numbers:
349 8175
0495 122566
00 44 607 948 7843

Email addresses:
ahmed@yahoo.com
laurie.brown@ntlworld.com
bressangf@tiscali.it

7 Write down three phone numbers. Work in pairs and dictate the numbers to your partner. Then check that the numbers are correct.

8 Jeff arrives in a new country and goes to a job centre. Put the lines of his conversation with the secretary in the correct order (3 to 10).

1 We need your personal details for our files. First, what's your name, please?

2 Jeff Lloyd.

___ Yeah. 305 6697.

___ Sure. That's L-L-O-Y-D.

___ Sorry, could you say that again?

___ L-L-O-Y-D … Thanks. And what's your phone number?

___ J-E-F-F. Fine. Great. Could you also spell your surname for me, please?

___ J-E-F-F.

___ 305 6697.

___ How do you spell 'Jeff'?

11 Just one more thing. What's your email address?

12 It's jlloyd@gmail.com

13 Great! Thank you.

9))) **1.7** Now listen to the conversation and check your answers.

10 Work in pairs. Practise the conversation in exercise 8. Use your own personal details.

Speaking: Personal details

11 Complete Membership Card 1 with your own details. Then, work in pairs. Student A: ask your partner questions and complete Card 2 with his/her details. Then Student B does the same. When you have finished, check that all the details are spelt correctly.

1

Membership Card

First name . . . .

Surname . . . .

Phone number . . . .

Email address . . . .

2

Membership Card

First name . . . .

Surname . . . .

Phone number . . . .

Email address . . . .

12 Some questions are *too* personal – it depends who asks them! Look at the questions below and the different people. Tick (✓) the boxes where you think it is alright for a person to ask you the question, and put a minus sign (–) if it is not alright. Do <u>not</u> answer the questions.

	Your aunt or uncle	Your boss	A neighbour	Your teacher	The police	Your doctor
How old are you?						
Are you married?						
Are you happy?						
Are you worried?						
Are you a very religious person?						
Is money a problem in your life?						
Is your job interesting?						
Are you in good health?						
What is your salary?						

13 Now work in pairs. Did you both tick the same boxes? Why?/Why not?

14 Play a game with your partner.

1 Write three sentences giving personal information about yourself (*I'm ...*). Two sentences should be true and one sentence should be false. Try to think of unusual information.

I'm in a basketball team.
I'm a salesperson.
I'm a good cook.

2 Say your sentences to your partner. He/She can ask four questions about each sentence. Then they must decide which sentence is false.

A: I'm in a basketball team.
B: What's the name of your team?
A: Blue Stars.
B: Are you professionals?
A: No, we're amateurs.
B: Where is your club?

15 Write down five numbers that have a special meaning to you. Then work in pairs. Ask questions to find out why those numbers are important to your partner.

A: 14. Mm ... Is it your house number?
B: No, it isn't.
A: Is it about your children?
B: Yes! My daughter is 14 years old.

TALKING POINT

- In your culture, what information do you usually share with work colleagues?

- Which personal numbers are difficult for you to remember?

Listening: The right person?

1 Work in pairs. You fly to a strange city. Somebody you do not know will pick you up at the airport. What problems can happen? Add your ideas to this list.

- you arrive at a different terminal
- you have no local contact telephone number

2 1.8 A driver from G.W. Electronics is picking up a visitor at the airport. Listen to their conversation. What is the problem?

3 Listen again and complete the sentences.

1 Could you _ _ _ _ me?

2 Could I have your name, _ _ _ _ _ _?

3 What do you _ _ _ _?

4 _ _ Nicola is your first name?
Yes, that's _ _ _ _ _.

5 Here, _ _ _ me help you with your luggage.

Requesting	Responding
Could I have your email address?	→ Of course. It's keiko@ hotmail.com
Can you spell your first name for me?	→ It's H-A-Z-E-M.
Could you pick up Jenny at the airport, please?	→ I'm sorry but I can't. There's an important meeting this afternoon.
Can you say that again, please?	→ No problem. T-R-I-S-T-A-N.

When we ask someone to do something for us, we often use *Can …?* or *Could …?*

We often add *please* at the end.

When we don't know the other person, or we ask for something big, we use *Could you …?* more often than *Can you …?*

4 Complete these requests with *Could I* or *Could you*.

1 _____ tell me how to get to the city centre?

2 _____ fill in this registration form, please?

3 _____ have a room on a non-smoking floor, please?

4 _____ show me your registration badge?

5 _____ have a programme in Russian?

6 _____ open that window for me, please?

5 Match each request above with the appropriate reply.

a Yes, of course. It's hot today!

b Here you are.

c Sure. And for how many nights?

d Well, it's a long way. I think it's best to take a taxi.

e Yes, but I think my details are already on your computer.

f I'm sorry, all our programmes are in English.

Speaking: Asking for help

6 Work in pairs. Take turns to make and respond to requests in different situations. Student A: Turn to File 2, page 108. Student B: Turn to File 32, page 116.

7 Think of some requests that can be useful in class. Add them to the list.

Student – Teacher
Could you say that again, please?
Could you write (that word) on the board, please?

Student – Student
Can I borrow your pen, please?
Can I use your dictionary, please?

8 Work in pairs. Compare your lists of 'English class requests'.

Reminder

Grammar reference page 142

We use contractions in conversations and in informal written English.

I'm a hairdresser.
We're from Turkey.

We often use *'re not* and *'s not* instead of *aren't* and *isn't*.

He's not Japanese.
They're not Greek.

We use full forms for short answers with *yes*.

Are you a designer? Yes, I am.

We use contractions for short answers with *no*.

Is Victor Serrano a model?
No, he isn't.

Board game: A day at a trade show

Play a game in pairs or in threes. You go to a fashion trade show to make some business contacts and to see some of your favourite models. The first person to finish the game is the winner.

Rules

1 Toss a coin to move. Heads, move one square, tails move two.
2 Follow the instructions on each square.
3 If you land on a square someone landed on before, move on to the next new square.

START
Registration Desk

1 The receptionist asks *Could you spell your surname for me, please?* What do you say?

2 The receptionist asks *What's your home address? What do you say?*

3 The receptionist asks *What's your work telephone number?* What do you say?

7 You walk up to someone interesting. Say 'hello' and introduce yourself.

6 You are at the cafeteria. You would like an espresso. What do you say?

5 You want to go to the cafeteria. You don't know where it is. Ask someone.

4 You need to make an urgent call. Oh no! Your phone battery is flat. **Penalty**: Spell your name backwards.

8 You drop your coffee! **Penalty**: Choose three people in your family. Say what their jobs are.

9 Ask someone two questions about themselves.

10 You have no business cards on you! **Penalty**: Count in sevens to 70: 7, 14, 21, …

11 Is the person sitting next to you Pamela Elson, the supermodel? Ask her!

15 Ask your teacher two personal questions about themselves. Don't be too personal!

14 Tell someone three things about yourself.

13 Success! A Brazilian manager wants to do business with your company. Move forward three squares.

12 Someone needs your email address. Spell it for them.

16 Someone asks you which countries are in today's show. Tell them the names of eight countries.

17 Someone walks up to you and says *Hi! I'm Liz Gray.* What do you say?

18 You finish a conversation with someone. Ask for their business card.

FINISH
Well done!

2

A Present simple 1
B Present simple: questions
C **Communication strategies** Showing interest
D **Interaction** Are you a people person?

Getting together

Present simple 1

Word focus: Special occasions

1 Work in pairs. Match each special occasion (1–6) to a picture (A–E). Then tell each other which three special occasions you like best.

1 a college reunion
2 an anniversary
3 a birthday
4 a wedding reception
5 New Year

2 Match the verbs with the correct words and phrases. Use a dictionary if necessary.

1 wrap —
2 wear
3 clean and decorate
4 do
5 cook
6 invite
7 book
8 send

a a lot of shopping
b friends and relatives
c presents
d cards
e a restaurant
f the house
g special food
h new clothes

3 Work in pairs. Tell each other how you prepare for a special occasion in your family.

For a wedding we cook a lot of special food.

Reading: Everybody's birthday

4 In this magazine article, Linh Tran, a marketing manager from Hanoi, talks about New Year in her country. Find out which of the things in exercise 2 Vietnamese people do before or during New Year.

New Year in Vietnam

In Vietnam, our New Year is not on 1 January. It takes place* late January or early February, it depends on the moon, and it lasts* three days or more. We call this festival Tết. It is also our spring festival, and it is the top event of the year.

We prepare for Tết weeks before. We do a lot of shopping because shops close during the celebrations. We also clean and decorate the house, buy new clothes for the children and cook special holiday food.

On New Year's Day, children wear their new clothes and wish their parents and grandparents a happy new year. Then they receive a red envelope with 'lucky money' in it. We believe red is a lucky colour, but we don't use white or black decorations.

Tết is also everybody's birthday, because in Vietnam you are one year old on the day when you celebrate your first Tết!

After New Year's Day, we visit friends and relatives. Many people go to temples, play games, or watch dragon dancers and other street performances.

And during Tết, we don't say bad things and we don't do bad things!

takes place: happens
lasts: continues to happen for a period of time

5 These statements are false. Look at the article again and correct them.

1 Tết lasts three weeks or more.

2 People clean and decorate their clothes before Tết.

3 Children get a red envelope with a photo of their grandparents in it.

4 People believe white is a lucky colour.

5 On New Year's Day, people visit friends and relatives.

6 After New Year's Day, people don't go out.

Grammar: Present simple 1

6 Look at the table. Then look at the article again to complete the examples.

Present simple with *I, you, we* and *they* (+, –)

We use the present simple to talk about …
1 things that we do regularly.
I/You/We/They **buy** *a lot of food before New Year.*
In Vietnam, shops ¹_____ *during New Year celebrations.*

2 long-term situations.
I/You/We/They **live** *in Vietnam.*

3 things that are generally true.
People ²_____ *for Tết weeks before.*

To form negatives, we use *don't.*
I/You/We/They **don't get up** *late on Sunday.*
People ³_____ _____ *white or black decorations.*
During Tết, people ⁴_____ _____ *bad things and they don't do bad things.*

>> For more information on the present simple, see pages 142–143.

Listening: Get together now?

7 Work in pairs. Think about a special occasion you do not like very much, and tell each other why. Add your ideas to the list.

I don't like _____   *I am always so busy!*
very much because …   *I can't relax.*
                                          I miss* some of my friends / relatives.
                                          I spend a lot of money.
                                          It's a lot of hard work. / It's boring.
                                          _____
                                          _____

miss: if you miss your friends or relatives, you feel sad because they are not with you

8))) 1.9 Listen to the interviews with Rob and Jill. Look at the list in exercise 7 and find one reason why each speaker doesn't really like festivals and celebrations.

9))) Listen to Rob and Jill again and complete these sentences.

1 We _____ _____ those big dinners where you just sit, eat and drink all day long.

2 A lot of our colleagues _____ _____ to work when there's a holiday.

3 We _____ to work during the holiday season because we _____ more money.

4 I _____ _____ very happy when I'm not together with all my children and grandchildren.

5 We _____ the computer on all day long. We chat, or we just smile or just _____ _____.

Writing: A PowerPoint presentation

10 Write some notes for a short presentation about a festival or celebration which is unique to your country and which you like. Here are some ideas to help you.

The [*festival / event*] I want to talk about is … [*what's the name of this event?*] in … [*which city / country?*].

It takes place _____ [*when? e.g. in winter / in May*]. and it lasts _____ [*how long? e.g. one day / two days*].

On that day, people celebrate _____ [*what?*].

People prepare for this event _____ [*how long?*] before. For example, they _____ [*how do they prepare?*]. They also _____.

On that day, people _____ [*how do they celebrate? what do they do?*].

I like this celebration because _____.

---

11 Use the notes you wrote in exercise 10. Write some PowerPoint slides to accompany your presentation.

Speaking: Giving a mini-presentation

12 Work in pairs or in small groups. Take turns at making your presentations.

TALKING POINT

- In your country, on what other occasions do people get together and celebrate?

- In Vietnam, red is a lucky colour, black and white are not. In your country, which colours have a special meaning?

Word focus: Getting together after work

1 Discuss these questions.

In your country, how often do people get together with colleagues after work? What do they do? Where do they go?

2 Match the sentence halves to make definitions of the phrases in *italics*.

1 If you *dress formally*,
2 If you *discuss a problem*,
3 If you *enjoy yourself*,
4 If you *socialize with colleagues*,
5 If you *answer the phone*,

a you go out with them to have fun.
b you have fun, you have a good time.
c you pick it up when it rings.
d you talk about it with somebody.
e you wear special clothes, e.g. for an important occasion.

Listening: Life after work

3 🔊 **1.10** Listen to an interview with Laura, a software designer. Tick (✓) the correct boxes in the table below.

Do you ...	Yes	No	It depends
1 socialize with colleagues at their homes?			
2 dress formally or informally on those occasions?			
3 discuss problems you have at work?			
4 make phone calls on your mobile?			
5 enjoy yourself?			

4 🔊 **1.11** Listen to Laura's answers to other questions. Match each answer 1–5 to the correct question.

a Do you spend a lot of money? ___
b Do you talk about your private life? ___
c Do male and female colleagues socialize together? ___
d Do you play sports or play games together? ___
e Do you go home late? ___

Grammar: Present simple: questions (yes/no)

Present simple: questions (yes/no)

Do	I	need to answer all the questions?	Yes,	I you we they	**do.**
	you	go out every weekend?			
	we	arrive before nine o'clock?	No,	I you we they	**don't.**
	they	spend a lot of money?			

! In short answers, we use *do/don't*, not the verb.
Do you arrive before nine o'clock?
~~Yes, I arrive.~~   ~~No, I don't arrive.~~

>> For more information on present simple questions, see page 143.

5 Read the information in the table.

6 Work in pairs. Talk about the times when you get together with colleagues after work. Student A: ask Student B the questions in exercise 3. Student B: ask Student A the questions in exercise 4.

Reading: It's the journey, not the destination …

7 Business meetings take place in an office. In pairs, think of more interesting, unusual places for meetings. Write down your list.

8 Read the article about an unusual place for meetings. Is the place on your list?

9 Complete the questions with words from the box.

How long   What   Where   Why

1 _____ do companies book dinner trains for meetings and parties?
Especially in North America.

2 _____ do people like dinner trains?
Because they can have a good meal and admire spectacular scenery.

3 _____ do passengers spend* on board dinner trains?
Two to four hours.

4 _____ do people do on board dinner trains?
They eat, have fun or work.

spend: if you spend an hour / a week / a month, etc. somewhere, you stay there for that period of time.

It's the journey,

Do you sometimes dream of a very special place for a party? You are not alone!

That is why a lot of people, especially in North America, now have some celebrations on board a 'dinner train'. Dinner trains are often beautiful, old steam trains which have a restaurant car and take their passengers on a return journey* across spectacular scenery*. The return journey is usually two to four hours. The trains do not run very fast, they do between about 20 and 40 kilometres per hour. But for the people who book them, it is the journey itself that's important, not the destination.

Grammar: Present simple: questions (wh-)

10 Look at the examples in the table. Then complete Rule 1 with the items from the box.

> do
> subject (e.g. *you*, *they*, *people*)
> question word (e.g. *how*, *who*)

Present simple: questions (wh-)

What			do on Friday evenings?
Where		I	spend the weekend?
Why		you	stay at home?
Who	do	we	have dinner with?
How		they	go to work?
How long			want to stay?

Rules

1 The word order in *wh-* questions is

   1 _____   2 _____   3 _____

2 We do not answer *wh-* questions with *yes* or *no* – we need to give some information about *what*, *where*, *why*, *how*, etc.

>> For more information on present simple questions, see page 143.

11 Complete the mini conversations. Look at the table in exercise 10 if you need help.

1 A: _____ ___ you work with?

   B: With Clara and Federico.

2 A: _____ ___ _____ do on your wedding anniversary?

   B: I have a meal with my wife in a special seafood restaurant I know.

3 A: _____ ___ you spend New Year's day?

   B: At home!

4 A: _____ ___ _____ want to learn English?

   B: Because I want to travel.

12 Work in pairs. Ask each other the questions in exercise 11. Give your own answers.

Speaking: Time at work and time off work

13 Work in pairs. Take it in turns to ask each other questions about your daily life. Student A: Turn to File 3, page 108. Student B: Turn to File 33, page 116.

not the destination ...

People go on those trains to enjoy a good meal and the slow journey, and also to look out of the window and enjoy the scenery. Some people even have wedding receptions and birthday parties on them.

But dinner trains are not just restaurants on wheels: companies now book them not only for staff parties and company anniversaries, but also for business meetings!

return journey: a journey to a place and back again

scenery: the things that you see around you in the country

TALKING POINT

What special places can you use for celebrations in your country?

Listening: Developing a conversation

1))) **1.12** In the lunch break, Helen meets a new colleague (David), in the company cafeteria. Listen to two conversations. Which one do you prefer? Why?

2))) Listen to Conversation 2 again and write in the missing words below.

Helen: *Hi! Is this seat free?*
David: *¹_____. Go ahead.*
Helen: *Do you work in Accounts, too?*
David: *No, I don't. I'm in IT.*
Helen: *²_____?*
David: *Yes, I'm the new graphic designer.*
Helen: *³_____, that's ⁴_____. ... Do you have lunch here every day?*
David: *⁵_____, not every day. Sometimes I just have a sandwich at my desk.*

3 To sound friendly and to show that we are interested in the conversation, we do not answer just *yes* or *no*. We give some more information to keep the conversation going. Match these questions and answers.

1 Do you go to work by car?
2 Do you go out a lot in your free time?
3 Do you travel a lot?
4 Do you do a lot of sport?
5 Do you read the papers?
6 Do you watch TV a lot?

a Well, I play tennis, and I go swimming at the weekend.
b Well, I watch gangster films and football.
c Yeah. I read *The Financial Times* online every day.
d Well, I go abroad two or three times a year.
e No. ... Well, I visit friends, but I don't go to restaurants.
f No, I take the bus or the metro.

> ⚠ *Well* can be a very useful word when you answer a question. It gives you time to think, and it tells your listener that you want to explain something.

4 Work in pairs. Practise the questions and answers in exercise 3. Give your own answers.

5))) **1.13** Listen and match the answers (a–f) that you hear with the correct questions (1–6).

1 Do you speak any foreign languages?
2 Do you go to bed late?
3 Do you drive a lot?
4 Do you work on Saturday?
5 Do you have a long summer holiday?
6 Do you surf the internet a lot?

6 Work in pairs. Ask each other the questions in exercise 5. Give your own answers. Do not answer just *yes* or *no*! Use *Well* if you need some time to think.

7 When people give us extra information, we react to this information to show interest. Study these dialogues and match them with the strategies (a–d) people use to do this.

1 A: We celebrate New Year on a train.
  B: On a train?
2 A: I always listen to music on my way to work.
  B: Really?
3 A: My best friend plays in a jazz band.
  B: Oh, that's interesting.
4 A: We spend our weekends on a farm.
  B: Mm. And what do you do there?
5 A: Our next staff party is in a castle.
  B: In a castle? Which one?

Showing interest	
To show interest in the conversation, we can:	**Dialogue:**
a ask an extra question	_____
b repeat some words	_____
c use phrases like *Really?*, *That's interesting*, etc.	_____
d use a combination of the above	_____ and _____

8 Work in pairs. Take turns telling each other about your favourite place for a holiday. Use the strategies in exercises 3 and 7 to show interest.

Speaking: The conversation game

9 Work in pairs. Student A: choose a conversation starter; Student B: express interest; Student A: respond; Student B: react with an extra question, etc. Then change roles. How long can you keep the conversation going in a natural way?

Conversation starters
I read a lot in my free time.
I visit my friends every weekend.
This is a photo of me with my parents.
My colleagues are fantastic.
I don't like this.
I want to celebrate my New Year abroad.

Reminder

Grammar reference page 143

We use the present simple to talk about regular activities.
I go to work by car.
We use the present simple to talk about long-term situations.
They live in Vietnam.

We use the present simple to talk about things that are always true.
During Tết, we don't say bad things.

Speaking: Questionnaire

1 Complete the questionnaire in pairs and discuss your answers.

Make a note of your answers and of your partner's answers, too. Perhaps you will learn something about yourselves!

2 Turn to File 4, page 108. Add up your partner's score and read your results together.

3 Tell the class whether you agree or disagree with the results, and why.

Me, you and them

1 Two friends invite you and some other people to dinner at the weekend. You do not know the other people. What do you do?

a … I go and have dinner with my friends but I only talk to them.

b … I say I am busy. I do not want to have dinner with people I don't know.

c … Great! I accept the invitation. It's good to get to know other people.

2 How do you like to spend your time off?

a … With your best friend or your family.

b … With a group of friends.

c … Alone.

3 How do you meet new people?

a … I just wait. There is always someone who wants to meet me.

b … I use Facebook or other online social networking sites.

c … I go out with friends and go to clubs where I can enjoy my hobbies.

4 How many times do you go out with friends in a year?

a … 0–15 times.

b … I do not go out with friends, we visit each other at home sometimes.

c … 15 times or more.

5 How many people from work or college have your private phone number?

a … Everybody. My phone number is on Facebook, Bebo and Hi5.

b … Nobody.

c … Only my friends.

6 What do you usually do on a long bus or train journey?

a … I try to talk to other passengers.

b … I talk on my mobile phone because I get a lot of business and private calls.

c … I turn on my iPod, play games, read or sleep.

7 You are in a shopping centre at the weekend. You see your English teacher. Do you …

a … hide behind other customers, then leave quickly?

b … walk up to him/her, say 'hello', and start a conversation?

c … smile, say 'hello' from a distance, then walk away?

8 Which of these sentences is the most true for you?

a … When I have some time off, I want to be with other people.

b … Friendship is very important. We all need two or three best friends.

c … It is so good to be alone after a week's work!

3

A Present simple 2
B *like, love* and *hate*
C **Communication strategies** Same or different?
D **Interaction** Choosing a candidate

A dream job

Present simple 2

Word focus: Jobs and people

1 Discuss this question.

Which is more important to you, a well-paid job, an interesting job or a job for life? Why?

2 Match the jobs to pictures (A–J).

1 an accountant

2 an air traffic controller

3 a head teacher

4 a lawyer

5 a lecturer

6 a librarian

7 a mechanic

8 a nurse

9 a personal assistant (PA)

10 a surgeon

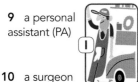

3 Read the story and answer the questions after each part.

A day in the life of Tom Gray

'Get up, you're late again!' Tom's mother shouts*.
Tom is still in bed. Tom doesn't want to get up. He thinks about his new iPad and smiles. Nobody knows about his iPad. Only his mother knows. Even Mrs Sodul doesn't know about it!
shout: to say something very loudly

1 Who is Mrs Sodul? 2 How old is Tom? What does he do?

It's time to go. There are a lot of schoolchildren on the bus. A teenager shouts into his mobile phone. A young girl looks at Tom and says something rude*. But Tom doesn't get angry* with her.
  'Mrs Sodul doesn't like rude pupils,' he thinks. 'I want to tell her about you today. I don't remember your name, but I know you are in the same class as my niece*.'
rude: not polite
get angry: became angry
niece: the daughter of your brother or sister

3 Who is Mrs Sodul? 4 How old is Tom? What does he do?

Eight thirty. Tom enters the school building. He sees the Headteacher's office, but he doesn't stop. He doesn't think it's a good idea to talk to her right now. 'Mrs Sodul is always so busy at this time,' he thinks.
  At the end of the corridor, he opens the last door. It is a small, dark* room with four desks and some bookshelves.
  Behind the bookshelves is another desk, a very small desk with a name card on it which says in big letters 'Tom Gray – Accounts Assistant'.
  Tom sits. He opens his briefcase. Then, on the middle of his desk, he puts his beautiful iPad, the birthday present he got from his 75-year-old mother yesterday.
  A new day begins …
dark: when there is not a lot of light

5 Who exactly is Mrs Sodul? 6 How old is Tom, do you think?

7 What does he do? Do you think he likes his job?

Do you like the story? Why/Why not?

4 Answer the following questions with *Yes, he does* or *No, he doesn't.*

1 Does Tom live with his mother?

2 Does he always get up on time?

3 Does he get angry with the children on the bus?

4 Does he want to tell the head teacher about one of the children?

5 Does he work in the same office as Mrs Sodul?

6 What does he do? Do you think he likes his job?

Do you like the story? Why?/Why not?

Grammar: Present simple 2

5 Read the information. Then <u>underline</u> five verbs (+) in the 3rd person singular in the story.

Present simple with *he, she, it* (+)

He works in an office.	*He* gets up late.
He lives with his mother.	*She* stays at home.

Spelling

I/You/We/They	study / fly / try. finish / watch. go / do. have.	He/She	studies / flies / tries. finishes / watches. goes / does. has.

6 Complete the rules and the examples below. Look for other examples in the story and in exercise 5 if you need help.

Present simple with *he, she, it* (–, ?)

To form negatives, use [1]_____; to form questions, use [2]_____.

He [3]_____ *want to talk to the head teacher at 8.30.*

When [4]_____ *Tom arrive at work?*

[5]_____ *he want to change his job?*

In short answers, we use *does / doesn't*, not the verb.

Does he *like* his job?   Yes, he **does**. / No, he **doesn't**.

~~Yes, he likes.~~   ~~No, he doesn't like.~~

>> For more information on the present simple, see pages 142–143.

7 Complete the article. Use the present simple forms (+ or –; singular or plural) of the verbs in brackets.

The number 1 stressful job

Photojournalists, air traffic controllers, librarians, surgeons, … Who has the most stress at work?

Psychologist Saqib Saddiq says that librarians [1]_____ (have) the most stressful job. Why? How is that possible?

A photojournalist often [2]_____ (travel) to dangerous places, but a librarian [3]_____ (spend) every day in a quiet room. A surgeon [4]_____ (look) inside people's bodies, but a librarian only [5]_____ (open) books. An air traffic controller [6]_____ (manage) new situations every day, but a librarian [7]_____ (see) the same old books all the time.

What, then, is so stressful about a librarian's job?

To find out, Mr Saddiq interviewed a lot of librarians. Here are the things that librarians [8]_____ (say) about their job:

'Libraries are boring places.'

'A librarian [9]_____ (do) a lot of different things: every day at work is the same, week after week.'

'Other people always [10]_____ (tell) us what to do.'

People in dangerous jobs, e.g. police officers, get a lot of help and training, but librarians are all alone with their stress because we [11]_____ (think) they [12]_____ (have) an easy job.

8))) 1.14 Listen to the radio programme and check your answers.

Speaking: Other people's jobs

9 Work in pairs. Student A: Turn to File 5, page 109. Student B: Turn to File 34, page 117.

10 Choose a dream job. Write down the name of the job. Don't show it to anyone.

Work in pairs. Ask each other questions to find out your partner's dream job.

Use some of the questions from exercise 9. Ask other *yes/no* questions if necessary.

TALKING POINT

• What jobs in your country pay a lot of money?

• What jobs are very useful to society?

In my country, I think being a(n) … pays a lot of money.

I think being a(n) … is very useful to society because …

Word focus: At work

1 Match each phrase (1–8) to the appropriate picture (A–H).

1	my boss	**5**	meeting clients
2	our photocopier	**6**	untidy desks
3	being late	**7**	helping my colleagues
4	loud ringtones	**8**	queuing in the cafeteria

A ☐

B ☐

C ☐

D ☐

E ☐

F ☐

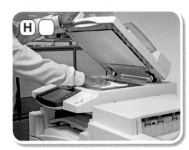
G ☐

H ☐

Grammar: *like, love, hate*

5 Match each sentence to the correct smile.

1	I *love* Saturdays.	:-(
2	She *likes* working with other people.	:-))
3	We *don't like* arriving late for meetings.	:-((
4	They *hate* long meetings.	:-)

6 Look at the four examples in the table and complete the rules.

---
like, love, hate

*1 Do you like work**ing** at weekends?*
2 She doesn't like untidy desks.
*3 I love watch**ing** other people work!*
4 Luigi hates slow computers.

After *like, love, hate* we often find …

a) a noun (or a noun phrase, as in examples ¹_____ and ²_____)

or …

b) a verb ending in ³_____ (as in examples ⁴_____ and ⁵_____).

>> For more information on the *-ing* form of verbs, see pages 158–159.

Listening: Likes and dislikes

2 🔊 **1.15** Listen to Enrica, a marketing manager, and to Sergei, an accountant. What do they (dis)like? Write 'E' (= Enrica) or 'S' (= Sergei) next to the things in exercise 1 that they talk about.

3 🔊 Listen to Enrica on Track 1.15 again. Are these statements true (T) or false (F)?

1 Enrica likes talking about what she likes or doesn't like.

2 She doesn't like the photocopier.

3 She doesn't like the cafeteria.

4 Her assistant's desk is very untidy.

4 🔊 Listen to Sergei on Track 1.15 again and complete the sentences.

1 I _____ _____ being late for work.

2 I _____ my boss, she's great.

3 The colleagues in my department are great, too. I _____ _____ them.

7 Work in pairs. Ask each other questions about your …

workplace / college

boss / teachers

office / classroom

meetings

spending time in the cafeteria

your computer

writing emails, etc.

> **A:** *Do you like your boss?*
> **B:** *Yes, I do. She/He is very nice.*
> **A:** *Do you like your office?*
> **B:** *Yes, I do. It's great. / No, I don't. It's very dark!*

Reading: Pet hates in the office

8 We all have our 'pet hates' – small things that we don't like. What are your pet hates in your workplace or college?

> *Some people don't answer their phone. I think that's terrible!*
> *I hate receiving spam emails.*

9 Read the blog about other people's pet hates in the office. Are their pet hates the same as yours?

10 Three of these statements are false. Rewrite them to make them true.

1 Roberto likes wearing informal clothes at work.

2 Noriko likes having coffee at the office.

3 Firas hates talking with colleagues.

4 Steve doesn't like his colleagues.

5 Marianne's manager never says 'Well done!'

6 Steve doesn't think it's OK to smoke at work.

11 Work in pairs. Look at the blog again. Then discuss these questions.

Which problems are small problems? Which ones are big problems? Why?

I think I'm very lucky because I work for a great company and the people in my department are very nice. I really like them. But in the other departments, some people don't say 'Hello', and I don't like that. We're all from the same company, so for me we are one big family.
  Another thing I don't like at the office is the coffee. It's terrible!

Noriko Matsuno, Osaka

Some colleagues at the office send me emails asking for information. I hate that. Why don't they come and talk to me? It's so good to talk with colleagues.

Firas Al Sayed, Damascus

In my country, I wear jeans and a T-shirt at work, because I work better when I can relax. But here the manager wants me to wear formal clothes every day. Why? I don't understand.

Roberto Gil, São Paulo

My number 1 pet hate: some people never say 'Thank you'. I think that's terrible. Our manager, for example. Our new project is very successful, but he never says 'Well done!'*

Marianne Leclerc, Brussels

I am happy. I love my boss and my colleagues. But I have one or two pet hates. For example:
* some colleagues use all the paper in the photocopier and then they go away
* some people wait for the lift with you and only go one floor
* a lot of people stop working to have a cigarette (I don't smoke, I work!)
* some people never say 'Please' or 'Thank you'. I hate that!
Just one more thing. Some people have a lot of pet hates and are never happy. Now I think *that's* really, really terrible.

Steve Gowing, Manchester

You say 'Well done!' when you want to tell someone that you are very pleased with their work.

Speaking: Empty chair

12 Work in pairs. Make a list of 8 to 12 questions to find out what people like / don't like about their workplace / college.

> *Do you like working with other people?*
> *Do you like your manager / lecturers?*
> *What do you like best about your workplace / college?*
> *Are you happy with the holidays you get?*

13 Work in a new pair. For this game, imagine that you are your partner, and your partner is you. Take turns at asking each other the questions from exercise 12. Remember when you answer: you are your partner!

> *A: Do you like working with other people?*
> *B: Yes, I love it.*

When you finish asking your questions, tell your partner how well he/she knows you.

The empty chair

TALKING POINT
* What is REALLY important at work / college?
* Think of a slogan for a company / college T-shirt beginning with the words *'All you need is …'*.

Listening: Something in common?

1 Work in pairs. Tell each other how you feel about the following situations:

- making business phone calls
- staying at the office after 6 p.m.
- working flexible hours*
- working in a team

flexible hours: changing from day to day

2))) **1.16** Davide and Sarah tell each other about their new jobs at Rihla, a travel agency. Number the topics in exercise 1 in the order in which they talk about them.

3 Decide if these statements are true (T) or false (F). Listen again if necessary.

1 Sarah thinks the salespeople are nice.

2 Davide says the best thing in his job is talking to customers on the phone.

3 Both Sarah and Davide like working in a team.

4 Davide hates going out in the evening.

5 Sarah only goes out on Saturdays.

4))) Listen to Track 1.16 again and complete these sentences.

1 D: … I think the salespeople are really nice.
   S: _____ too.

2 S: And I _____ talking to customers on the phone …
   D: Really? I _____. In fact, I _____ doing business on the phone.

3 S: … I just _____ working in a team.
   D: _____ _____. You know, I really hate working alone.

4 D: … I'm _____ too happy about the flexible working hours …
   S: _____ neither. Four hours last Tuesday, and then twelve hours the next day!

5 D: … I want to go out with my friends.
   S: _____? I never go out on weekdays.

5 Study the sentences in exercise 4. Do Davide and Sarah have the same or different opinions and feelings?

1   *Same*

2 _____

3 _____

4 _____

5 _____

The same or different?

To show interest in a conversation, people often say when their opinions and feelings are the same, or when they are different.

1 Same:

A: I'm tired.	B: Me too.
A: I'm not very happy about the hours.	B: Me neither.
A: I like travelling abroad.	B: Me too.
A: I don't like our computer system.	B: Me neither.

2 Different:

A: I'm hungry.	B: Really? I'm not.
A: I'm not good with computers.	B: Really? I am.
A: I like our company logo.	B: Really? I don't.
A: I don't like the view from our office.	B: Really? I do. I think it's beautiful.

Speaking: The same or different?

6 A company newsletter asks what staff like and dislike. Complete these sentences with *like / don't like* to make them true for you.

1 I _____ writing letters.
2 I _____ surfing the internet.
3 I _____ Mondays.
4 I _____ taking work home.
5 I _____ listening to music when I work.
6 I _____ reading business reports.
7 I _____ texting.
8 I _____ long holidays!

7 Work in pairs. Take it in turns to read and respond to the sentences in exercise 6.

> A: I like writing letters.
> B: Really? I don't. I hate it!

> **!** When adding information, we use *and* in positive sentences. In negative sentences, we use *or*.
> She likes texting **and** writing letters.
> He doesn't like reading reports **or** surfing the internet.

Reminder

Grammar reference
pages 142–143 and 158–159

With *he*, *she* and *it*, the verb in the present simple ends in *-s*, *-es* or *-ies*.
He works in an office.

With *he*, *she* and *it*, we use *doesn't* not *don't* + verb in the negative.
She doesn't travel a lot.

After the verbs *like*, *love* and *hate*, we can use a noun or a verb ending in *-ing*.
I love Saturdays.
She likes working with other people.

Word focus: Finding a job

1 Complete the definitions with the words in the box. Use a dictionary if necessary.

> apply   CV   fill in   look for

1 A _____ is a list of your education and jobs. You show it to companies when you try to get a job.

2 If you _____ for a job, you ask for a job by writing a letter, sending your CV, etc.

3 If you _____ something or someone, you try to find that thing or person.

4 If you _____ a form, you write the information that someone wants in the spaces on that form.

2 Read the job vacancies. Do you have the experience Rihla wants? What do you / don't you like about the job?

VACANCY*

Rihla is a new and exciting travel agency with offices in 15 different countries.
We now need an energetic* **Tour Manager** for our new office in Costa Rica.

The candidate:
- has experience in the tourist industry
- has a lot of travel experience
- speaks English, Spanish and another language

The job:
- answering customer phone calls; writing and answering emails and faxes
- planning holidays with customers over the phone
- meeting and doing business with customers face-to-face
- working irregular* hours, sometimes seven days a week
- a lot of driving

Salary: very good, depending on experience and qualifications
To apply, please send a letter and your CV to naseem@rihlaworld.co.uk

---

vacancy: a job that is available for someone to do
energetic: working a lot and not feeling tired
irregular: happening at different times; not regular

Listening: A job interview

3))) **1.17** Rita Oliveira applies for the job of Tour Manager and goes for an interview. Listen and circle the correct answers in the table below.

	Rita			
experience in tourist industry	yes	some	no	
travel experience	yes	some	no	
languages	5	4	3	2
driving	:-))	:-)	:-(	:-((
working irregular hours	:-))	:-)	:-(	:-((
writing emails, faxes, etc.	:-))	:-)	:-(	:-((
doing business face-to-face	:-))	:-)	:-(	:-((
doing business over the phone	:-))	:-)	:-(	:-((

4))) Listen again and decide if these statements are true (T) or false (F).

1 Rita works in a hotel in the summer.

2 She doesn't know South America.

3 She doesn't like driving.

4 She is free at weekends.

Speaking: Choosing a candidate

5 Two other candidates, Harish and Yun, apply for the job of Tour Manager. Work in pairs. Ask and answer questions about the two candidates. Student A: Turn to File 6, page 109. Student B: Turn to File 35, page 117.

6 Work in pairs. Compare your notes about Rita, Harish and Yun. Choose one person for the job of Tour Manager. Who do you choose? Why?

7))) **1.18** Now listen to John Rivas, a manager at Rihla, talking about the candidate who gets the job. Do you agree with him? Why?/Why not?

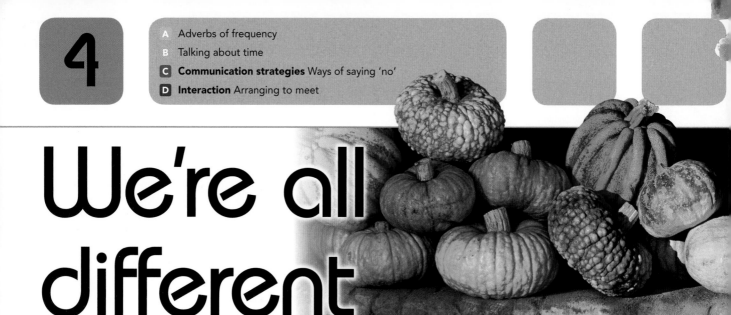

4

We're all different

Adverbs of frequency

Reading: The power of difference

1 Work in pairs. Discuss these questions.

A lot of people go abroad to study or to work. What is exciting about living abroad for a few years? What can be difficult?

2 We all have ideas about people from other countries. Read the blog posts and find out what some people think of those ideas. Are these statements true (T) or false (F)? Correct the ones that are wrong.

1 Günter is always late for meetings.

2 The Greeks think the Swiss are always on time.

3 Claudio hates Italian food and pizza.

4 Colin believes that all people are the same.

3 Read the blog posts again. Find the opposites of these words.

1 never   _____

2 the same   _____

3 on time   _____

4 love   _____

4 Work in pairs or in small groups. Write down other pairs of opposites you already know.

Hi

I'm Swiss, but I work in Turkey. I have a question. I'm usually on time for meetings, but I'm sometimes two or three minutes late, and then my Turkish colleagues laugh. But they don't laugh when other people are late. I don't understand. Can you help?   **Günter**

Hi Günter

Hm. Interesting. I think I know the answer to your question: maybe your colleagues think all Swiss are always on time because in Switzerland you have fantastic clocks and watches? Everybody thinks the Swiss are never late. Well, that's what we think in Greece!   **Ana**

Hello

I agree with Ana. I'm from Italy, but I work in China. I love it here, but my Chinese friends often ask me why I don't drink coffee or why I don't like pizza. I love Italian food, but I hate pizza. And when I go out, I usually drink tea, not coffee. Italian people are not all the same!   **Claudio**

That's a great post, Claudio! I work in China, too, and every day, my ideas about Chinese people change. Now I don't see a 'nationality', I see a lot of different individuals. I think I'm lucky to have a job abroad: I learn a lot about myself, too.   **Colin**

Grammar: Adverbs of frequency

5 Read the article again and find three other adverbs. Put them in the correct place in the chart.

always   ¹___   ²___   ³___   hardly ever   never
100%•---------•---------•---------•---------•---------•0%

6 Look at the examples in the table below and complete the rules with the words *before* or *after*.

Adverbs of frequency

We use adverbs of frequency (e.g. *always*, *never*) to say how often we do something, or how often something happens.

My Chinese colleagues **often** *ask me questions.*

I **usually** *drink cola or lemonade.*

It is **never** *easy to talk about culture.*

They think all Swiss are **always** *on time.*

1 We usually put the frequency adverb _____ the verb.

2 We usually put the frequency adverb _____ the verb be.

Questions

How often *do you meet people from other countries?*

>> For more information on frequency adverbs, see page 144.

7 Rewrite these sentences to make them true for you, using the best adverb of frequency each time. Then add two sentences of your own.

> *I meet people from other countries.*
> *I* **don't often** *meet people from other countries.*

1 I meet people from other countries.

2 I work at weekends.

3 I give my business card when I meet someone for the first time.

4 I am the last person to leave the office.

5 I am late for meetings.

6 I dream of living in a different culture.

8 Work in pairs. Take turns at guessing your partner's sentences in exercise 7.

> *A: You sometimes meet people from other countries.*
> *B: True.*
> *A: You hardly ever work at weekends.*
> *B: Sorry, that's not correct. I often work at weekends.*

TALKING POINT

What are good ways to learn about other countries and cultures?

Speaking: Discovering cultures

9)) **1.19** Work in pairs. Look at these statements about doing business in other cultures. Decide which three statements are false. Then listen and check your answers.

1 In China, people always give their business cards with both hands.

2 In Italy, business lunches are usually very short.

3 In Russia, people don't always wait for you to finish speaking for them to start speaking.

4 In the United Arab Emirates, it is always bad manners to eat with the left hand.

5 In Brazil, people sometimes ask you personal questions about your salary or your religion.

6 In Turkey, the person who invites you out for dinner always pays for the meal.

7 In South Korea, people sometimes ask you to sing a song at the end of an evening out.

8 In Germany, bosses usually keep their office doors open.

9 In India, business meetings often begin with 'small talk', i.e. a friendly conversation about personal or unimportant topics.

10 In Japan, people usually use first names in business meetings.

10 Work in pairs. Use the statements in exercise 9 to talk about business life in your country. Make changes when necessary.

In my country, we don't usually give our business card with both hands.
OR
In my country, we usually give our business card with the right hand.

Writing: Cultural information

11 You work on an international team. Read the email from one of your colleagues abroad. Send an email to answer all the questions.

> Dear ...
> My boss wants me to work in your country next year. I'm very pleased about that, but I need some information before I go. Could you please answer these questions?
> • How often do you have meetings? How long do they usually last?
> • Do visitors always give / receive presents?
> • Do colleagues usually socialize after work?
> Thank you in advance.
> All the best
> Jan

> Dear Jan
> Thanks for your email. Here is some information
> _____
> _____
> I hope this helps.
> Best wishes
> _____

Listening: What's on?

1 Tick (✓) the activities you do at the weekend. Add two more activities.

Activity	You	Your partner	Activity	You	Your partner
1 go for a walk	......	......	8 play computer games	......	......
2 visit art galleries	......	......	9 relax with friends	......	......
3 go dancing	......	......	10 go to concerts	......	......
4 go to the cinema	......	......	11 stay in and watch TV	......	......
5 go to a café	......	......	12 work in the garden	......	......
6 do housework	......	......	13 _____	......	......
7 play sport	......	......	14 _____	......	......

2 Ask your partner questions to find out what activities they do at the weekend. Tick (✓) the things that they do. Find three things that you have in common.

Do you go to concerts?
Yes, I do. / No, I don't.   I do too! / Me too!

3 Talk to another pair about the things that are the same and different about you and your partner's weekends.

We both play sport at the weekend.
He usually goes dancing but I stay in and watch TV.

4 Look at the magazine adverts and choose one activity you like and one activity you don't like.

5 🔊 **1.20** Listen to four conversations about activities. Match the conversation to the information in the adverts. Listen again and complete the information in the adverts.

6 Ask and answer questions about the activities in *What's on?*

1 dance class / Friday?
   Is the dance class on Friday?
   No, it's at the weekend.

2 concert / Thursday?

3 gardening club / start / July?

4 When / advanced skiing class?

5 What time / dance class / Sunday?

WHAT'S ON?

1

Learn to dance at the weekend!

Salsa, Flamenco, Tango. evening classes on
¹ _____ at 7 p.m. and ² _____ classes on Sunday at
³ _____ p.m.

2

Autumn concert dates:
Khaled

on ⁴ _____ 21ˢᵗ and Saturday 22ⁿᵈ ⁵ _____ at ⁶ _____ p.m.

Phone today to get your ticket!

3

Try a different sport today! Don't wait for winter to learn to ski.
Come to the Holiday Adventure centre in Dubai

⁷ _____ groups.
Beginners' class every
⁸ _____ at 10 a.m.
advanced class every
⁹ _____ at 6 p.m.

4

Do you want a beautiful garden in the spring and
¹⁰ _____ ?

Come to the ¹¹ _____ club at Ardale Agricultural college. Classes start in ¹² _____ and May.

Grammar: Prepositions of time

7 Look at the adverts again and <u>underline</u> examples of *in*, *on* or *at*.

8 Complete the box with *in*, *on* or *at*.

Preposition	Time
1	four o'clock, three thirty, midnight, midday the weekend, night
2	January, February, March the morning, the afternoon, the evening 1999, 2005, 2012
3	Sunday, Monday, Tuesday 20th February, 26th August, 4th October 2011

> ⚠ 1999 *nineteen ninety-nine*
> 2005 *two thousand and five*
> 2012 *two thousand and twelve* or
> *twenty twelve*

9 Sophie Miller, a sales director, arranges for her sales team to go on an activity holiday. Complete her email to her secretary with *in*, *on* or *at*.

Hi Gerald,
I arrive in Cannes ¹___ Sunday ²___ 5 p.m. Are the banks open ³___ the weekend because I need euros? We can go shopping ⁴___ Monday morning. ⁵___ the afternoon our team has a meeting. Our activity course starts ⁶___ Tuesday 6th May. The team goes climbing ⁷___ 11 a.m. ⁸___ the evening there is a party for all the people on the course. I want to see Cannes ⁹___ night – they say it's a very beautiful city. See you ¹⁰___ Sunday!
Regards
Sophie

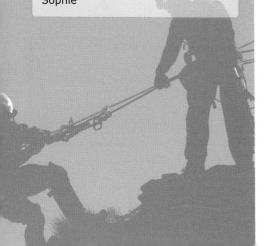

Word focus: Telling the time

10 Match the different ways of saying the time.

What time is it?

1 It's four o'clock in the morning.
2 It's quarter past four.
3 It's half past nine.
4 It's quarter to nine.
5 It's twenty-five past eleven.
6 It's twenty to eleven.

a It's eleven twenty-five.
b It's eight forty-five.
c It's four a.m.
d It's ten forty.
e It's four fifteen.
f It's nine thirty.

11 Work in pairs. What is a good time to do these things? Tell your partner a different time for each activity.

Do exercise?
Go to the cinema?
Start a party?
Finish a party?
Have a meeting?
Have your last cup of coffee of the day?
Go for a swim?
Go shopping?

Speaking: My week

12 Work in pairs. Take turns to ask and answer questions. When you answer your partner's questions, use an adverb of frequency and say a time.

Student A
What time / wake up / Mondays?
What time / read emails / mornings?
When / have dinner / Wednesdays?
What time / go out / evenings?
When / have / first coffee / morning?

Student B
What time / get up / Sundays?
When / have break / afternoons?
When / leave work / Fridays?
What time / go to bed / Saturdays?
When / meet friends / weekend?

TALKING POINT   Tell your partner how you usually relax after work or college.

Listening: What do you *really* think?

1))) **1.21** Listen to two meetings. Which meeting is more successful? Why?

2))) **1.22** Listen to parts of Conversation 2 and write in the missing words.

1 A: I'm sure you want to see our new company magazine.

   B: Great. _____ _____ look at it during the break?

2 A: Now, before we finish, are there any questions?

   B: _____ , _____ think we have all the information we need. _____ you.

3 A: Is 9:30 next Thursday convenient?

   B: __' __ _____ Thursday is a bit difficult. But we are free on Wednesday morning.

3 Work in pairs. Match the questions and answers.

1	Coffee?	a	Sorry. We are closed.
2	Do you like your new job?	b	I don't know. I don't think so.
3	Can you come tomorrow morning?	c	Sorry, I have other plans. But I'm free on Saturday.
4	Could I just have a look around?	d	No, thank you.
5	Do you know Paris?	e	No, not very well.
6	Is Jim here today?	f	I'm afraid I don't. It's boring.

Reading: Where 'no' isn't an answer

4 Discuss this question.

When you are in a meeting, do you say 'yes' or 'no' directly? Why?/Why not?

5 Read the story about an international business negotiation. What do you think the problem is?

Kurt Knebel works for a large pharmaceutical company in Germany. He is now in a meeting in Kuala Lumpur. He wants a new contract for his company in Frankfurt. The meeting goes well, so Kurt feels good. The Malaysian business people smile and nod. They often say 'yes' and agree with Kurt.

When he is back in Germany, Kurt tells his boss about the successful negotiation.

But three days later, the phone rings. It's one of the Malaysian managers from the meeting. He wants to discuss the dates. And the price is not quite right, he says.

Kurt doesn't understand. He remembers the smiling faces and people saying 'yes' in the meeting. Why does the manager want to make changes now? They have an agreement, don't they?

Speaking: Don't say 'no'!

6 Work in pairs. Student A: you can ask your partner ten *yes/no* questions. You win the game if/when you can make your partner use 'no' in an answer. Student B: you want to answer 'no' to each question, but you cannot use the word 'no'.

Then, change roles.

   A: Are you the manager?
   B: I'm not. / I'm afraid I'm not. / Well, not really.
   A: Could you help me?
   B: Sorry, I'm very busy just now.

Reminder

Grammar reference page 144

We use adverbs of frequency to say how often we do something or to say how often something happens.
I **hardly ever** read the papers.
Gunter is **always** late for meetings.

We often use the prepositions *in*, *on* and *at* in time phrases.
See you **on** Monday **at** ten o'clock.
The conference is **in** June.
Some time phrases have no preposition.
Let's meet next week.

Speaking: Different ideas of time

1 Do you usually arrive for appointments a) early, b) on time, c) late?

2 Match the photos with what Aisha and Fernando say. What problems could happen when they arrange to meet?

A

B

1 *I'm hardly ever on time. There always seems to be a problem. But it's OK, the people that I arrange to meet always wait for me!*

2 *I think it's very important to arrive on time for appointments. I always check traffic reports so that I'm not late. I usually arrive early for meetings.*

3 Is your idea of time more like Aisha or Fernando? Do any of your friends or colleagues have a very different idea of time to you?

Listening: Let's meet

4 1.23 Listen to Aisha and Fernando's phone conversation and complete the notes.

Message
Meet Fernando
Re: New designs for the _____
on _____ at _____

5 It is the day of the meeting. What do you think happens? Look at this text message. What does it say?

> Write new
> **Sorry. Am L8. C U in 30 mins.**
> Continue   More

6 1.24 Listen to the conversation when Fernando and Aisha meet.

1 Who is late? Why?

2 What phrase can you use when you are late?

3 What is the response?

Speaking: Are you free?

7 Work in groups of four. You are in a meeting with members of your team. Look at your diaries to arrange a morning or afternoon to have regular team meetings every week. Student A look at the diary below. Suggest a day to have the meeting. Student B: Turn to File 7, page 109. Student C: Turn to File 36, page 117. Student D: Turn to File 47, page 121.

Can we meet on
What about } *Monday morning?*
Are you free on

Sorry, I usually have a meeting on Tuesday morning.

	Morning	Afternoon
Monday		
Tuesday	IT meeting with production	
Wednesday		
Thursday	IT team meeting	
Friday		Website meeting

8 It is the day of the next meeting.

1 Student A and B arrive late. Apologize and give a reason why you are late.

2 Student C and D respond to the apology.

Review 1-4

1 Complete this text with the correct present form of *be* (+ / – / ?). Use short forms where possible.

Ana Steiner and Dan Hill ¹_____ married with two children. She ²_____ from Germany and he ³_____ from Scotland. They ⁴_____ both medical doctors, and they live and work in Argentina. ⁵_____ they happy in South America? 'This new life ⁶_____ great for all of us,' says Ana, 'but of course it ⁷_____ always easy. For example, Dan's Spanish ⁸_____ very good, so he takes lessons after work and at weekends. It can be difficult to work and study at the same time, and Dan ⁹_____ often very tired. Our children ¹⁰_____ at school and have a lot of friends, and their Spanish ¹¹_____ better than ours. I ¹²_____ very happy about that. But we ¹³_____ sure what is best for them at home. It ¹⁴_____ great if they can speak Spanish, German and English, but how can they learn to speak three languages well?'
A lot of families ¹⁵_____ in the same situation. Ana wants to start a blog, so she and Dan can share ideas with other people. 'It ¹⁶_____ good to talk!' says Ana.

2 Complete this text with the verbs in the box in the present simple (+ / –).

ask   earn   live   love   see   spend   talk   travel   want   work

My friend Rick ¹_____ in California with his wife and their two children. He ²_____ in the computer industry and he ³_____ his job. He ⁴_____ a very good salary, but he ⁵_____ very often, maybe just once or twice a year, and then only to New York or to Canada on business. So we ⁶_____ each other very often. We ⁷_____ on Skype every weekend or just email. But next year, I ⁸_____ to go to the States and ⁹_____ some time with him and his family. 'California is a fantastic place. Why don't you come and live here?' Rick sometimes ¹⁰_____. But I'm not sure. I love travelling, but it can be difficult to be away from home for a long time!

3 Complete each question with *Do/Does, Is/Are* or a question word.

1 _____ Nikola your first name?

2 _____'s your surname?

3 _____ do you spell that? One 'f' or double 'ff'?

4 _____ your husband in the fashion business as well?

5 _____ you work in IT, too?

6 _____ time do you usually get up?

7 _____ Gina like travelling?

8 _____ they nice?

9 _____ do Vietnamese people like red?

10 _____ do you want to go this summer? Bali? Goa? Blackpool?

11 _____ you free on Tuesday morning?

4 Rewrite these sentences with the adverbs in brackets.

1 Jean and Edith are at home in the evening. (*always*)

2 I write reports. (*sometimes*)

3 Barbara is not late. (*usually*)

4 Jeff goes out after work. (*hardly ever*)

5 I am the first person to arrive at the office. (*never*)

6 Do you go abroad? (*often*)

7 Luka doesn't travel by plane. (*usually*)

8 Do they work on Sunday? (*always*)

5 Complete these questions using the verbs from the box and the word(s) in brackets.

be   go   last   speak   spend   take place

1 A: (you) What time _____ _____ usually _____ to bed?
  B: Well, around eleven o'clock.

2 A: (I) _____ _____ late?
  B: No, don't worry. We start at 9:30.

3 A: (the film) How long _____ _____ _____ _____?
  B: About two hours, I think.

4 A: (the festival) When _____ _____ _____ _____ _____?
  B: At the end of June.

5 A: (your wife) _____ _____ _____ _____ a lot of money?
  B: Yes. But she earns a lot, too.

6 A: (your children) _____ _____ _____ _____ Arabic?
  B: Just a little.

6 Complete this crossword puzzle.

Across

4 My husband is an _____ manager. He organizes conferences and trade shows.

6 A formal word for *job*.

9 I need to phone right now. It's _____!

10 Do you _____ your name with one 'r' or double 'r'?

Down

1 'Are you from France?' 'That's right. Yes, I'm _____.'

2 Pamela and Dan are often together at f_____ shows.

3 Excuse me. Is Gabor your _____ or your first name?

5 Pamela Elson is an Australian m_____.

7 My email _____ is elio@t-com.it

8 It's OK. You're not late. Don't _____.

7 Put each word in the box into the correct group according to its stress pattern.

> Brazil business cinema computer evening Germany manager midnight occasion per cent performance Poland report reception return Saturday

Oo	oO	Ooo	oOo
Turkey	Japan	Italy	tomorrow

8 Complete these sentences. Choose the correct prepositions.

1 Liz is hardly ever _____ time, but the people she arranges to meet always wait _____ her.

2 We're interested _____ the yoga course that starts _____ March.

3 This week, Alex starts work _____ eight _____ the evening.

4 I'd like to buy two tickets _____ the concert _____ Saturday.

5 _____ the weekend, I often go _____ the cinema.

6 When I look _____ those photos, I always get angry _____ Peter.

7 Could we have a room _____ a non-smoking floor, please?

8 When I'm _____ very good friends, we talk _____ everything.

9 Write down the times. You need one word per blank.

1 08:40 It's _____ _____ nine.

2 07:05 It's five _____ _____.

3 16:15 It's _____ _____ four.

4 21:30 It's _____ _____ nine.

5 09:45 It's _____ _____ ten.

6 5 a.m. It's _____ o'clock _____ the _____.

10 Match each sentence (1–10) with the most suitable response (a–j).

1 Tea?

2 Do you like your hotel?

3 Excuse me. Is this seat free?

4 I don't like our new cafeteria.

5 I love Sam Rigley's new film.

6 I'm tired.

7 My friend Rick works in California.

8 Excuse me. Could you tell me the time?

9 Could you say that again, please?

10 Could I have your phone number?

a Erm … Half past eight.

b Oh, that's interesting. What does he do?

c Really? I'm not.

d No, thank you.

e Well, it's OK, but my room is very small.

f Sure. Sean. S-E-A-N.

g Yeah. Go ahead.

h Of course. Here's my business card.

i Me neither.

j Really? I don't.

5

A Comparative adjectives
B Superlative adjectives
C **Communication strategies** Offering help
D **Interaction** The best way to help?

Time of your life

Comparative adjectives

Listening: Working together

Miles

Chris

1))) 1.25 Look at the pictures of Miles and Chris. How old do you think they are? Who is the manager? Listen and see if you are right.

2))) Listen to Miles on Track 1.25 again and complete the sentences.

1 His _____ is younger than him.

2 He wants to retire when he's _____.

3 He is a _____ employee now.

4 He is a _____ colleague.

3 Match a word in exercise 2 with a word or phrase below.

a stop work

b worker

c a person in the same company

d boss

4))) Listen to Chris on Track 1.25 again and underline the words he says. Do you agree?

1 It's easier for *older / younger* people to learn new things.

2 It's *easier / more difficult* to manage older people.

3 It's *better / worse* to be a young manager than to have a young manager.

Grammar: Comparative adjectives

5 Look at the examples. Complete the comparative adjectives in the table.

Comparative adjectives
*My employees are **older than** me.*
*I'm **happier** now **than** at 21.*
*Experience is **more important than** age.*
*I'm a **better** employee now.*

Short adjectives			Long adjectives	
old	+ er	older	important	more important
young		1 _____	difficult	3 _____
nice	+ r	nicer		
happy	y + ier	happier	**Irregular adjectives**	
easy		2 _____	good	better
			bad	4 _____

When we compare two things we use the word 5 _____ after a comparative adjective.
*Miles is **older than** Chris.*

>> For more information on comparative adjectives, see page 157.

6 Match the adjective to its opposite. What is the comparative form of the adjectives?

1 rich   a unfriendly

2 slow   b low

3 small   c large

4 modern   d quiet

5 comfortable   e near

6 far   f uncomfortable

7 friendly   g boring

8 noisy   h long

9 short   i poor

10 high   j traditional

11 interesting k fast

Reading: A better place to work?

7 What things are important in a job? Add more to this list.

salary, colleagues …

8 Read about Horizons and NP Solutions and answer the questions.

a Give three examples of Horizons projects.

b Who does NP Solutions help?

9 Work in pairs. Read what Alisha and Charles say about the company they work for. Compare offices, salaries, work hours and colleagues.

Speaking: A good person for the job?

10 Work in pairs. Jess is looking for a job as a project leader. Read the information. What company is better for her, Horizons or NP Solutions? Why?

Jess wants an exciting job. She likes to help people and is happy to travel and work long hours. She thinks that an interesting job is more important than a high salary. She wants good colleagues and a comfortable office. After work, Jess likes to play sport and go out with friends.

11 You want to work as a project leader. Compare Horizons and NP Solutions with your partner. Student A: Give reasons why Horizons is better. Student B: Give reasons why NP Solutions is better.

Horizons is better because the office is more modern than NP Solutions.
NP Solutions has a higher salary than Horizons.

Company name: **Horizons**

Horizons is a new and exciting company that helps community projects around the world. We speak to local people to discover how they want to make their community better. Then we work with international businesses that want to help. Some companies give money and others send workers with special skills. Our projects include building schools and hospitals, training workers and we also organize concerts and events to raise money.

Do you want to work for Horizons? We want project leaders to work in Asia, Africa and Europe.

Alisha: Horizons Project Leader
I work for Horizons and I think it's a great company. My colleagues are friendly and the work is always interesting. I'm a project leader and my salary is €35,000. I start work at 8.30 and I usually finish at 6.30. We have an hour for lunch. The company gives employees an apartment near the office so I cycle to the office every day. I work in a large, modern office with ten people. My colleagues are friendly but sometimes it's noisy. Every day is different. Sometimes I'm in the office all day and sometimes I travel to different communities or meet business people who want to help with the projects.

Company name: **NP Solutions**

NP Solutions is a company that helps rich and famous people to have a great time. Our project leaders work with International film stars, singers, business people and royalty. Our clients like everything to be perfect when they visit a new city. We help them to stay in excellent hotels, visit lovely places and meet famous people. The project leaders organize the trips and travel with the clients. They work with interesting people, travel to beautiful locations and have an exciting job.

Do you want to work for NP Solutions? We want project leaders to work in Dubai, The United States and Australia.

Charles: NP Solutions Project Leader
I work for NP solutions. I'm a project leader and my salary is €43,000. I start work at around 7:30 a.m. I don't have time for lunch. Usually I finish work at 4 p.m. for two or three hours and then I start work again at 7:30 in the evening. I often organize parties for clients or go to the theatre and concerts. Sometimes I see the same concerts two or three times a month and that's boring but the clients are often interesting. I usually get home at 11:30 p.m. My office is quiet and comfortable but my colleagues aren't always friendly because they are very busy. When I travel for business, the company gives employees an apartment and a car. It usually takes about an hour to drive to work.

TALKING POINT
- Is a high salary more important than an interesting job?
- Is it worse to have long working hours or a long journey to work?
- Is it better to have friendly colleagues or a quiet office?

Listening: The best time?

1 People do things at different times in their life. Put these things in the order that people usually do them in your country.

___ get married
___ retire
___ start school
___ get a job
___ go to university
___ start a family

2 What is a good age to do these things? Compare your answers with a partner.

Six is a good age to start school.

3 🔊 **1.26** Look at the photos (A–C) below. Listen and match a speaker to a photo. Who do you think is the oldest speaker and who is the youngest speaker?

4 🔊 Listen again and <u>underline</u> a word in *italics* to complete the sentences.

1 This is the *worse / worst* time to lose something like this.

2 She's the *lovely / loveliest* girl in the world.

3 This isn't the *better / best* way to start married life.

4 It's the *greatest / great* feeling in the world.

5 This is the *most / more* exciting time of my life.

Grammar: Superlative adjectives

5 Look at the examples in exercise 4 and complete the examples below.

short adjectives	long adjectives
old → ¹ old___	important → ³_____ important
easy → ² eas___	**irregular adjectives**
big → biggest	good → ⁴_____
	bad → ⁵_____
We usually use the word ⁶_____ in front of superlative adjectives.	

>> For more information on superlative adjectives, see page 157.

6 Complete the sentences. Use a superlative adjective.

1 It's the _____ (good) time of your life. You can play all day.

2 The _____ (difficult) thing is to find time for work and family.

3 My son is the _____ (noisy) person in the house. He listens to music all day.

4 I play with my grandchildren and have time to travel, that's the _____ (important) thing.

5 All you do is eat, sleep and cry – it's the _____ (easy) time in your life!

6 You aren't old but you aren't young. But for some people it's the _____ (interesting) time.

Word focus: Time of your life

7 There are different times in our life. Match these words to the sentences in exercise 6. Do you agree with the descriptions?

a baby   d adult

b child   e middle-aged person

c teenage   f elderly person

8 Underline the plural words. Regular plural words end in an -s. Which of these plurals are not regular?

Our community has 15 babies and 50 children. There are 25 teenagers. There are 110 adults. Sixty of these are middle-aged people and 30 are elderly people.

Speaking: The right time?

9 What is the best and worst time of life to do these things? Add three more things to the table. Compare your ideas with your partner.

	You	Your partner
Have a pet		
Travel for a year		
Learn to drive		
Be rich		
Fall in love		
Start a business		
_____		
_____		
_____		

10 Work in groups.

• Each person writes five interesting things to do before you are 70.

• Discuss your ideas in the group.

• Report the ideas to the class.

Two people want to …
One person thinks …
Everyone thinks it's a good idea to …
Nobody thinks …

TALKING POINT When is the most exciting time of life? Why?

Listening: Offering help

1 Who do you think needs most help in your community? Tick (✓) three that you think are most important. Compare your ideas with your partner. Give reasons for your choices.

- elderly people
- children
- people with no job
- people with no home
- teenagers
- animals

2 🔊 **1.27** Listen to five conversations. In which conversation doesn't the speaker need help?

3 🔊 Listen again and complete these sentences.

	Offering	Responding
1	I'd like to donate these to your _____.	That's very _____ of you.
2	Would you _____ me to give you marketing advice for your new company?	That's really _____. Thank you.
3	I'm a gardener. _____ help you every week.	Thanks for the _____, but I'm fine.
4	Do you _____ volunteers to visit people?	That's really _____ thanks.
5	Can I _____ your organization deliver food? I have two hours free every Thursday.	Thursdays are _____. Thanks.

Speaking: Can I help?

4 Look at the photos. What help are people giving?

5 Work in pairs. Choose one of the organizations to help.

- Decide what help you want to offer.
- Can you help for an hour, a day, every week?
- Roleplay offering help and responding.

1 We want people to help plant flowers in the local park.

2 We arrange business advice for small companies.

3 We want volunteers to visit elderly people.

4 We deliver food to poor families in the town.

5 We help unemployed people to learn new skills.

6 We want help cleaning and painting a house for homeless people.

Reminder

Grammar reference page 157

We use comparative adjectives when we compare two things.
*It's **better** to give time **than** money.*

We use superlative adjectives when we compare three or more things.
*The **best** plan is to raise money for charity.*

Speaking: Raising money

1 Discuss these questions with a partner.

1 What are the most popular charities in your country?

2 Do you think older or younger people give more to charity? Read the information and tell each other about your group. Are you surprised?

Student A: Turn to File 8, page 110. Student B: Turn to File 37, page 117.

2 Look at these photos of raising money for charities. Can you think of more ways to raise money?

3 Work in groups of three. Read about the charity or organization. Student A: read the information on this page. Student B: Turn to File 9, page 110. Student C: Turn to File 38, page 118.

Student A:

PROFESSIONAL CARE

Professional Care is a charity for professional people. We make most of our friends at work. When we retire it is more difficult to meet new people. Professional Care helps you to meet other retired business people.

Can you help?

We need volunteers to help make tea and coffee on the days that Professional Care meets. We also want to raise money to build our own meeting place.

4 Tell your group about your charity. Explain why you think your charity is the best. Discuss the points below.

1 Compare the three charities and decide which one to help.

2 Decide the best way to help the charity you choose. Do you want to help with time or donate things?

3 What is the best way to raise money to help your charity?

5 Tell the class about your charity. Explain how you want to help.

6

A *there is / there are*
B Imperatives
C **Communication strategies** Asking for help
D **Interaction** Welcome to the trade fair

You are here

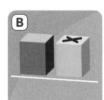

there is / there are

Reading: A great place to stay

1 What facilities do you like to have when you go on holiday? What facilities are useful on a business trip?

2 Look at the photo. What is it? What facilities do you think it has on it? Read the article and find out if you are right.

This cruise ship is called *The Oasis of the Seas* and it cost around $400 million to build. That's a lot of money, but there isn't another ship like it. The facilities are amazing. There are about 25 *restaurants*. There is a *theatre* with more than 1,300 seats. Passengers who enjoy sport can play basketball, climb or play golf. There are five *pools* and there is a *gym* near one of the pools. Here you can go to an exercise class or relax in the spa. There is a *park* with more than 12,000 plants and trees in the centre of the ship. You can walk on *deck* and visit the shops and cafés opposite the park. Business travellers can use the *conference hall*. There are *lifts* to take guests to the 18 decks. There are up to 6,296 passengers and 2,291 staff on the ship. It's a great venue for a special holiday but don't forget your map!

3 Read the article again and find a place in *italics* in the article where you can do these things.

1 eat dinner
2 do exercise
3 swim
4 walk
5 see plants and trees
6 see a show
7 travel up and down
8 have a meeting

4 Find these numbers in the article. What do they refer to?

1 One thousand three hundred
2 Two thousand two hundred and ninety-one
3 Six thousand two hundred and ninety-six
4 Twelve thousand
5 Four hundred million

5 Where are these places on the ship?
a the park   b the gym   c the shops and cafés

Word focus: Prepositions of place

6 Match the words to the pictures.

behind   in front of   in the centre   near   next to   opposite

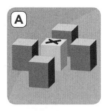

7 Work in pairs. Take turns to ask and answer the questions.

1 What is next to the room you are in at the moment?
2 What is the name of the person opposite you?
3 What is in front of the building you are in?
4 What is behind your chair?
5 Name three things that are near you.
6 Name four shops or businesses in the centre of town.

Grammar: *there is / there are*

8 Look at the examples in the table. Choose the right words in *italics* to complete the rules (1 and 2). Then find more examples of *there is / there are* in the article.

there is / there are
+
There's a park. (*There is a park.*)   **There're** four pools. (*There are four pools.*)
–
There isn't another ship like it. (*There is not another ship like it.*)   **There aren't** three theatres. (*There are not three theatres.*)
?
Is there a cinema? — **Yes, there is. / No, there isn't.**
Are there two spas? — **Yes, there are. / No, there aren't.**

There is water in the pool. **There is a cinema. There are trees** in the park.

1 We use *there is / there are* with singular nouns and uncountable nouns.

2 We use *there is / there are* with plural nouns.

>> For more information on *there is / there are*, see page 154.

9 A passenger on a cruise ship asks a receptionist for information. Complete the dialogue using the correct form of *there is / there are*. Practise the conversation with a partner.

Passenger: Excuse me, ¹___ ___ a gym on this ship?
Receptionist: Yes, ²___ ___ two gyms near here. I can show you on your map.
Passenger: Great, ³___ ___ any gym classes this morning?
Receptionist: I'm sorry, ⁴___ ___ any classes until this afternoon.
Passenger: OK, ⁵___ ___ any other sports activities this morning?
Receptionist: Sure, ⁶___ ___ a tennis lesson that starts at 10 a.m.

Speaking: Choosing your accommodation

10 Work in pairs. You want to arrange a short break with some friends. Answer the questions below.

1 What facilities do you want the holiday accommodation to have?

2 Look at the photos and the information below. Which type of holiday accommodation is best for your group?

Cecile and Mark have two children.
Tomas has problems walking.
Greg, Lukas and Naasir like sports activities outside.
Yuko and Miranda like swimming.
Vanda and William like relaxing.
Katrina and Paulo are vegetarian.
Petra likes doing exercise.

Now choose a location for your short break.

Writing: Asking for information

11 Choose one of the places in the pictures for your short break. Write an email to the manager.

- Say how many people are in your group.
- Say when you want to go on holiday.
- Ask questions about the facilities.

Useful phrases
Can I have some information about …
There are … people in our group.
We want to go on holiday on …
I have some questions about the facilities.
Thank you for your help.

TALKING POINT Do you think it's a good idea to go on holiday with friends from work or university?

Word focus: Directions

1 How do you get from the room that you are in now to the exit of the building?

2 Match the phrases and the directions.

> go past   go straight on   it's at the end of …
> it's on the corner   take the second left   turn left   turn right

(A) (B) (C) (D) (E) (F) (G)

3 Work in pairs. Ask for and give directions to places in the building where you are now.

> *Where's the kitchen?   Go out of the door and turn right. Go to the end of the corridor and it's opposite reception.*

Listening: You are here

4 What places are there in a town or city? Add five more places to the list.

mall, cinema, school, park, bank, supermarket, library …

5))) **1.28** Look at the map. Do you know all the places on it? Listen to four conversations. Follow the directions and mark the places in the boxes on the map. Each time start where it says 'You are here'.

> bank   conference centre   The Garden Hotel   hospital

6))) Listen again and complete the sentences with the words in the box.

> corner   first   from   me   near   next   opposite
> past   right   straight   take   tell   to   turn   where

1 Excuse _____. Can you _____ me the way to the conference centre, please?

2 Go past the library and turn _____. The conference centre is _____ the Sun Hotel.

3 Excuse me, is there a bank _____ here?

4 Turn left and go _____ on. Turn right and there is a bank on the _____ of the street.

5 _____'s the Garden Hotel, please?

6 OK, take the _____ right and go to the end of the road. _____ left and the Garden Hotel is _____ to Zen's Restaurant.

7 Excuse me, how do you get _____ the hospital _____ the station?

8 Go _____ the supermarket and _____ the first left. The hospital is opposite the park.

7 Work in pairs. Take it in turns to ask for and to give directions to these places. Start from 'You are here'.

Student A: You want directions to a) a gym, b) the park.

Student B: You want directions to a) an internet café, b) the cinema.

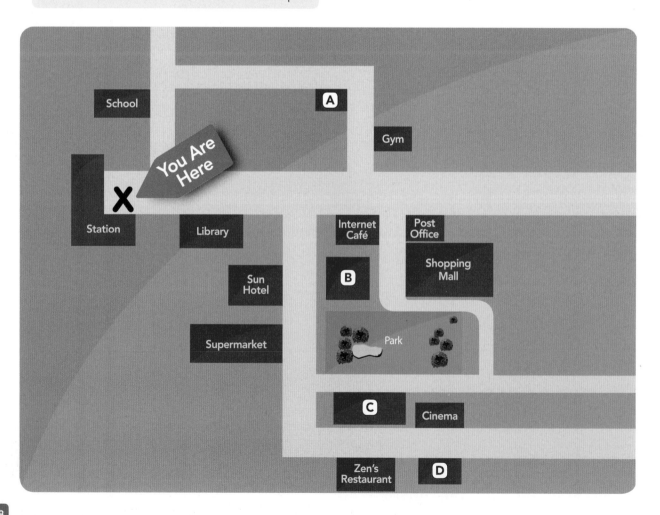

Grammar: Imperatives

8 Look at the examples in the table and complete the rules. Then look at exercise 6 again and underline more examples of the imperative.

Imperatives
We use the imperative to give an order or an instruction.
+ **Cross** the road. not ~~To cross~~ the road.
– **Don't turn** left. not Don't ~~to~~ turn left.
1 In positive sentences: we use the base form of the verb without _____.
2 In negative sentences: we use _____ + the base form of the verb without _____.
! When it is not an order or an instruction, we generally add polite words and phrases. ~~Tell me the way~~ to the conference centre. **Can you** tell me the way to the conference centre, **please**?
>> For more information on imperatives, see page 144.

9 Complete the email to a colleague who is visiting your office for the first time. Use the correct form of the verbs in the box.

> ask   cross   go   not take   see   turn

Hi Gregor

Here are directions from the station to my office in Marine Avenue:

¹_____ left at Station Road. ²_____ past the university and turn right. ³_____ the road. ⁴_____ the first left, take the second left. My office is on the corner.
⁵_____ the receptionist to call me.

⁶_____ you on Friday.

Speaking: Where is it?

10 Draw a map of the part of the town where you work, live or study. Tell your partner what is/isn't in the town.

> There's a station. There isn't a cinema.
> There are three supermarkets.

11 Ask for directions to get to and from some of the places on your partner's map.

> I'm at the station. Can you tell me the way to the college, please?
> How do I get from the station to the college?

Then answer your partner's questions about some of the places on your map.

TALKING POINT

When you are lost, do you prefer to ask directions, use a map or use modern technology to find your way?

Listening: Help!

1 Why do these people need help?

2 🔊 **1.29** Listen to four people at a conference. What does each speaker want to find? Match the speaker with the photos.

3 Which speaker doesn't get the information he/she wants? Why?

4 🔊 Listen again and complete these sentences.

Asking for help	Agreeing to help
1 Can you __help__ me? How do I register for the conference?	2 _____, no problem.
3 Can you tell me where the toilets are, _____?	4 Yes, _____.
5 Can you _____ me who the speaker is at the next seminar?	6 Oh _____. It's Malcolm Gladwell.

5 Do the speakers use these phrases to thank (T) someone or respond to thanks (R)? Can you add more expressions to the list?

You're welcome, My pleasure, Glad to help, Cheers, Great, thanks, Many thanks …

Speaking: Can you help?

6 Work in pairs. Practise asking for help, thanking and responding to thanks in these situations.

1 Student A: You want to find a café near here.

   A: Excuse me, is there a café near here?
   B: Yes, go out of the building and turn right. The café is at the end of the road.
   Or
   No, there isn't a café near here. But there's a good restaurant opposite the station.
   A: Thanks.
   B: No, problem.

2 Student B: You want to find where to get a taxi.

3 Student A: You want to know when the seminar starts.

4 Student B: You want help to spell an English word.

5 Student A: You want to use your partner's pen.

6 Student B: You want help with your bags.

Reminder

Grammar reference
pages 154 and 144

We use *there is / there are* to say that
something or someone exists.
There is a park.
There aren't three theatres.
Is there a pool?

We use imperatives for orders and
instructions.
Turn left / right.
Go straight on.

Rules

1 Toss a coin to move. Heads move one square, tails move two.
2 Follow the instructions on each square and use your imagination to act out the conversations.
3 When you land on a square that your partner is on, move to the next new square.
4 The first person to reach *Finish*, wins.

Board game: Trade Fair

1 Do you go to any of these in your work? Use a dictionary to help you with any new words.

> conferences   seminars   trade fairs
> training courses   workshops

2 Imagine you are at an international trade fair. Choose the country that the trade fair is in.

3 Play a game in pairs or small groups. Read the rules and then play the game.

START

1 Say three facilities you can find in a hotel.

2 At the hotel You're at reception. Ask about sports activities in the hotel.

3 At the hotel Ask for directions to the pool.

4 At the hotel Ask how to get to the trade fair from the hotel.

9 At the trade fair Ask for information about the next seminar.

8 Say three ways to say 'thank you'.

7 At the trade fair Ask where to get a coffee.

6 At the trade fair Ask someone where to get a badge.

5 Say two things you usually do when you arrive at a trade fair.

10 At the trade fair Ask what time the next workshop starts

11 At the trade fair Ask someone where to get lunch.

12 At the trade fair Stop someone and ask to look at their conference programme.

13 At the trade fair You want to buy a book by one of the speakers. Ask for help.

14 Say four prepositions of place.

19 At the hotel You lose your room key. Ask for help.

18 At the hotel You're a vegetarian. Ask about restaurants.

17 At the trade fair Ask to use a pen.

16 At the trade fair Ask the way to the meeting point.

15 At the trade fair You want to find the toilets.

20 At the hotel Ask for help about two things in your hotel room.

21 At the hotel Ask reception to arrange a taxi to the airport at 9:30.

22 At the hotel Ask for help with your bags.

FINISH

7

A Countable and uncountable nouns
B *some* and *any*
C **Communication strategies** Making suggestions
D **Interaction** Asking about products

Buying and selling

Countable and uncountable nouns

Listening: The survey

1))) **1.30** Café Starbean is a company that sells drinks. What does the employee want the woman to do?

2))) Listen to the questions and write the woman's answers.

---

1 Does she prefer hot drinks or cold drinks?

....

2 How much tea does she drink every day?

....

3 What tea does she usually choose, black or green?

....

4 How many cups of coffee does she drink?

....

5 What other hot drinks does she buy?

....

6 What cold drinks does she buy?

....

---

3 Work in pairs. Take turns to ask your partner the questions.

> *Do you prefer hot drinks or cold drinks?*

Grammar: Countable and uncountable nouns

4 Look at the rules and answer these questions.

a Look at the food and drink nouns in the survey again. Which rule (1 or 2) describes each one?

b Look at the sentences from the listening and complete rules 3 and 4.

Countable and uncountable

1 Countable nouns can be singular or plural. We can use *a* or *an* with singular countable nouns.
a cup → two cups

2 Uncountable nouns cannot be plural.
water → ~~waters~~
We can't use *a* or *an* with uncountable nouns.

3 We use *How* _____ with countable nouns.
4 We use *How* _____ with uncountable nouns.
How much *tea does she drink every day?*
How many *cups of coffee do you drink?*

>> For more information on countable and uncountable, *How much* and *How many*, see pages 154–155.

---

5 Are these words countable or uncountable?

> bread cakes drinks food lemon milk sandwich

6 Complete the sentences with *a*, *an* or no article (Ø).
1 There is _____ cup of coffee for you on the table.
2 Do you want _____ milk in your tea?
3 I prefer to have _____ water in the morning.
4 In some countries drinking tea is _____ event.
5 Is there _____ sandwich for me?
6 Do you want me to buy _____ cakes for the party?

7 Choose the correct words in *italics* to complete the questions.
1 *How much / How many* hot drinks are on the menu?
2 *How much / How many* milk do you want in your tea?
3 *How much / How many* time does he spend at the coffee machine?
4 *How much / How many* bottles of drink are in the fridge?

Word focus: Food and drink

8 Look at the words in the food and drink table. Complete the table with the headings in the box.

> dairy fish fruit hot drinks meat
> soft drinks vegetables

A	B
1	chicken, lamb, beef
2	salmon, tuna, cod
3	carrot, onion, potato
4	apple, orange, banana
5	cheese, yogurt, butter
6	hot chocolate
7	fruit juice, mineral water, cola

9 Work in pairs. Talk about food in the table. Which foods do you have for breakfast? Which foods do you eat as a snack?

Speaking: A healthy choice?

10 Work in pairs and discuss these questions.

1 Which food and drink is a healthy choice?

2 How many times a day / week is it a good idea to eat and drink these things?

11 Ask and answer questions to complete the information about Karl and Nina. Student A; Turn to File 10, page 110. Student B: look at the information below.

Student B:

Ask questions and complete the information about Karl.

1 Karl eats meat _____ times a week.
How much meat does Karl eat?

2 He eats oranges _____ day.

3 He drinks _____ glass/es of water a day.

4 He drinks fruit juice _____ times a week.

Now answer your partner's questions about Nina.

1 Nina eats rice five times a week.

2 She eats salad four times a week.

3 She drinks a bottle of water every day.

4 She eats fish six times a week.

12 Ask your partner five questions about what they eat and drink. Which of your partner's food and drink choices do you think are healthy?

How much water do you drink every day?

> **TALKING POINT** Is it sometimes difficult to choose healthy food? What things make it difficult to make healthy choices when we eat?

Listening: The mystery shopper

1 🔊 **1.31** Listen to a mystery shopper talk about her work. Does she like her job? Why/Why not?

2 Are these statements true (T) or false (F)?

1 She always tells people that she is a mystery shopper.

2 She asks questions about products.

3 She writes her report in the shop.

4 The company gives the report to the sales assistant.

3 🔊 **1.32** Listen to the mystery shopper talk to a sales assistant. Answer the questions.

1 What sort of shop is it?

2 What does she want to buy?

4 🔊 Complete these questions. Listen again to check.

1 What _____ is it?   It's small.

2 What _____ is it?   It's rectangular.

3 What's it _____ of?   It's plastic.

4 Does it come in any   It comes in brown and black.
   other _____ ?

5 Do you think the mystery shopper gives the sales assistant a good report? Choose a word in *italics* and complete the report.

Write new

Aa

Report for Fabio Furniture

1 The sales assistant at Fabio Furniture is *helpful / unhelpful*.

2 The customer service is *good / bad*.

3 The sales assistant is *polite / impolite*.

Continue   **More**

6 🔊 **1.33** Listen to the mystery shopper in another shop. Is the sales assistant polite? Who says these things, the customer (C) or sales assistant (S)?

1 How can I help?

2 Certainly.

3 Does it come in any other colours?

4 I'll think about it.

5 Thanks for your help.

6 You're welcome.

Word focus: Describing products

7 Look at the list of words 1–4 and answer the questions.

1 Choose the correct heading for each list.

colour material shape size

1 small, medium, large

2 rectangular, square, triangular

3 black, white, brown

4 wood, plastic, glass

2 Now add these words to the lists. Can you add any more adjectives?

big blue green metal oval paper round tiny

> ! We say *It's made of **wood***, but *It's a **wooden** desk*.

8 Take turns to describe the object to your partner. Student A: Turn to File 11, page 110. Student B: Turn to File 39, page 118.

Grammar: *some* and *any*

9 Look at the examples from the listening. Complete the rules with *some* or *any* in the table below.

some and any

*I want to buy **some** furniture.*
*Do you have **any** desks?*
*We **don't** have **any** desks.*

1 We use _____ in questions and negative sentences with plural countable nouns and uncountable nouns.
2 We use _____ in positive sentences.

>> For more information on *some* and *any*, see page 155.

10 Complete the sentences with *some, any* or *a.*

1 Do you have _____ lamps?

2 We have _____ new chairs.

3 They don't have _____ furniture that I like.

4 She has _____ desk next to the window.

5 I have _____ information about their products.

6 Does he have _____ lamp in his office?

Speaking: What is it?

11 Work in pairs. What objects can you see in these photos?

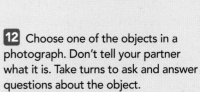

12 Choose one of the objects in a photograph. Don't tell your partner what it is. Take turns to ask and answer questions about the object.

> *A: What's it made of?*
> *B: It's made of glass.*
> *A: What size is it?*
> *B: It's small.*
> *A: Is it the lamp?*
> *B: Yes.*

TALKING POINT   Is it a good idea to have an office in your home? Why?/Why not?

Listening: What can we do?

1 Where do you buy clothes? Do you prefer to shop with other people?

2 Look at pictures A–E. What are the people wearing? What colours are the clothes?

3)) **1.34** Listen to three conversations and answer questions.

1 What clothes do they talk about?

2 Where are the people in Conversations 1 and 2?

3 In Conversation 3 who is speaking?
  a a customer and shop assistant
  b a supplier and a buyer
  c two office workers

4)) Listen again and complete the sentences.

Suggestion	Response
How ^{1}_____ green? You ^{3}_____ try a smaller size.	→ I'm not ^{2}_____ about green. → ^{4}_____ a good idea.
Say it is available	**Say it isn't available**
We have it ^{5}_____ blue. We have red in ^{6}_____.	^{7}_____, we don't have it in stock. I'm ^{8}_____ we don't have them in brown.

5 Work in pairs. Look at the pictures A–E again.

1 What suggestions do you think the shop assistants make in B, C and D? What do you think the customer says in A and E?

2 What responses do you think the customers give to the suggestions?

Reminder

Grammar reference
pages 154–155

We can use *a/an* with singular nouns.
We don't use *a/an* with plural nouns with countable and uncountable nouns.
*Is there **a** sandwich for me?*
Do you want milk in your tea?

We can use *some/any* with nouns.
*Do you sell **any** soft drinks?*
*I want **some** information about your products, please.*
We can use *How much/How many*.
***How many** suppliers are there?*
***How much** time do we have?*

Reading: Come to the Expo

1 Look at the photos of food and drink. Name the food or drink. What are the different containers called?

2 Read the information about the Expo and answer the questions. What companies in your country could go to it?

1 How many suppliers are at the Expo?

2 Who can you meet there?

3 What industry is the Expo for?

> ### INTERNATIONAL
> ## FOOD AND DRINK EXPO
> —— AT THE ——
> ### INTERNATIONAL EXPOCENTRE, WARSAW, POLAND
>
> * Visit the food and drink industry's number 1 event.
> * Come and enjoy great food and drink.
> * Visit over 600 suppliers.
>
> **It's the perfect place for buyers and suppliers to meet.**

Listening: I have some questions

3))) 1.35 A buyer talks to a supplier at the Expo. Listen and complete the conversation.

A: Hi, I have some ¹_____ about your products.

B: Certainly, how ²_____ I help?

A: I want to ³_____ some olives from Spain.

B: ⁴_____, we don't have any Spanish olives in stock at the moment. How about some from Turkey?

A: Are the olives in tins or ⁵_____?

B: They're in ⁶_____ jars.

A: Hmm, I'm ⁷_____ sure. I prefer tins. They're easier to transport.

B: Oh, I ⁸_____.

A: What ⁹_____ are the jars?

B: We sell small and ¹⁰_____ sizes. Here is a list of our prices.

A: OK, I'll ¹¹_____ about it, thanks.

4 Work in pairs. Practise the conversation.

Speaking: Explain what you want

5 You are at the Expo and you want to meet a new supplier. Take turns to be the buyer and supplier and have a conversation. Use the information below for Conversation 1.

The buyer	The supplier
You have some questions for the supplier.	Offer to help.
You want mineral water from Japan.	Choose a response. a You have mineral water from Japan. b You don't have mineral water from Japan. Suggest mineral water from Korea.
Plastic or glass bottles?	Choose a response. a glass b plastic
Choose a response. a You prefer the bottle in this material. b You prefer another material.	Choose a response. a I see. b That's good.
Ask about the size of bottle.	Choose a response. The water is in a small bottles. b big bottles.
Choose a response. a You want this size. b You don't want this size.	Offer a list of prices.
Say you'll think about it and thank the supplier.	Say thank you and goodbye.

6 Change roles. Turn to File 12, page 110 for Conversation 2.

7 Think of a company you know and roleplay a conversation between a buyer and supplier about their products.

8

A Modal verbs: *can, have to, should*
B Modal verbs: question forms
C Communication strategies Giving instructions
D Interaction Surviving in a strange city

A question of survival

Modal verbs: *can, have to, should*

Reading: Always read the signs!

1 Work in pairs. Discuss these questions.

1 What do these signs and notices mean?

2 What other signs and notices can you find (1) at or near your workplace or college? (2) when you go on holiday?

2 Here is a quiz about workplace signs and notices. Choose the correct meaning from the list for each picture.

What does this sign mean?

· ·

a You can't press this button if there is a fire.

b You can smoke here.

c You can't park here on weekdays.

d You can't enter this place now.

e You don't have to pay for parking at the weekend.

f You have to press this button if there is a fire.

g You should smoke.

h You can't wear a hat and boots.

i You shouldn't enter this place now.

j You have to wear a hat and boots.

1 ☐

2 ☐

3 ☐

4 ☐

Grammar: Modal verbs: *can, have to, should*

3 Complete the examples in the table with the modal verbs in the box.

> can   can't   doesn't have to / don't have to
> has to / have to   should   shouldn't

Modal verbs: *can, have to, should* (+/–)	
It's OK. / It's possible.	You ¹_____ smoke here.
It's not OK. / It's not possible.	You ²_____ park here.
It's necessary.	Workers ³_____ wear boots. He/She ⁴_____ wear a hard hat.
It's not necessary.	You ⁵_____ pay for parking at the weekend. He/She ⁶_____ wear a hard hat in the office.
It's a good idea.	We ⁷_____ pay attention to all signs.
It's not a good idea.	We ⁸_____ forget to read notices.

> **!** *can* and *should* never take *-s*.
> She **should** read the notices.
> He **can** park here.

>> For more information on modal verbs, see page 152.

4 Here are some ideas for the workplace. Choose the best modal verbs to complete the sentences.

1 Everybody wants to help when there is an accident, so companies *can't / should* offer free first-aid courses.

2 Staff *can / don't have to* take short breaks when they want. It's good for them, and it's good for productivity, too.

3 The company offers five different training courses every year. Employees *don't have to / can* choose which courses they want to take. They *don't have to / shouldn't* pay for the courses, the company pays for them.

4 Employees who smoke aren't happy that they *have to / can* go outside for a cigarette break. There *shouldn't / should* be a special area for them inside.

5 Employees *can't / don't have to* eat their lunches at their desks because the equipment gets very dirty.

6 Staff meetings *don't have to / shouldn't* last longer than 45 minutes.

5 Work in pairs or small groups. Discuss the ideas in exercise 4. Agree on the two best ideas.

Listening: I feel ill

6 In pairs, match the photos (1–6) and the health problems (a–f). Check with a dictionary or with your teacher if necessary.

a neck pain
b headache
c shoulder pain
d eye problem
e backache
f wrist pain

7 ♫ **1.36** Listen to six people talking about health problems at work. Write the correct letter (a–f) next to each name.

1 Goran   **3** Jeff   **5** Rosa
2 Pete   **4** Richard   **6** Kate

Word focus: Health problems

8 ♫ When you feel ill, there are different expressions you can use to talk about your problems. Listen to the conversations again and complete the expressions.

1 I've got a _____.
2 I have a pain in my _____.
3 My _____ hurt.
4 I've got _____.
5 I have a pain in my _____.
6 My _____ hurts.

Speaking: My job, my health

9 Work in pairs. Look at the expressions in exercise 8. Tell each other about health problems at your workplace.

> *I sometimes have a pain in my legs because …*
> *My colleagues often have headaches because …*

10 Work in pairs. One of you has a problem, the other makes a suggestion. Take it in turns to be A and B.

> *A: I'm not very well.*
> *B: I'm sorry to hear that. What's the matter?*
> *A: …*
> *B: Well, I think you should …*

> **TALKING POINT**
>
> What do you do for your own health and safety when you are on holiday?

Reading: Risks and rewards

1 Work in pairs. Look at the photo of an oil rig and discuss this question.

Imagine there is a good job for you on an offshore oil rig. Do you take it? Why?/Why not?

2 In pairs, guess the answers to these questions.

1 How much does a workman earn per day on an offshore oil rig (in US$)?

2 How long can workers stay on an offshore oil rig?

3 Read the information leaflet about working on an oil rig. Check your answers to exercise 2.

4 Find the words and phrases in the leaflet with these meanings.

1 fun   e_____

2 pays for all travel costs   c_____ all travel e_____

3 level of quality   s_____

4 work more hours after your usual working hours   d_____ o_____

5 Answer these questions.

1 Do oil rig workers have to pay for their travel expenses?

2 Does everyone have to do a survival course to work on an offshore oil rig?

3 Do oil rig workers have to do overtime every day?

4 Can oil rig workers spend a whole month offshore?

Working on an oil rig

Offshore oil rig jobs are often difficult and dangerous, but companies also want their workers to have an enjoyable time. For example, the bedrooms are sometimes of the same standard as in a 4- or 5-star hotel, the food is often excellent, and the company usually covers all travel expenses.

Safety standards are very high. Everyone has to wear special clothes, attend regular safety meetings and take part in regular safety exercises. In some countries, you have to do a survival course before you can work offshore.

The working day is usually 12 hours, and sometimes you have to do two or three hours overtime. Workers often have two weeks on*, then two weeks off*. So they can be on holiday six months a year! Nobody can stay on an oil rig for longer than three weeks.

Salaries are good. A cleaner earns $900 per week, and a workman earns from $1,000 to $1,500. A technician or engineer's salary is often three or four times as high.

on / off: working / not working

An offshore oil rig

Listening: Expert advice

6 Two young men, Bob Hill and Rajit Gupta want a job on an oil rig to earn a lot of money quickly. They go to a career fair to talk to an expert. What questions do they ask?

7))) **1.37** Listen to the conversation at the career fair. Do Bob and Rajit ask any of your questions from exercise 6?

8))) Listen to the conversation again and complete these questions.

1 ___ I _____ ___ buy safety clothes myself?

2 How much luggage _____ we take, by the way?

3 _____ I leave my mobile phone at home, too?

4 How much money ___ we _____ ___ take with us?

9 Match each question in exercise 8 to two possible answers.

a Just enough to buy some sweets and soft drinks.

b Not really. But it's best to use a payphone.

c Well, you can't take anything big.

d No, you don't.

e Maybe that's a good idea.

f You don't need any. You can use your credit card.

g No. The company buys them for you.

h Just one middle-sized bag.

10 Work in pairs. Test your memory! Look at these items. Put a tick (✓) if you can take them on board and a cross (✗) if you can't.

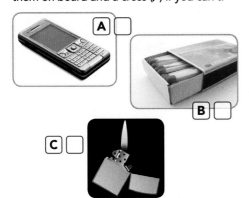

A ☐ B ☐ C ☐ D ☐ E ☐

Grammar: Modal verbs: question forms

11 Look at the table. Complete the examples and the rules.

Modal verbs: question forms	
¹___ we smoke on board?	Yes, you **can** smoke in the smoking room. But you **can't** smoke outside.
²___ we take our laptop? Do we ³___ ___ take a lot of money?	Well, maybe you **shouldn't**. No, you **don't**.

1 With *can* and ⁴___ , we just change the word order to make questions, and we do **not** use *do* in short answers.

2 With *have to*, we use ⁵___ (or *does*) to make questions and short answers.

>> **For more information on modal question forms, see page 152.**

Speaking: Rights and responsibilities

12 Work in pairs. Ask and answer questions about the things you *can / can't* do and *have to / don't have to* do at your workplace. Use the modal verb in brackets.

A: *Do you have to wear special safety clothes at work?*
B: *No, I don't. But I wear special glasses when I work on the computer.*

1 wear special safety clothes (*have to*)

2 do overtime (*have to*)

3 smoke (*can*)

4 take a day off when you want (*can*)

5 take part in safety exercises (*have to*)

6 send and receive personal emails (*can*)

Writing: Dos and don'ts

13 A friend wants information about your workplace. Write an email telling them about some of the things you *can* and *can't* do and *have to* and *don't have to* do. Tell them why they should apply for a job with your company.

Hi _____
Good to hear from you after all this time.
_____ is a great company to work for.
You don't have to _____ . Sometimes you have to _____ , but I think that's the same in a lot of companies.
You can't _____ , but that's not a problem. The good thing is that you can _____!
I think you should apply for the job – the _____ is really great.
Good luck and all the best
_____

TALKING POINT

• What are your biggest responsibilities at work or in your family?
I have to …
Sometimes, I also have to …

Listening: Could you show me how to do it?

1 Work in pairs. Do you agree with these statements? Why?/ Why not?

1 Giving instructions is easy, following instructions is difficult.

2 When you explain something, showing is better than telling.

2 Think of something *physical* you can do. Then, work in small groups and take turns to teach each other.

3 Match the verbs in the box to the illustrations.

beep   flash   lock   press

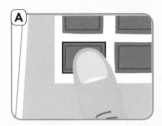
A

B

C

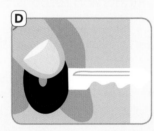
D

4 🔊 **1.38** Listen to two people telling Frieda how to set a burglar alarm. Which explanation do you prefer? Why?

5 🔊 Listen to conversation 1 on Track 1.38 again and complete the sentences.

Giving instructions

Explaining the order of steps:

¹_____, make sure all windows and doors are closed.

²_____, ____ _____ _____ enter your user code.

³_____ _____, the red light flashes and the keypad beeps.

And that's it!

When people give instructions, they often explain in what order to do things. They also check that the other person understands.

Finally, they don't often say *Do this, Do that,* but they use 'you': *You have to do this.*

Checking understanding:

A: OK?   B: Yes. Fine.

A: Do you have any   B: No, that's all very clear.
questions?   Thank you.

A: Any questions?   B: Yes. I'm not sure what happens
                         when the red light stops flashing.

6 In pairs, prepare a set of instructions for Frieda. What does she have to do when she comes home? What happens to the keypad?

First, you unlock the door.

Speaking: Let me show you

7 Work in pairs. Imagine you have to explain how to write and send an SMS message. With your partner, agree on the order of all the different steps. Student A: Turn to File 13, page 111. Student B: Turn to File 40, page 118.

Reminder

Grammar reference page 152

We use *can* to say that something is possible, and *can't* if it isn't.
*You **can't** park here.*
We use *have to* to say that something is necessary, and *don't have to* to say that it is not necessary.
*Everyone **has to** wear special clothes.*

We use *should* to say that something is a good idea, or the right thing to do, and *shouldn't* if it isn't.
*I **should** stay at home tomorrow.*

Word focus: Means of transport

1 Work in pairs. List all the means of transport that you know (e.g. *car*, *plane*, etc).

2 Some verbs are often used with particular means of transport. In four of the five sets below, cross out the word which does not normally go with the verb.

to go somewhere by	car bus foot train metro
to get into / out of	a taxi a bike a car
to catch / miss	a taxi a bus a train a plane a ferry
to take	a ferry a plane a taxi a train the metro
to get on / off	a train a car a bike a plane a boat

3 Work in pairs. Tick (✓) the sentences that are true for you. Correct the ones that are not.

1 When I'm in a city I don't know, I go everywhere by metro.

2 From where I live, I can't take a bus to the airport.

3 I believe everybody should get on their bike and leave their car at home.

4 Sometimes taking the ferry in the morning is the best part of the day.

5 You can take a plane from our capital city to a lot of other cities in our country.

6 Before I go to a strange city, I search the internet and find out about public transport.

Listening: Easy business travel

4 Work in pairs. Your company sends you to Cairo for a month on an exchange programme. What information do you need? Write down your questions.

Do I have to have a visa?
What kind of clothes should I take?

5 🔊 1.39 Listen to a radio programme for travellers to Cairo. Which of your questions from exercise 4 does the programme answer?

6 🔊 Choose three topics from the list below. Then listen again and take notes on those three topics.

1 travelling from the airport to the city centre

2 travelling around Cairo

3 tipping

4 the weather

5 free time activities

Speaking: Strange cities

7 Your company sends you to different cities. Ask your partner for information. Student A: Read the information below. Student B: Turn to File 14, page 111.

Student A: you have to go to Shanghai in January. Ask your partner for some information. Here are some ideas:

- take warm clothes?
- take a train or a bus from the airport to the city centre?
- give tips?
- get a visa?

Do I have to take warm clothes?
Can I take a train or a bus from the airport to the city centre?

Now turn to File 41, page 118.

Review 5-8

1 Find seven adjectives in the word squares which you can use to describe an office or a room. Read across →, down ↓ and diagonally ↘.

m	v	r	a	t	i	n	g	w	e	l	c
o	l	s	d	o	z	i	a	s	a	t	m
d	a	r	m	x	o	y	p	n	b	o	o
e	r	o	e	a	r	m	o	d	e	r	n
s	g	w	r	m	l	i	n	p	e	v	o
c	e	v	i	e	t	l	q	o	b	q	i
l	m	u	e	i	s	a	u	u	i	p	s
a	q	u	d	h	u	z	i	f	l	o	y
n	d	a	t	a	k	t	e	f	b	u	t
t	r	e	y	r	k	w	t	l	s	d	e
t	m	o	x	y	i	u	z	e	m	r	n
c	o	m	f	o	r	t	a	b	l	e	v

2 Complete these sentences. Choose the correct comparative or superlative.

1 Is Zurich *further / furthest* than Geneva?

2 It's the *most / more* expensive watch in the shop.

3 Is the Amazon the *longer / longest* river in the world?

4 Your computer is *fastest / faster* than mine.

5 This isn't the *best / better* place to have a meeting.

6 The staff are *friendliest / friendlier* in this company.

7 He's the *most / more* interesting speaker at the conference.

8 House prices are *higher / highest* in Tokyo than in Lisbon.

3 Write the plurals of these words.

1 baby _____

2 child _____

3 person _____

4 man _____

5 adult _____

6 woman _____

7 teenager _____

4 Complete the questions and responses in this questionnaire. Put *much, many, some* or *any* in each gap.

How ¹____ water do you use in your business?
We use a lot of water because we clean our company cars three times a week.

How ²____ company cars do you have?
Ten and we want to buy two more.

Do you have ³____ other company vehicles, for examples trucks or delivery vans?
We have ⁴____ delivery vans but we don't have
⁵____ trucks.

How ⁶____ delivery vans do you have?
Five, at the moment.

Do you want us to send you ⁷____ ideas about ways to save water in your company?
Yes, please. Do you have ⁸____ information with you today?

Yes, here are ⁹____ brochures and you can find
¹⁰____ more information on our website.
Thanks for your help.

5 Write sentences with the same meaning as the statements. Use *can, can't, should, shouldn't have to* and, *don't have to*. The first one is done for you.

1 It's OK to use the internet.
You can use the internet.

2 It's a good idea to go on a first-aid course.
You _____.

3 It's not OK to eat at your desk.
You _____.

4 It's necessary to wear a name badge.
You _____.

5 It's not a good idea to use mobile phones here.
You _____.

6 It's not necessary to work this weekend.
You _____.

6 Look at the map and use prepositions of place to complete the sentences.

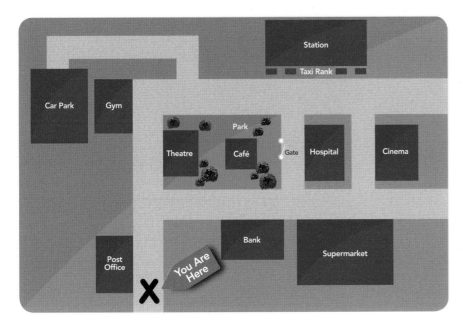

1 The bank is _____ the supermarket.

2 The taxi rank is _____ the station.

3 There's a car park _____ the gym.

4 There's a café _____ of the park.

5 There's a bank _____ the park.

7 Look at the map again and use it to complete this conversation about directions. Put one word in each gap.

A: ¹_____ me. Is ²_____ a café near here?

B: Sure, ³_____ past the post office and ⁴_____ right. ⁵_____ the first left and go ⁶_____ ____. Opposite the ⁷_____ there's a gate to the park and there's a good café in the centre of the park.

A: Great. ⁸_____ for your ⁹_____.

B: You're ¹⁰_____.

8 Match each phrase 1–6 with the most suitable response (a–f).

1 Do you have it in brown?   a It's square.

2 Is the juice in bottles or cans?   b It comes in small bottles.

3 It's too big.   c It comes in small, medium or large.

4 What shape is it?   d Sorry, we don't have any other colours in stock.

5 Does it come in any other sizes? e Plastic and glass.

6 What's it made of?   f You could try it in a smaller size.

9 Underline the word that has different word stress.

1 Oo   headache health shoulder backache

2 oO   problem discuss forget donate

3 oOo   important instruction equipment overtime

4 Ooo   exercise dangerous survival difficult

10 Match the words to what they describe.

1 juice / coffee / water   a shape

2 plane / ferry / car   b accommodation

3 apple / orange / banana   c drinks

4 oval / rectangular / triangular   d fruit

5 villa / motel / camping   e transport

9

A much / many, a lot of / lots of
B have got, need / need to
C Communication strategies Reacting to news
D Interaction On the move

Favourite places

much / many, a lot of / lots of

Reading: Discover Coimbra

1 Work in pairs. Discuss these questions.

1 What makes a city a great place to live in? Look at the list below. Is there anything you want to add?

	A: _____	B: _____
Architecture		
Climate		
Culture (music, theatre, films, museums, etc.)		
Eating out		
History		
Nightlife		
Personal safety		
Public transport		
Other?		

2 Work alone first. In column A, write the name of a city you like. Give each item in the list from 1 to 5 stars. Then tell your partner about your favourite city.

3 With your partner, choose another city that you both like. Write its name in column B. How many stars do you want to give each item in the list?

2 Read this article from an online travel guide about Coimbra, a city in Portugal. Do you want to go there for a holiday? Why?/Why not?

3 Answer these questions.

1 Why do some people call Coimbra 'the City of Students'?

2 Why can May or October be a good time to go to Coimbra?

3 Why is the city less lively during the summer?

4 Why can Coimbra be interesting for both young and older people?

Discover Coimbra

Coimbra is a very old city on the River Mondego between Porto and Lisbon in central Portugal. There is a lot of history in Coimbra, and there are a lot of beautiful old buildings.

But it is also a lively and exciting place. Some people call it 'the City of Students' because there are a lot of international students. The University of Coimbra, one of the oldest in Europe, is really the heart of the city. The students organize a lot of street parties which everyone finds interesting. For example, in October there is a party to welcome the new students, and then there is another one in May which lasts about a week.

So if you like dancing and partying, that is a very good time to go. But if you want a quiet holiday, go during the university summer holidays because there isn't much activity in Coimbra then.

Coimbra has something for everyone: history, culture, nightlife and great food. And there is lots of sunshine, too!

If you are a music-lover, it is also a great place to enjoy or discover the *fado*, a typically Portuguese style of music.

Grammar: *much / many, a lot of / lots of*

4 Read the text again and complete the examples in the table below.

> **much / many, a lot of / lots of**
>
> **+** There are ¹___ ___ ___ beautiful old buildings.
> And ²___ ___ ___ of sunshine, too!
>
> **–** There isn't ³___ activity in Coimbra then.
> There aren't **many** students in summer.
> There aren't **a lot of** tourists in winter.
>
> **?** Are there **many** restaurants? / Are there **a lot of** restaurants?
> Is there **much** noise at night? / Is there **a lot of** noise at night?
>
> **1** We use *many / a lot of / lots of* with countable (plural) nouns.
> **2** We use *much / a lot of / lots of* with uncountable (singular) nouns.
> **3** We can use *many / a lot of / lots of* in both + and – sentences (but *many* is quite formal in + sentences).
> **4** We don't use *much* in + sentences.
>
> >> For more information on *much / many, a lot of / lots of*, see page 156.

Speaking: My places

6 Work on your own. How many sentences can you make about the area where you live? Start with these words:

> In my area, there's a lot of …
> There are a lot of …
> There isn't much …
> There aren't many …

7 Work in pairs. Take it in turns to tell each other about the area where you live. Then ask each other some questions to get more information.

> Are there any restaurants in your area?
> Are there many …?
> Are there a lot of …?
> Is there much …?

8 Do you want to stay in your area or move to your partner's (or another) area? Why? Prepare to tell the group.

5 Read these postings from the Lifestyle Travel Forum on the internet. Choose the correct option in *italics*.

bluekiwi 29 April 16:55 Posts: 23	Hi fellow travellers! We are from New Zealand and we don't know much about Europe. We want to spend one week in Portugal in July. Can anyone tell us the cost of transport and accommodation there? Are there ¹*many / much* trains and buses to travel around? And what about eating out? Do we need ²*many / a lot of* money? Kiwipedia says there isn't ³*many / much* nightlife in Coimbra. Is that true? Thank you in advance for your help and advice!!! View profile Send message Report problem
startrek64 To: bluekiwi 1 May 20:46 Posts: 175	Hello, July is a very good time to visit Portugal if you like hot weather. Of course there are ⁴*lots of / a lot* tourists then, so make sure you book a room early. You have luxury hotels, of course, but also ⁵*lots of / much* cheap accommodation. Last year I paid €50 per night for a double room with a beautiful view. About the nightlife, I don't agree. It's true there aren't ⁶*a lot / many* students in July, but there are ⁷*a lot / lots* of concerts and also cafés with terraces where you can just sit and have a drink. And you can mix with the local people – they are very nice and they always have ⁸*much / a lot of* time for their guests. Enjoy yourself! This answer is the opinion of a Lifestyle Travel Forum member and not of Lifestyle Travel Forum LLC. Was this answer helpful? Yes No View profile Send message Report problem
NoMercy To: bluekiwi 2 May 00:25 Posts: 1,243	In my opinion, you ask ⁹*a lot of / much* stupid questions. Just google 'Coimbra' or 'Portugal', and you get all the answers. Or if you want, I can recommend one or two guidebooks – there are ¹⁰*lots of / many* them at Amazon.com. This answer is the opinion of a Lifestyle Travel Forum member and not of Lifestyle Travel Forum LLC. Was this answer helpful? Yes No View profile Send message Report problem

TALKING POINT   Where is life better, in a small town or in a big city? Why?

Word focus: Home sweet home

1 Work in pairs. Discuss these questions.

1 What is your favourite room in your house or flat? Why?

2 In which rooms do we usually find these things: a cooker, a bed, a TV, a shower, a desk?

3 How many other things can you name for each room?

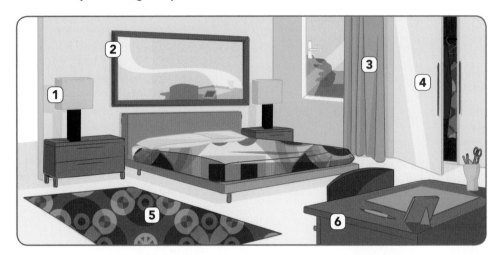

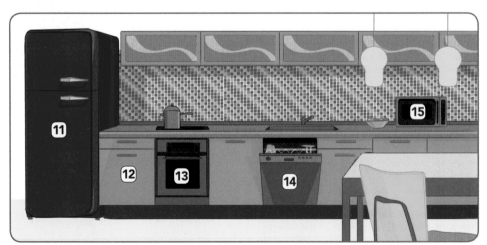

2 Find these things in the kitchen, living room and bedroom. Write a number in each space.

__ armchair	__ cooker	__ cupboard	__ curtains
__ desk	__ dishwasher	__ fridge	__ lamp
__ microwave	__ mirror	__ plant	__ rug
__ shelves	__ sofa	__ wardrobe	

3 Imagine that you move into a new house and you have nothing. Which three things from the list above do you want first? Why?

Listening: What's your favourite room?

4 ◁)) **2.1** Listen to four conversations. In which room is each conversation taking place?

5 ◁)) Listen again. Are these statements true (T) or false (F)?

1 Renata lives alone.

2 The curtains in Nedim's room are beautiful.

3 Jack spends a lot of time in the garage.

4 Meiying doesn't need to buy a dishwasher.

Grammar: *have got, need / need to*

6 ◁)) Listen to Conversations 1 and 2 on Track 2.1 again and complete the sentences in the table.

have got
I can see ¹___'__ ____ lots of CDs. This is a nice room, Nedim. And ²___'__ ____ a terrace!
We can use *have got* when we talk about possession and when we describe things or people. **+** You**'ve got** an interesting sofa. (= You **have** an interesting sofa.) **–** They **haven't got** a garage. (= They **don't have** a garage.) **?** **Has** your room **got** a nice view? (= **Does** your room **have** a nice view?)
>> For more information on *have got*, see page 145.

7 ◁)) Listen to Conversation 3 on Track 2.01 again and complete the sentences in the table.

need / need to
Well, we've got two cars. ³___ ____ ___ look after them. ⁴__ ____ ____ some help?
If you **need to do something**, you have to do it because it is necessary. If you **need something**, you want to have it; it is necessary for you to have it.

8 Test your memory. Who says these things, Renata, Nedim, Jack or Meiying?

1 I've got all the things I need.

2 I don't need curtains. I don't like them.

3 It's very old. I need to buy a new one.

4 We need a very big fridge because we are a big family.

5 In this room I've got all the peace and quiet I need.

9 Work in pairs. Take it in turns to describe a room that you know well (e.g. your office, your study, etc.). Don't say which room it is – your partner has to guess.

> It's got …
> I've got a lot of …
> I need to …

Speaking: The ideal office

10 Work in pairs. Plan your 'dream office'. Discuss the following points.

- Where is it? In the city centre? In a quiet part of town? Why?

  > Our office is in … because …

- What has it got?

  > It's got a large …
  > It's got some …
  > It's got a lot of …
  > There aren't any … because …

- What else do you need? Why?

Draw a large plan of your dream office and prepare a mini presentation.

Writing: Expecting a guest

11 A friend needs a place to stay when you are away next month. They can stay at your place. Write an email to give them some information about the following.

- the area where you live

- your house / flat

- the room where they can stay

- anything else you think they need to know.

TALKING POINT What's most important for you in a house or flat?

Listening: What's your news?

1 Discuss these questions with a partner.

1 What do you talk about during breaks at work / at college?

2 What are your favourite conversation topics? Which topics do you dislike most?

2 🔊 2.2 Listen to five conversations and decide if they are about good news, bad news, or a mix of good and bad news.

	Good news	Bad news	Good and bad news
Conversation 1			
Conversation 2			
Conversation 3			
Conversation 4			
Conversation 5			

3 🔊 Before you listen to Conversation 1 on Track 2.2 again, try to put the lines in the correct order. Then listen and check.

- ☐ Wow! A weekend in Paris! That's wonderful. You're a lucky man.
- ☐ What? Why not?
- ☐ The bad news is, I can't go.
- ☒ *1* Hi Liz! How are you?
- ☐ That's a shame. Can't you go next weekend?
- ☐ I'm alright. You know what? My wife wants to go to Paris this weekend.
- ☒ *9* I'm afraid not. It's my mother's birthday next weekend.
- ☐ I have to be at a trade show in Frankfurt from Friday afternoon till Monday morning.
- ☐ Fine, thanks. And you?

4 🔊 To react to news, we often use expressions with 'That's ...'. Listen to Conversations 2–5 on Track 2.2 again and complete the examples in the table opposite with the phrases from the box.

> That's too bad. That's cool. That's great.
> That's interesting. That's nice. That's terrible!

Reacting to news

Conversation 2

A: My office is very big and it's got a beautiful view.

B: ¹_____ Can you see the river and the old town?

A: Yes, I can. And another thing: there are only two other people in this large office.

B: ²_____ Are they nice?

Conversation 3

A: I've got a lot of books about Turkey, as you can see.

B: Mm. ³_____ Do you want to go on holiday there?

A: And I know Antalya. I've got some friends there.

B: ⁴_____ Do they know about your plans?

Conversation 4

A: It's my boss. He's always so rude to me!

B: ⁵_____ What do you want to do?

Conversation 5

A: I don't like our new cafeteria.

B: Really? ⁶_____ What's the problem with it?

> ⚠️ As the examples above show, very often we not only react to news, but we also ask a follow-up question to show interest in the conversation.

5 Look at exercises 3 and 4. Which three expressions with 'That's ...' do we use to react to bad news only?

Speaking: Showing interest

6 Work in pairs. Student A chooses the first conversation starter; Student B reacts and asks a follow-up question; Student A responds.

Then Student A and Student B change roles. Student B chooses the second conversation starter, etc.

Conversation starters

1 I want to go to Japan this summer.

2 There are a lot of nice restaurants in my area.

3 I've got a big problem with my holiday plans.

4 I can't go anywhere this weekend.

5 There aren't any supermarkets in my area.

6 I want to learn Chinese.

> *A: I want to go to Japan this summer.*
> *B: That's great! How long do you want to stay?*

7 Now have more mini conversations with your partner using conversation starters that are true *for you*.

Reminder

Grammar reference
pages 156 and 145

We use *much / a lot of / lots of* with uncountable nouns.
*They don't need **a lot of** time.*
We use *many / a lot of / lots of* with plural nouns.
*She's got **lots of** friends in Japan.*
We don't usually use *much / many* in positive sentences.

We use *have got* to talk about possessions and to describe things or people.
*You**'ve got** an interesting sofa.*
We use *need to* when you have to do something because it's necessary.
*We **need** a big fridge.*
*Meiying **doesn't need to** buy a dishwasher.*

Reading: Changing location

1 Work in pairs. Discuss this question.
When you choose a place for after-school or after-work activities, how important is the location of the place to you? Why?

2 Read this report about a school. How many problems has the school got?

The School of Modern Languages of Redhill University is an excellent place to study. There are language classes during the day for the university students, and in the evening for the general public. The school is very successful, and there are a lot of students from other places near Redhill. In summer, international students also enjoy all the beautiful places of interest near the school.

But there are some problems. The school building is very small – there are only 15 rooms and they need 25, maybe more next year. The rooms are on four different floors, and nobody likes that. The university students are happy because the school is in the centre next to the other departments, but a lot of evening students from other places complain that it is very difficult to find a parking place. Parking is also a problem for staff. It takes 20 minutes to walk to the metro station and 10 minutes to a bus stop, and there is only one bus every hour. The school is in a very expensive part of town, where flats and houses cost a lot of money, so teachers live in the suburbs, sometimes quite far away from the school.

That's why the school now wants to move to a different location.

3 Find the words in the report that mean the same as these words and phrases.
1 very, very good
2 doing very well
3 the different levels in a building
4 to say that you are not happy about something
5 apartments
6 areas away from the centre of a city

Listening: Long Park (Site #1)

4))) **2.3** Listen to two of the school directors talking about a building in Long Park and make notes to complete the card below.

Long Park (Site #1)

Distance from city centre:	_____ km
Transport:	Trains: _____ Buses: _____
Number of rooms:	_____
Number of parking places:	_____
Flats and houses:	_____
Other useful information:	_____ _____

Speaking: Barbridge (Site #2) and Peakside (Site #3)

5 Work in pairs. Ask and answer questions about two other sites to complete your cards. Student A: Turn to File 15, page 111. Student B: Turn to File 42, page 118.

6 Work in pairs. Compare your notes about Long Park, Barbridge and Peakside. Choose the best location for the school. Which site do you choose? Why?

7))) **2.4** Listen to Mina Nasir, one of the school's directors, talking about the site that they choose for the school. Do you agree with the directors' choice?

10

A Past simple *be*
B *too small / not big enough*
C **Communication strategies** Telephoning
D **Interaction** Customers' expectations

finding solutions

Reading: The worst hotel in the world?

1 Discuss this question.

You plan to stay at a new hotel. What do you want to know about it?

2 Read a travel writer's review of a hotel for young people. Does she answer any of your questions in exercise 1?

3 Answer these questions.

1 Why are KesselsKramer's advertisements clever?

2 Were the advertisements right about the staff?

3 What was wrong with the room?

4 Why don't the guests complain very often?

4 Discuss this question.

Do you want to stay at the Hans Brinker Hotel? Why?/Why not?

Staying at 'the worst hotel in the world'

'No swimming pool, no tennis court, no car park, no mini bar, no room service.' The Hans Brinker Hotel in Amsterdam is 'the worst hotel in the world', said KesselsKramer, a Dutch marketing agency, in their advertisements. The idea was: 'Say your hotel is very bad, so your guests cannot be disappointed.'

But was it really a terrible hotel? I wanted to know, so last year I was at the Hans Brinker for one night. Some of the advertisements say that the staff are rude and unfriendly. But in my opinion the guys at the check-in desk weren't bad.

Now, what about the rooms? OK, my room was small and there were already five people in it, so it was hot. But the advertisements were right: there is 'eco-friendly air conditioning in every room', – a window! Then, there wasn't a chair in the room. There was just a photo of a chair on the wall. Very funny! There was a shower … but no hot water. But my bed was clean and comfortable.

So ... was that really the worst hotel in the world? I wasn't sure. But the advertisements were very clever: today, the Hans Brinker is a big success. It has guests from all over the world, and the guests hardly ever complain.

Grammar: Past simple *be*

5 Read the article again and <u>underline</u> all the examples of the verb *be* in the past. Then, complete the table below.

Past simple *be*

The past simple of *be* has two forms: [1]_____ and [2]_____.

+	–
I [3]_____	I was not ([4]_____)
You / We / They [5]_____	You / We / They were not ([6]_____)
He / She / It [7]_____	He / She / It [8]_____ (wasn't)

?	
[9]_____ I / he / she / it?	
[10]_____ you / we / they?	

Short answers	
Were you late?	**Yes, I was. / No, I wasn't.**
	Yes, we were. / No, we weren't.

>> For more information on the past simple *be*, see page 148.

6 Complete the conversation with *was* or *were*.

A: So, how [1]_____ your stay at the Royal Hotel?

B: Well, the people [2]_____ very nice, and the facilities [3]_____ very good. I really liked their business centre. And the swimming pool [4]_____ great, too. So I can't complain. But ...

A: [5]_____ there a problem?

B: Yes, there [6]_____ . I couldn't use the gym!

A: Really? Why not?

B: Because of the strange opening hours. It [7]_____ open from ten to four.

A: I can't believe it! That's when you [8]_____ at work.

B: Yes, I had a nine to five working day. So ... goodbye fitness!

7 Complete the sentences with *is, are, was, were* (+, –, or ?).

1 A: Excuse me. I need to talk to the manager. Where _____ he?
    B: I don't know, but he _____ here at ten o'clock.

2 Last year, we _____ at the Imperial. Our room _____ OK, but the food _____ very good.

3 Don't stay at the Astoria! The reviews say it _____ cheap, but the people _____ very rude.

4 I phoned you yesterday, but you _____ at work. Where _____ you?

5 A: You _____ in room 115. Here _____ your key.
    B: Thank you.

8))) 2.5 Listen and check your answers to exercise 7.

Speaking: Hotel experiences

9 Complete the questionnaire below with the correct past forms of *to be*.

HOW WAS YOUR STAY?

What _____ the name of the hotel?
_____

Where _____ it?   _____

When _____ you there?   _____

_____ you on holiday or
on business?   _____

_____ the staff polite?
Score: 0 1 2 3 4 5 6 7 8 9 10

_____ the room clean?
Score: 0 1 2 3 4 5 6 7 8 9 10

How _____ the bed?
Score: 0 1 2 3 4 5 6 7 8 9 10

How _____ the breakfast?
Score: 0 1 2 3 4 5 6 7 8 9 10

How _____ the facilities?
Score: 0 1 2 3 4 5 6 7 8 9 10

Overall score _____ / 50

10 Work in pairs. Student A: You speak first. Use the questionnaire above to interview Student B about a very bad hotel. Write B's answers and scores. Student B: Turn to File 43, page 119.

11 Student B: It's your turn to interview Student A about a very bad hotel. Write Student A's answers and scores in the questionnaire above. Student A: Turn to File 16, page 111.

12 Work in pairs. Look at your questionnaires. Which hotel is worse, yours or your partner's? Why?

TALKING POINT Think of a hotel where you stayed. What was good about it? What was not so good?

Word focus: Something is not right

1 Do you have problems with these things? How often? Tick (✓) the right boxes.

	Sometimes	Often	Never
your computer			
internet shopping			
public transport in your town			
your office cafeteria			
banks and other services in your town			

2 Work in pairs. Discuss your answers to exercise 1.

3 Match the sentences (1–8) to the pictures (A–H).

1 My desk is *not big enough*.

2 *There's something wrong with* my mobile.

3 *I've got a problem with* my printer.

4 A page is *missing*.

5 All trains are *delayed*.

6 The photocopier *doesn't work*.

7 My computer is *too slow*.

8 That chair is *broken*.

4 Complete the sentences with a word or phrase in *italics* from exercise 3.

1 I can't set my new burglar alarm because the instructions are _____ .

2 We don't like the cafeteria because it's _____ . There are only six tables for 30 people.

3 _____ my Skype connection. I can see you, but I can't hear you!

4 Oh no! The lift _____ and my office is on the ninth floor.

5 His plane was _____ because of the bad weather.

6 Sorry, you can't use that CD player. It's _____ .

Grammar: *too* + adjective / *not* + adjective + *enough*

5 Look at exercise 3 again and answer these questions.

1 Which phrase in *italics* means the same as *too small*?

2 Which phrase in *italics* means the same as *not fast enough*?

6 Complete the rules with the words from the box.

before   complain   happy   wrong

1 We use *too* + adjective and *not* + adjective + *enough* to talk about things and situations that we are not ¹_____ with, when we want to ²_____ or criticize.

2 With *not / enough*, the adjective goes ³_____ *enough*. So ~~The water was not enough warm~~ is ⁴_____ . We say *The water was **not** warm **enough**.*

7 Work in pairs. What is the problem in each illustration?

Reading: That's not good enough!

8 Discuss these questions.

1 What things do people usually buy on the internet?

2 What problems do people sometimes have with internet shopping?

9 Read the post from a shoppers' blog. In pairs, complete the text with the phrases from the box.

not big enough   too big   too busy   too short   too small

I have no complaints about VB Crooks & Co's products. We order a lot of clothes from them and we are never disappointed. But I want to complain about their customer service.

My husband is ¹_____ to go shopping, so I often buy clothes for him online. He is a big man and he always takes size XXL for everything. Because the new jeans in the online catalogue were a good price, I ordered three pairs in three different colours.

It says XXL on them but they are too small and the legs are ²_____. I call customer service to tell them about the problem. A rude man answers the phone and says: 'You ordered XXL, that's what you got. XXL means extra extra large.' So I answer: 'I'm not stupid! Of course I know what XXL means. And I also know that the jeans are ³_____ and the legs are not long enough.' Then the guy says: 'Maybe your husband is ⁴_____ then.' Can you believe it?

ELZA, VANCOUVER

> Notice the difference:
> to complain (verb)   a complaint (noun)
> *She wants to **complain** about bad service.*
> *She wants to make a **complaint** about bad service.*

Listening: What's the problem?

10 🎵 **2.6** Listen to five phone calls of people complaining about products. Write the number of the call after the product.

a air conditioning   ___

b digital camera   ___

c jeans   ___

d orange juice   ___

e radio   ___

11 🎵 Listen again. What is the problem with the product in each telephone call?

1 _____

2 _____

3 _____

4 _____

5 _____

Speaking: Nothing is perfect

12 Work in groups. Here are four things that office workers and students often complain about. Think of four more to add to the list.

- there is not enough light
- there is too much noise
- the chairs are not comfortable enough
- the desks are too small
- _____
- _____
- _____
- _____

13 In your groups, decide together which are the three biggest problems. Then, think of possible solutions.

14 Think about a room where you spend a lot of time. Tell each other what you like / don't like about it.

> *My office is big enough for me, but my computer is too old.*
> *My living room is too dark, there aren't enough windows.*

TALKING POINT

Do you find it easy or difficult to complain about things? Why?

Listening: Are you really sorry?

1 Discuss this question.

Why do people phone Customer Service?

2))) **2.7** Listen to two phone conversations. Which one do you prefer? Why?

3 In what order does the person from Customer Service in Conversation 2 do these things?

a apologize again / thank customer ___

b suggest a solution ___

c say 'goodbye' ___

d introduce himself / herself / greet someone ___

e apologize ___

4))) Listen to Conversation 2 on Track 2.7 again and complete these sentences.

Customer Service		Customer	
Introduction: **Greeting:**	CBA Customer Service. ^{1}_____ morning.		
		Greeting: **Introduction:** **Explain problem:**	Hello. Ana Baranowska ^{2}_____. It's ^{3}_____ my DVD player. I have a problem with it.
Apologize: **Suggest a solution:**	Oh, I'm very ^{4}_____ to hear that. We ^{5}_____ give you your money back.		
		Say 'thank you':	Thanks for your ^{6}_____.
Apologize again: **Thank customer:** **Say 'goodbye':**	Once again, sorry ^{7}_____ this problem. And thank you for ^{8}_____. Goodbye.		
		Say 'goodbye':	Goodbye.

5))) **2.8** Listen and choose the best response (a, b or c) for each of these sentences.

1 Hello. This is Luk Wai Man. _____

2 How can I help you? _____

3 Can I speak to Jan Peters, please? _____

4 There's something wrong with my new TV. _____

5 Can you give me some more information? _____

6 Can you say that again, please? _____

7 Thanks for your help. _____

6 Look at the sentences in exercise 5. Write 'C' if it is the customer speaking or 'CS' if it is Customer Service.

1 ___ 2 ___ 3 ___ 4 ___ 5 ___ 6 ___ 7 ___

Speaking: Getting the message right

7 Work in pairs. Student A: Turn to File 17, page 112. Student B: Turn to File 45, page 119.

8 Work in pairs. Look at exercise 4. Student A is the customer, Student B is from Customer Service. Roleplay the telephone conversation.

- Use your own names.

- Think of a different product.

- Offer a different solution.

Then swap roles.

Reminder

Grammar reference page 148

When we talk about problems, we can use sentences like these:
My radio is broken.
I have a problem with it.
It doesn't work.
It's too small. / It isn't big enough.

We can say 'sorry' by apologizing like this:
Oh, I'm sorry to hear that.
I'm very sorry about that.

Listening: How can I help you?

1 Discuss these questions.

1 Do you go to fitness classes? Why?/Why not?

2 What do customers expect from a fitness club?

2 Skyline is a company with 12 fitness centres in different towns. Now it has a new centre in your town, too. Look at the advertisement. What do you like about the centre?

3))) 2.9 Some Skyline customers are very unhappy and complain to Mr Bagley, the centre manager. Listen and number the complaints in the order in which you hear them.

a The groups are too large. ___

b The showers aren't clean. ___

c The membership system is not flexible enough. ___

d The instructor is often late. ___

e There aren't enough exercise machines for everyone. ___

New in your town: **Skyline** Fitness Centre
New Cymex® body-building machines to make your body strong and beautiful

Class size: maximum 10 people per group
Location: large room in quiet part of town
Facilities: showers / sauna / salad bar
Come and meet Joe Reno, your personal fitness instructor
Membership: only £80 per month (= 3 one-hour classes per week)
Centre Manager: Sam Bagley / **Tel**: (045) 382 4791
Email: sam.bagley@skyline.com

Writing: Could we have a meeting?

4 Work in pairs. Sam Bagley writes an email to the general manager, Alex Cruse. Put the lines of the email in the correct order (1–9).

___ But there are also customers who are disappointed with our facilities.

___ Our new fitness centre is a success and we have a lot of happy customers.

___ Could we have a meeting next week to discuss these complaints?

_1_ Dear Mr Cruse,

___ Could you let me know as soon as possible when you are free.

_9_ Sam Bagley

___ Those customers often come to me with their complaints.

___ With best wishes,

___ We also need to discuss possible solutions to these problems.

Speaking: Finding solutions

5 Work in pairs. Think of different solutions to the problems in exercise 3. Agree on the best solution to each problem.

A: *The groups are too large. I think the maximum is ten people.*
B: *That's right. Maybe we could have more groups, so we don't lose money.*
A: *What about a bigger room?*

6 Sam Bagley has a meeting with Alex Cruse. Work in new pairs. Student A: Turn to File 18, page 112. Student B: Turn to File 44, page 119.

Turning points

Past simple 1

Reading: Head teacher

1 Who was your favourite teacher at school?

2 Read about Babar Ali and answer the questions.

1 Find words in *italics* with a similar meaning to these sentences.

  1 The teacher in charge of a school

  2 Things you study at school, for example Maths and English

  3 Work that you do in the home, for example cleaning

  4 Special clothes people wear to look the same

  5 Teaching or learning at school or college

  6 A time when an important change starts to happen

2 Look at the article and answer the questions.

  1 Babar Ali was born in

  a) India   b) China

  2 His friends couldn't go to school because they were

  a) rich   b) poor

  3 Babar Ali helped his friends to

  a) read and write   b) play and sing

  4 He wanted to help other poor children so he started a

  a) business   b) school

  5 The children that go to Babar Ali's school

  a) pay money   b) don't pay money

3 Work in pairs and answer the questions.

  1 What subjects does Babar Ali learn and teach?

  2 What other subjects do you know?

Babar Ali

B ABAR ALI was born in West Bengal, in India. Seven years ago, he started his own school.

Every morning, Babar Ali got up and helped with the *housework*. Then he travelled 10 km to school. He was a good student and listened to his teachers.

Babar Ali's friends wanted to learn but they couldn't go to school. Their parents didn't have enough money to pay for their travel, books and *uniform*. That was the *turning point* for Babar Ali. He decided to help his friends. Every day he arrived home from school at 4 p.m. He talked to them about the things he studied at school and he showed them how to read and write.

That decision changed Babar Ali's life. More and more children asked Babar Ali to teach them. He decided to help poor children to have an *education*. When he was nine years old, he started a school in his parents' garden. He didn't ask for money, he wanted the school to be free for all children. His students learned the same *subjects* that Babar Ali learned at his school, like Science and Maths.

Now he is sixteen and he is *head teacher* of his own school. The school has 800 students and ten teachers. All the teachers at Babar Ali's school are young and they are also students at school or college.

Grammar: Past simple 1

3 Look at the article again and <u>underline</u> the regular past simple verbs.

4 Write the past simple form of these verbs. Use the article to help you.

1 start _____ 6 listen _____
2 help _____ 7 want _____
3 show _____ 8 arrive _____
4 talk _____ 9 decide _____
5 learn _____ 10 ask _____

5 Look at the information about regular past simple verbs and complete the rules.

> **Past simple 1: Regular verbs**
>
> *Babar Ali's friends **wanted** to learn.*
> *He **arrived** home at 4 p.m.*
> *He **studied** at school.*
>
> With regular past simple verbs we …
> 1 add ¹_____ to the base form of the verb
> 2 add ²_____ when the base form ends in -e
> 3 change y to ³_____ when the base form ends in -y
>
> **Negative**
>
> *He **didn't ask** for money.*
> Use ⁴_____ (*did not*) + the base form of the verb.
>
> >> For more information on the past simple, see pages 148–149.

6 Complete the information with the past form of the verbs.

Stephanie
I ¹_____ (not like) school. I ²_____ (enjoy) Science and Music but I ³_____ (hate) Sports. My friends and I ⁴_____ (talk) in the lessons and my teacher often ⁵_____ (shout) at us. I ⁶_____ (not listen) to anything my teachers said. I ⁷_____ (want) to be a rock star.

Malik
I ¹_____ (love) school. My favourite lesson was Maths but I ²_____ (not enjoy) History I ³_____ (learn) a lot from my teachers. I ⁴_____ (work) hard and I ⁵_____ (pass) all my exams. A lot of universities ⁶_____ (offer) me a place so I ⁷_____ (decide) to go to college.

7 What happened next? Who do you think did these things?

travelled to Australia   worked in a bank
learned Japanese   opened a restaurant

8))) 2.10 Listen to Stephanie and Malik talk about what they did next. Were you right? What was the turning point in their lives?

Word focus: Talking about the past

9 Put these time phrases in order closest to now. Start with the phrases close to now.

___ two years ago   ___ last night
___ yesterday morning   ___ the week before last
___ last week   ___ five years ago
___ the day before yesterday ___ last month

10 Work in pairs. Tell your partner about these things.
- something you watched on TV last night
- somewhere you visited last year
- something funny that happened last week

Speaking: Life events

11 Work in pairs. Look at the pictures and symbols. What life events do they show? Think of more life events. What symbols can you use for them?

12 Look at the life events below. Write three events on a time line in the order that they happened in your life. Tell your partner about the events and when they happened.

As a child	As an adult
The first house you lived in	When you learned to drive
A place you visited on holiday	Your first job
Favourite subjects at school	Places you travelled to
Born ◄─────────────────► Now	

TALKING POINT

What did you want to be when you were at school? Did your ideas change? Why?

Listening: Can you remember?

1 How do you remember important events in your life? Do you write in a diary, keep photographs or do something else?

2 Do you have a good memory? Tick (✓) the things that are easy for you to remember and put a cross (✗) next to the things that are difficult to remember.

1 Names ☐

Who is she?

2 Numbers ☐

3 Objects ☐

4 Actions ☐

5 Faces ☐

3))) **2.11** What is in the photos? Listen and match the photos to the speakers. Did any of the information surprise you?

A

B

4 Answer these questions.

Speaker 1

1 How many things did the writer lose?

2 Where did the writer find the things?

Speaker 2

3 Where did he meet the scientist?

4 What nationality were the scientists who did the test?

5))) Put the verbs in brackets into the past tense. Listen to Speaker 1 on Track 2.11 again to check.

Speaker 1

Did you lose anything today? Don't worry, you're not alone. We all lose things. These are some of the things that I ¹_____ (lose) last month: keys, my phone, a bag, my wallet, an important document and my passport. I ²_____ (find) them all again. The document ³_____ (be) in my office and the rest were at home. I ⁴_____ (read) a report that ⁵_____ (say) that people ⁶_____ (spend) an hour a day looking for things. Imagine what you could do with an extra seven hours a week!

6 What could you do with an extra seven hours a week?

Grammar: Past simple 2

7 Write the past simple form of these irregular verbs that Speakers 1 and 2 used. Look at the audio script in the back of the book to check.

1 lose _____
2 find _____
3 read _____
4 say _____
5 spend _____
6 go _____
7 meet _____
8 tell _____
9 do _____
10 think _____
11 give _____
12 get _____

8 Look at the examples and complete the rules.

Past simple 2: questions	
Did you lose anything?	*Yes, I did. /No, I didn't.*
Where did she meet the scientist?	*She met him at a party.*
To make past simple questions use _____ + the base form of the verb.	

>> For more information on past simple questions, see page 148.

9 Complete the dialogue with the correct form of the verbs.

Cara: I ¹_____ (go) on a training course last week.

Luke: Really? ²_____ you _____ (have) a good time?

Cara: No. I ³_____ (lose) my bag and my car keys at the hotel.

Luke: What ⁴_____ you _____ (do)?

Cara: I ⁵_____ (tell) the hotel manager.

Luke: ⁶_____ he _____ (find) your bag?

Cara: Yes, he ⁷_____ (do). But he ⁸_____ _____ (not find) my car keys.

Luke: That's terrible. How ⁹_____ you _____ (get) home?

Cara: I got a train and my friend ¹⁰_____ (meet) me at the station.

Luke: I'm glad you ¹¹_____ (get) home OK.

Speaking: How do you learn?

10 Do you prefer to learn things by seeing, hearing or doing? Ask your partner the questions in the quiz.

11 Find out what type of learner your partner is. Did they choose mostly a, b or c? Turn to File 55, page 123. Tell your partner the type of learner they are and listen to what they say about you. Do you agree with the results?

What type of learner are you?

1 How did you learn a new word in the last lesson?

a I wrote the word down.

b I repeated the word so that I knew how to say it.

c I thought of a picture of the word.

2 When you relaxed last weekend what did you do?

a I played sport or went for a walk.

b I listened to music.

c I read a book, watched TV or went to the cinema.

3 The last time you learned a new skill what did you do?

a I wanted to try it myself.

b I listened to instructions and talked about it.

c I watched someone show me how to do it.

4 The last time you had a new pin number how did you learn it?

a I wrote the number down.

b I said the number.

c I saw the numbers in my mind.

TALKING POINT   Work in pairs or small groups. Think of ways to learn the irregular verbs from today's lesson.

Listening: An interview

1 What was the last interview you had? What did you do to prepare?

2)) **2.12** Langford Industries are interviewing Robert and Duncan for a new job. Listen to both interviews. Is Robert or Duncan's interview best? Why?

3)) Listen again to Duncan's interview on Track 2.12 again and answer the questions.

1 What are qualifications?

   a information about where you worked in the past

   b information about your education and training

2 What are Duncan's qualifications?

4)) Listen to Duncan again and complete the questions.

1 _____ questions	2 _____ questions
1 _____ you have a good journey here?	6 What did you _____ after that?
2 Do you _____ a drink?	7 What do you _____ about our company.
3 Did you _____ for a degree?	8 What department did you _____ in?
4 Do you _____ what Langford Industries does?	9 _____ training did you do?
5 Did you train staff in your _____ job?	10 What other qualifications do you _____ ?
	11 Why _____ you study finance management?
	12 _____ do you want to work for Langford Industries?

Speaking: Open and closed questions

5 English speakers often use open and closed questions. A closed question can be answered with *yes*, *no* or a short answer. An open question invites a longer answer. Write *open* and *closed* in the correct column in the table above.

6 Circle *Open* or *Closed* to answer the questions.

1 Which is useful to find out facts, figures and dates? *Open / Closed* questions.

2 Which is useful to find out opinions and explanations? *Open / Closed* questions.

7 Look at the information about Christine Howard in this letter and the notes about her. Write six questions for an interviewer to ask.

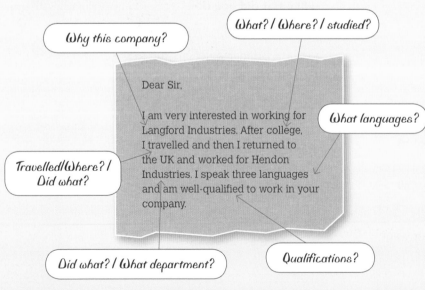

Why this company?

What? / Where? / studied?

Dear Sir,

I am very interested in working for Langford Industries. After college, I travelled and then I returned to the UK and worked for Hendon Industries. I speak three languages and am well-qualified to work in your company.

What languages?

Travelled/Where? / Did what?

Did what? / What department?

Qualifications?

Example: Where did you study?

8 Work in pairs. Think of some answers for Christine.

9 Roleplay the interview. Take turns to be Christine and the interviewer.

Reminder

Grammar reference
pages 148–149

We use the past simple to talk about finished actions and situations in the past.
He **studied** st school.
He **didn't ask** for money

We use *did/didn't* to form questions.
Did he **work** in Marketing?
Yes, he did. / No, he didn't.
Where did he **study**?
He studied in Milan.

Speaking: The best CV

1 Are these statements true or false? Compare your ideas with a partner. Turn to File 19, page 112 and check your answers.

1 A CV (Curriculum Vitae) is a document that has information about your education, qualifications and work experience.

2 Employers like CVs that are more than five pages long.

3 It's a good idea to check your CV regularly and write information about new qualifications and training.

4 It's a good idea to send a letter with your CV.

2 Look at part of a British CV below. Add these words to the headings.

Career   Curriculum Vitae   Education   Interests
Personal details   Skills

3 Ask and answer questions to complete the information about Jo Foyle's CV. Student A: Turn to File 21, page 113. Student B: Turn to File 46, page 120.

Example: What's Jo's telephone number?

4 What questions could you ask Jo at the interview?

5 Roleplay the interview. Take turns to ask and answer questions.

Jo

Writing: Write your CV

6 What are the differences between the CV on this page and how you write CVs in your country? What information do you include?

7 Write a CV to send to an employer. You can use information about you or write an ideal CV for your perfect job.

---

1 _____

2 _____

Sam Merton
Telephone: 055 03352
Mobile: 42913842
Email: MertonS@wfgmail.com

Sam

3 _____

| 2011 | MBA Insead Business School |
| 2005 | BA (Hons) Electronics, Edinburgh University |

4 _____

| 2007–2011 | Ventura Electronics, Australia |
| 2005–2007 | Arlington Construction, Canada |

5 _____

I can speak Russian, German and English.
I can write electronics and design computer programs.

6 _____

Photography, skiing and tennis.

12

A Present continuous
B Present continuous or present simple?
C Communication strategies What do you call it?
D **Interaction** Company presentation

Getting away

Present continuous

Listening: It's a mobile world

1 Work in pairs. Discuss these questions.

1 What do you do at the airport when you are waiting for a connecting flight or when there is a delay?

2 How could you use your mobile phone while you are waiting?

2 Sarita phones Alan, a colleague from Bluestar Travel Group. Put their conversation in the correct order.

☐ **A:** Well, I'm working on it right now. But I need some more information from Shin for the graphs. What is she doing? Could you phone her?

☐ **S:** Hi Alan! Where are you?

☐ **S:** Sorry to hear that. What about the report?

☐ **S:** Yes, of course. But I think she's sleeping. It's 2:30 a.m. in Seoul!

☐ **A:** Hi Sarita. I'm at the airport. I'm waiting for my flight. I think there's a delay.

3))) **2.13** Listen and check your answers.

4 Are these statements true (T) or false (F)? Correct the ones that are false.

1 Alan is waiting for his luggage.

2 Sarita is sleeping.

3 Shin isn't working.

4 Alan is writing the report.

5 Sarita is waiting for her flight.

6 Alan isn't having lunch.

Grammar: Present continuous

5 Look at the table below and complete the rules with the items from the box.

> be -ing now

Present continuous: (+ / – / ?)

+	I'm **working** on the report. She's **talking** to Alan. We**'re waiting** for our flight.
–	He **isn't sleeping**. They **aren't waiting** for a train.
?	**Are** Shin and Alan **working** on the same project? **Is** Alan **watching** a video?

	Yes, they are.
	No, he isn't.

We use the present continuous to talk about actions happening ¹_____ or around now. We make the present continuous with ²_____ and the ³_____ form of the main verb.

>> For more information on the present continuous, see page 146.

6 🔊 **2.14** Listen to Alan phoning Debra, his wife, from the airport. Number the sentences below in the order in which you hear them.

☐ There's a guy who's reading the papers.

☐ What's everyone doing?

☐ Some kids are playing computer games.

☐ She's looking for another seat.

☐ We're expecting a long delay.

☐ What's happening?

Word focus: have + noun

7 🔊 Listen to Track 2.14 again and complete these sentences.

1 Still waiting for my flight. I'm just _____ _____ _____ around the lounge.

2 Yeah. I think they're _____ _____ _____ time.

> ⚠ We can use *have* with many nouns.
> **have** *a walk* (= walk)   **have** *lunch* (= eat lunch)
> **have** *a drink* (= drink something)   **have** *a look* (= look)

8 Complete the sentences with the words from the box.

> break breakfast sandwich swim

1 When I'm on holiday by the sea, I want to have a _____ every day.

2 I don't feel well if I don't have _____ before going to work.

3 When I work on my computer, I try to have a short _____ every hour.

4 I usually have a _____ for lunch. If I eat a lot, I feel sleepy.

9 Work in pairs. Look at exercise 8. Discuss which sentences are true for you and correct the ones that aren't.

Speaking: Guess what I'm doing

10 Work in pairs. Take it in turns to mime actions and to guess what the actions are. Ask *yes* or *no* questions only. Student A: Turn to File 22, page 113. Student B: Turn to File 50, page 121.

> A: Are you going somewhere?
> B: No.
> A: Are you waiting for someone?
> B: No. Not exactly.
> A: Are you waiting for a train?

11 Work in pairs. Take it in turns to make true or false sentences about the photos on pages 74–75. Your partner has to repeat the sentence if it is true. You score one point if …

a your partner repeats a sentence which isn't true.

b your partner doesn't repeat a sentence which is true.

Writing: An email to a friend

12 You are waiting for your flight. Write an email to a friend. Include the following information:

- where you are and what you're doing
- why there's a delay
- what some of the other people are doing.

Remember to ask what your friend is doing.

> **TALKING POINT**   Think of some people you know in other countries. What are they doing at the moment?

Reading: Flying the skies

1 Work in pairs. Discuss this question.

What do you like/dislike about travelling by air? Why?

2 In pairs, check if you know the meaning of these words. Check with a dictionary or with your teacher if necessary.

airfares   to invest   an opportunity   to pay extra   a trend

3 Air travel is changing. Read the magazine article and find out how.

4 Answer these questions.

1 Why do people travel by air?

2 What are three big changes in air travel?

3 What is 'à la carte pricing'?

4 What are the good and bad points of 'à la carte pricing'?

5 How is business travel changing?

Flying the skies ....

As we all know, air travel offers everyone fantastic opportunities. Business people often fly to other parts of the world to visit partners and customers. Tourists discover other countries and cultures during their holidays or even just a long weekend. And of course people also travel by air for a lot of other reasons.

But air travel is changing, and it is changing in many different ways. Airfares are going up, and some traditional airlines are also introducing 'à la carte pricing'. This means that travellers can choose which extra services they want, but they have to pay for them. For example, they have to pay for every piece of luggage that they check in, and they have to pay extra for a window or an aisle seat or for in-flight drinks or food.

Another recent trend is that the number of business people who travel internationally is falling. Instead, companies are investing more in new forms of communication technology such as videoconferencing. And in some countries, more business people are now travelling economy rather than first or business class.

The way people book their flight is changing too: in many countries, most travellers are now booking online.

Grammar: Present continuous or present simple?

5 Look at the magazine article on page 76. Then answer these questions.

1 Which tense is used in the first paragraph?

2 Which tense is mostly used in the rest of the article?

6 Look at the table. Complete the examples with words from the article. Then complete the rules.

Present continuous or present simple?

Business people often ¹_____ *to other parts of the world to visit partners and customers.*

People ²_____ *by air for a lot of other reasons.*

Air travel ³_____ _____ *in many different ways.*

Most travellers ⁴_____ *now* _____ *online.*

We use the present ⁵_____ to talk about things that are always or usually true.

We use the present ⁶_____ to talk about actions happening now or around now. For example, we use it to talk about present trends.

>> For more information on the present continuous and present simple, see page 146.

---

7 Complete this text. Use the present simple or present continuous form of the verbs in brackets.

It's 10:30 a.m. in Vancouver and Alan Steiner ¹ *is waiting* (wait) for his connecting flight at Vancouver International Airport. Alan often ² *travels* (travel) on business because he is the sales manager of Blue Star Travel Group, a tourism and travel company with offices in eight different countries. He usually ³ _____ (enjoy) flying but this morning he ⁴ _____ (not / have) a very good time because his flight is delayed. Besides, he always ⁵ _____ (feel) bad when he ⁶ _____ (have to) write a report, and his boss needed the report yesterday! Back at head office in Denver, Sarita Chopra ⁷ _____ (expect) Alan's email. But Alan hasn't got all the data he needs. In fact, he ⁸ _____ (wait) for information from the Seoul office. But right now, he is worried about something more urgent: someone ⁹ _____ (sit) in his seat, so he can't do any work. That's why he ¹⁰ _____ (enquire) about the business lounge.

Word focus: Present trends

8 Look at the the article *Flying the skies* again and complete these two sentences.

1 Airfares _____ _____ _____.

2 The number of business people who travel internationally _____ _____.

9 Work in pairs. Complete the table about trends (↗ and ↘) with the verbs from the box.

decrease   go down   increase   rise

↗	↘
go up	3 _____
1	fall
2 _____	4 _____

! We can also say that something *isn't changing* (→).
To say <u>how</u> something is rising, falling, etc., we use **slightly**, **gradually**, **sharply**, etc.

Airfares are rising **slightly**. →

The number of visitors is going up **gradually**. ↗

Last year prices increased **sharply**. ↗

Speaking: What now?

10 Work in pairs. Discuss the present trends in travel and tourism in your country.

- the number of foreign visitors
- the number of people who travel by plane
- the number of people who spend their summer holiday abroad
- airfares
- the cost of hotel accommodation
- our currency's exchange rate with the dollar.

11 Work in pairs. Take it in turns to describe and identify some imaginary graphs about air travel trends. Student A: Turn to File 23, page 114. Student B: Turn to File 49, page 121.

12 Work in pairs or in small groups. Tell each other about:

a your job or your studies, what you normally do at work or at college, what your usual duties are.

b a project you are working on now; things you are doing these days which you don't normally do.

I work in marketing.
At the moment, I'm planning advertisements for a new product.

TALKING POINT   What are some of the trends in train and car travel in your country?

Listening: Do you know what I mean?

1 Discuss these questions with a partner.

1 When you speak your own language, what do you do when there is a word you don't know or a name you can't remember?

2 Do you do the same when you are having a conversation in English?

2))) **2.15** Listen to four conversations and number the things in the photos below in the order in which they are mentioned.

(A)

(B)

(C)

(D)

3))) Listen again and complete these sentences.

Asking	Responding
I need one of those little cars … erm … ¹_____ do you call them?	²_____ you ³_____ a baggage trolley?
There were dozens of people around … erm … you ⁴_____, the ⁵_____ that goes round and round with all the luggage.	Oh, I ⁶_____. You mean the carousel.

4 Match the words (1–6) with the explanations (a–f). Then check your answers.

1 baggage reclaim

2 excess luggage

3 a flight attendant

4 jet-lagged

5 a stopover

6 a cash machine

a the feeling of being very tired after a long journey by plane

b a machine in a public place from which you can get money with a bank card

c a place where a plane stops during a journey

d the place where you get your luggage after a flight

e bags that are very heavy so you have to pay extra to take them with you

f someone who looks after passengers on a plane

5 Complete the conversations with words and expressions from exercises 3 and 4.

1 A: There's something wrong with my seat belt. Could you call the … erm … the guy in the uniform for me?
B: Oh, you _____ the _____? Sure. Here he comes.

2 A: Excuse me. I'm looking for those machines for money … erm … _____ do you call them?
B: You mean a _____. They're all on the first floor.

3 A: It was a 16-hour flight. Now I don't know if it's day or night and I'm very tired.
B: You mean you are _____? I know, the same happens to me whenever I fly to Singapore.

4 A: I checked my suitcase at home. It's 26 kilograms. Do you think I'll have to pay … erm … more money. _____ do you call that?
B: Oh, you mean _____. Yes, I'm afraid so. The limit is 20 kilograms.

5 A: It was not a direct flight. First there was Istanbul. You know, we stopped there for half an hour …. What do you call that?
B: Do you mean there was a _____ in Istanbul?
A: Yeah, that's right. And then we flew to Tashkent.

6 A: We arrived on time, but then I couldn't find the place, you know, the place where you collect your luggage. What do you _____ it?
B: Do you _____ baggage reclaim? I know, it's a very long walk.

Speaking: I can't remember the word

6 Practise the conversations in exercise 5 with a partner.

7 Work in pairs. Choose a conversation from exercise 5. Change one thing (e.g. a number, a place name, etc.). Learn your conversation and then roleplay it to the group. Can they identify what you changed?

Reminder

Grammar reference page 146

We use the present simple to talk about regular activities and things that are always true.
*Alan **works** in Denver.*

We use the present continuous to talk about things that are happening now or around now, or to talk about present trends.
*Alan **is working** on his monthly report.*

Reading: Not only sea, sun and sand

1 Discuss these questions.

1 What do you think the words and phrases in the box mean?

> adventure tourism   ecotourism
> gastrotourism   medical tourism

2 Match the photos and the different types of tourism above.

3 What do you think are popular destinations for these holidays.

2 In pairs, check if you know the meaning of these words. Check with a dictionary or with your teacher if necessary.

> competitive   headquarters   to employ
> to introduce   to provide

3 Read the leaflet about a travel company. Which two types of holidays does it offer?

Blue Star Travel Group (BSTG) is an international travel company which started in 2002.

Its headquarters are in Denver, and it has offices in Delhi, Seoul and Ho Chi Minh City. It employs 85 people. BSTG provides quality services at competitive prices and specializes in adventure holidays for people who love nature and want to discover the true way of life of the local people. This year, BSTG is introducing new exciting destinations in Burma and Cambodia. It had almost 1,500 customers last year, and this number is rising gradually. Sales too are going up.

4 Put the words in the correct order to make questions about BSTG. Then ask a partner the questions.

1 the company / did / when / start / ?

2 are / headquarters / its / where / ?

3 employ / it / how many / does / people / ?

4 does / and services / it / what / provide / products / ?

5 any / it / this year / introducing / new products / is / ?

6 customers / the trends / are / in sales and / what / in the number of / ?

Listening: Company profile

5))) 2.16 Listen to an interview with Layla Ajram, CEO of Heritage Travel, and complete the fact file.

Heritage Travel Fact File

Started in:	1 _____
Headquarters:	2 _____
Offices:	3 _____ , Damascus, Amman, 4 _____
Products and services:	traditional 5 _____ and cultural holidays as well as 6 _____ .
New product:	à la carte holidays for 7 _____ and teachers of 8 _____ and Architecture.
Present trends in sales and number of customers:	9 _____

Speaking: Tell me about your company

6 Take it in turns to roleplay an interview for a business magazine.

1 Student A: You are the CEO of Aquila Tours, a successful travel company. Turn to File 24, page 114. Student B: You are the interviewer. Turn to File 48, page 121.

2 Student A: You are the interviewer. Turn to File 25, page 114. Student B: You are the CEO of Pegasus Holidays, a successful travel company. Turn to File 51, page 122.

7 Work in pairs. Imagine you win a free holiday with any of the four travel companies (Blue Star Travel Group, Heritage Travel, Aquila Tours, Pegasus Holidays). Which one do you choose? Why?

1 Complete this text. Use the present simple or present continuous form of the verbs in brackets.

Wellness Holidays is an Irish travel company which started in 2005 and which 1_____ (specialize) in medical tourism and in yoga and meditation holidays. Its headquarters are in Cork, and it 2_____ (have) offices in Vancouver, Wellington and Goa. It 3_____ (employ) over 50 people and it is 4_____ (look for) two new tour managers to work at their Goa office. At the moment, the company 5_____ (work) on an environmental project with an international organization in India. This new project 6_____ (want) to give tourists the opportunity to do something useful for local communities. Besides, for the first time this year, Wellness Holidays 7_____ (introduce) meditation camps in Western Canada and in the Goa area. Two years ago, the company had about 1,000 customers. This number 8_____ (increase) gradually, and sales 9_____ (rise), too. 'Today more and more people 10_____ (need) a holiday without stress,' says chief executive Sean Lankford, 'and that's what we 11_____ (offer) every year.'

2 Complete this job interview. Write one word in each gap, including the verb in brackets. Use the past simple or the present simple.

I = Interviewer, C = Candidate

I: Where 1_____ you 2_____? (study)

C: At Bexhill College in Florida.

I: What 3_____ _____ _____ there? (study)

C: I studied Marketing and Business Communication.

I: Mm. That's great! And what department 4_____ you work for in your last company? (do)

C: I 5_____ in Sales & Marketing for three years. (work)

I: 6_____ _____ _____ _____? (do)

C: I 7_____ the new salespeople. (train) My job 8_____ to help them increase sales. (be)

I: That's interesting. I know you are bilingual in English and Turkish. What other languages 9_____ _____ _____? (speak)

C: I also speak German, and I want to learn Chinese.

I: Great. And 10_____ _____ _____ other qualifications? (have)

C: Yes. I have a diploma in Computer Science.

I: Excellent. Now tell me, Zeynep, 11_____ _____ _____ _____ _____ work for New Vision? (want)

C: Because I want to use my communication skills in advertising. And of course I enjoy working with people.

I: That's great. Erm ... 12_____ _____ _____ any questions? (have)

3 Complete this crossword puzzle.

Across

1 Don't work on your computer for hours nonstop. Make sure you have a _____ every 15 or 20 minutes.

4 Where are your holiday photos? Can I have a _____ at them?

5 If you have more than one piece of hand luggage, you have to pay _____.

7 Many companies _____ a lot of money in new forms of communication technology.

9 A recent _____ in business travel is that more people are now travelling economy.

11 Another word for *go down* or *decrease*.

12 The past form of 11 across.

Down

2 What's your currency's exchange _____ with the US dollar?

3 A flower, and the past form of 10 down.

5 If you are an _____ of the company, you can use the company cafeteria.

6 Would you like an _____ or a window seat?

8 The number of foreign visitors went up _____ from 2.5 to 4 million.

10 It's terrible! Prices _____ all the time, they never go down.

4 Complete the sentences. Use *too* or *not enough* and the best word from the box.

> big   busy   dark   early   expensive   far   fast   old

1   My feet hurt. These shoes are _____ _____ _____ .

2   £35 for a CD? Don't buy it. It's _____ _____ .

3   I can't see anything in this room. It's _____ _____ .

4   Sorry, I can't talk just now. I'm _____ _____ .

5   Jim is only 14. He's _____ _____ _____ to learn to drive.

6   You don't need to leave at five. It's _____ _____ . You don't want to sit at the station and wait for your bus for 45 minutes!

7   Rita never walks to work. It's _____ _____ .

8   I can't win the race. I'm _____ _____ _____ .

5 Read this interview. Choose the correct words in *italics*.

A: Hi, Tony. I know you love Brussels. So, tell me about your favourite city.

B: ¹*A lot of / Much* people say Brussels is boring, but of course I don't agree. It's true that there isn't always ²*much / many* nightlife, but if you work, you can't go out ³*much / a lot of* anyway. In my job, I don't have ⁴*many / much* free time.

A: But when you have ⁵*some / any* free time, are there ⁶*a lot of / lots* things to do?

B: Yeah, sure. For example, there are ⁷*much / many* concerts, both jazz and classical. Then, I like good food. I don't eat ⁸*many / a lot*, but I enjoy discovering new dishes, both Belgian and international ones. I like going to ⁹*lots of / a lot* different restaurants.

A: And what about the weather? Do you ever dream of being in a city where there is ¹⁰*much / a lot of* sunshine?

B: Well, what can I say? It's good to have dreams, and it's good to be in Brussels!

6 Complete these conversations with the verbs from the box. Use two different forms of the same verb each time.

> go   meet   read   see   spend

1   A: I ¹_____ to Egypt last summer.
    B: Mm. That's nice. Did you ²_____ to Sharm el-Sheikh?

2   A: It wasn't a cheap holiday. I really ³_____ a lot of money.
    B: How much did you ⁴_____ ?

3   A: Of course I ⁵_____ the pyramids.
    B: Great. Did you ⁶_____ the Great Sphinx of Giza as well?

4   B: Did you ⁷_____ any interesting people?
    A: Yes, I did. One day I ⁸_____ an old man who makes those boats, you know, those traditional boats for cruises down the Nile. What do you call them?
    B: You mean feluccas? Wow, that's cool.

5   A: Before leaving, I ⁹_____ a book about life on the Nile.
    B: That's interesting. Did you ¹⁰_____ anything else?

7 There is one extra word in each of these sentences. Correct each sentence by crossing out the extra word.

1   Why were you not at the office on yesterday morning?

2   I like pictures and diagrams because I learn best when I can to see things.

3   Why did you were study Finance Management?

4   Clara really enjoyed in her studies at Standon College.

5   A lot of young people from my country are go abroad to study for an MBA.

6   The Human Resources department bought new computers for their staff in last month.

8 Complete this conversation. Write one word in each gap.

E = Elio Deltell, C = Customer Service rep

E: ¹_____ afternoon. Elio Deltell here. Can I speak to Ms Berktay, ²_____ ?

C: Speaking. How can I ³_____ you, Mr Deltell?

E: Well, it's ⁴_____ my new printer. I've got a problem with it.

C: I'm ⁵_____ to hear that. Can you give me some ⁶_____ information, please?

E: Yes. It's the Arato Laserjet Pro. It makes ⁷_____ lot of noise. And when a page comes out, half of it is black.

C: Mm. I see. We can send our specialist to look at it after three o'clock ⁸_____ afternoon.

E: That's great. ⁹_____ for your help.

C: My ¹⁰_____ , Mr Deltell. Bye.

E: Bye.

9 Put the words and phrases from the box under the correct heading below.

> baggage reclaim   car parks   cooker   curtains
> degree   diploma   excess luggage   flats   flight
> qualifications   shelves   sports centre   stopover   suburbs
> training   wardrobe

Education	Home	Cities	Air travel
....	....	....	....
....	....	....	....
....	....	....	....
....	....	....	....

10 <u>Underline</u> the word that has different word stress.

1   Oo   safety   mobile   advice   housework

2   oO   complain   travel   decide   agree

3   Ooo   terrible   interesting   excellent   exciting

4   oOo   successful   beautiful   expensive   commercial

5   oO   invest   arrive   enjoy   study

6   Oo   delay   passport   journey   language

Money matters

will for predictions

Listening: The future of money

1 What ways can we pay for things in shops and on the internet?

2))) **2.17** A market researcher is asking questions about money in a survey.

1 Listen and complete the questions.

2 Listen again and tick the answers you hear.

3 Work in pairs. Answer the survey yourself. Then ask and answer the questions with your partner. How do you think we will pay for things in the future?

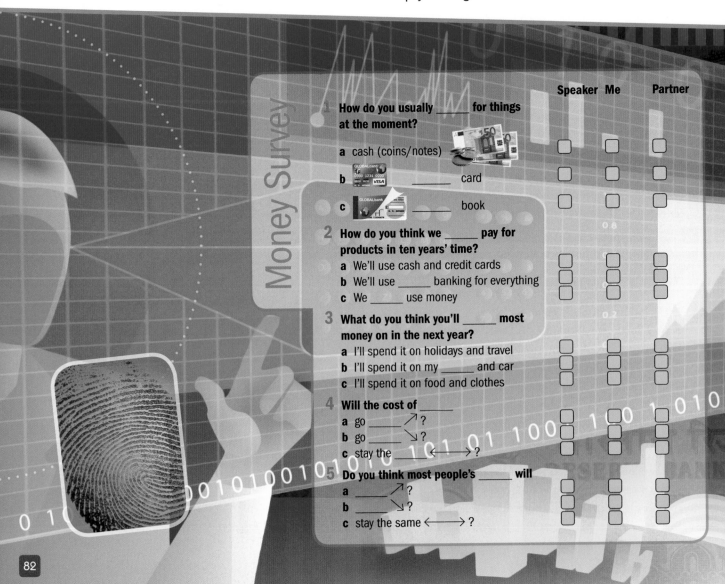

Money Survey

		Speaker	Me	Partner
1 How do you usually _____ for things at the moment?				
a cash (coins/notes)		☐	☐	☐
b _____ card		☐	☐	☐
c _____ book		☐	☐	☐
2 How do you think we _____ pay for products in ten years' time?				
a We'll use cash and credit cards		☐	☐	☐
b We'll use _____ banking for everything		☐	☐	☐
c We _____ use money		☐	☐	☐
3 What do you think you'll _____ most money on in the next year?				
a I'll spend it on holidays and travel		☐	☐	☐
b I'll spend it on my _____ and car		☐	☐	☐
c I'll spend it on food and clothes		☐	☐	☐
4 Will the cost of _____				
a go _____ ↗ ?		☐	☐	☐
b go _____ ↘ ?		☐	☐	☐
c stay the _____ ↔ ?		☐	☐	☐
5 Do you think most people's _____ will				
a _____ ↗ ?		☐	☐	☐
b _____ ↘ ?		☐	☐	☐
c stay the same ↔ ?		☐	☐	☐

Grammar: *will* for predictions

4 <u>Underline</u> examples of *will* or *won't* in the survey on page 82. Then complete the rules (1–4) in the table with the words below.

> start 'll will won't

will for predictions

We use *will* to say what we think will happen in the future.

1 We use _____ + the base form of the verb.
2 The contracted form of *will* is _____ .
3 In negative sentences we use _____ (*will not*).
4 To make questions we put *will* at the _____ of the sentence.

>> For more information on *will*, see page 151.

5 Complete the sentences with *will* or *won't*. Use contractions where possible.

1 The price of holidays _____ (not be) cheaper next summer.

2 In ten years, we _____ (use) internet banking.

3 People _____ (spend) more money on technology in the next five years.

4 _____ people still use cheques in shops next year?

5 We _____ (pay) for things by cheque in the future.

6 When _____ salaries increase again?

6 Ask your partner questions about these things.

Price of / cost of	cars houses electricity food computers mobile phones	go up go down stay the same	next month next year in five/ten years' time in the future

7))) 2.18 Listen to the speakers. <u>Underline</u> the words you hear.

1 I think *I'll / I* buy a house in the next five years.
2 *I'll / I* buy my clothes online with a credit card.
3 *I'll / I* listen to the financial news on the radio.
4 *We'll / We* spend all our money on restaurants.

Word focus: Money

8 Complete the table with the words about money. Use a dictionary to help you.

> earn save investment payee lender
> earnings loan pay investor savings

Verb	Noun – person	Noun – thing
bank	*banker*	*banking*
1	earner	
2 invest		
3 lend		
4		payment
5	saver	

9 Complete the sentences with one of the words in the table in exercise 8.

1 A: Will you invest in new technology?
   B: Yes, I will. It's a good _____ .

2 A: Will bankers make a lot of money next year?
   B: Yes, the _____ industry always makes money!

3 A: Most people's earnings won't increase for another two years.
   B: But people will _____ more in ten years' time.

4 A: Will you save money for the future?
   B: Yes, I have a _____ account at my bank.

5 A: Will the bank lend you money to buy a new car?
   B: No, they won't give me a _____ .

Speaking: Spending or investing

10 Work in pairs. You work for a market research company. Write six questions for a questionnaire about what people will spend and invest their money on in the future.

11 Join with another pair. Take turns to ask and answer the questions in your questionnaire.

TALKING POINT What things can you do to save money every day?

Reading: Get rich quick!

1 Read about three ways to make money. Do you think they are good ideas? Why?/Why not?

> **Send me $20 and I will send you magic words to turn it into $2,000.**

> **If you invest £150 every month, we'll give you £1,150 in ten months!.**

> If you send me your bank account details, I'll put €3 million in your account tomorrow.

2 Complete the fact sheet with one of these words.

> bank change dangerous email know
> money never ~~rich~~ tell

Stay safe on the internet

The internet has lots of ways to get
¹ _____rich_____ quick. Some are interesting and
some are silly but some are ² _____ .
Sometimes you'll get an ³ _____ from
someone you don't know. The email will say
'I'll send you money, if you send me your
⁴ _____ account *details*.' But the writer is a
criminal. If you send the information, they will take
your ⁵ _____. Here are some *tips* to help
your money stay safe on the internet.

★ Don't send information about your bank
account to a company that you don't
⁶ _____.

★ Credit cards and *debit cards* usually have a
secret number called a pin number. Don't
⁷ _____ anyone your pin number.

★ If you bank on the internet, you will have a
password. Don't tell anyone your *password*
and ⁸ _____ it often.

★ ⁹ _____ lend your bank card or credit
card to anyone.

3 Find a word in *italics* that means these things.

1 a secret word that allows you to use a computer or website
2 someone who does something that isn't legal
3 information
4 advice
5 a card to get your money from the bank

Word focus: *borrow* and *lend*

4 We use *borrow* and *lend* when we talk about something that we use and then return. Look at the examples and complete the rules.

> **borrow** and **lend**
>
> 1 Can I **borrow** a pen, please?
> 2 I'll **lend** you my dictionary.
>
> **a** We use _____ when we give something that we want back in the future.
> **b** We use _____ when we ask for something that we will return in the future.

5 Work in pairs. Say three things that you can *borrow* or *lend*? Look at the objects below. Use *lend* and *borrow* to ask for and offer these things.

> *Can I … / You can …   Please … / Thank you.*

Listening: Bank with us!

6))) **2.19** Listen to an advertisement on the radio and answer the questions.

1 What does the person want you to do?

2 What will they give new customers?

7))) Listen again and match the two parts of the sentence.

1 If you *open* an internet bank account with KDW Bank today,

2 If you save £2,000 a month,

3 We'll arrange foreign *currency*

a if you go on holiday.

b we'll give you a *free* MP4 player.

c you'll get three per cent *interest*.

8 Find a word in *italics* in exercise 7 that means these things.

1 You don't pay any money

2 Notes and coins they use in another country

3 Money the bank gives you for the money you have in your account

4 Start an account at a bank

Grammar: First conditional

9 Look at the examples in the table and match the information (1–3 to a–c) to complete the rules. Then choose the correct option in 4.

First conditional

Situation	Result
If I **save** £100 a month,	I**'ll have** £1,000 in ten months.
If I **save** £10 a month,	I **won't have** £1,000 in ten months.

Result	Situation
I**'ll need** foreign currency	**if** I **travel** on business.
I **won't need** foreign currency	**if** I **take** my credit card.

1 First conditional sentences are in	a *will/won't* + base verb.
2 The situation part uses	b two parts.
3 The result part uses	c *if* + present simple.

We can use *if* at the start of a sentence.

If I go to the shops, I**'ll use** my credit card.

(present simple)　　　(*will* + base verb)

We can also use *if* in the middle of a sentence.

I'll use my credit card **if** I go to the shops.

4 We use a comma (,) when the sentence begins with *will* / *if*.

We use the first conditional to talk about actions that have possible results in the future.

>> **For more information on the first conditional, see page 153.**

10 Underline the correct word to complete the sentences.

1 If you have a problem, *I'll help* / *I help* you.

2 *We'll start* / *We start* the meeting if everyone is here.

3 Will I get five percent interest if I *will open* / *open* an account?

4 The bank manager will see you if you *will have* / *have* an appointment.

5 If she *will go* / *goes* to Paris, she'll use Euros.

6 *They'll pay* / *They pay* by cheque if they buy a car.

Speaking: A new account

11 Work in groups. Sometimes banks offer customers products when they open a new account. What sort of products do they usually offer?

12 You work for a bank. There is a competition to see which team can produce the best radio or TV advertisement. Read the information and write the advertisement.

Our customers won't want pens and clocks! We want to offer them something different. Write an advertisement for the radio or TV and offer our customers something they won't find in any other bank.

- Say what you will offer new customers if they bank with you.

- Present your advertisement to another group.

- Which team offered the most unusual product?

TALKING POINT

Which banking activities do you prefer to do online and which do you prefer to do in a bank?

Listening: Buying online

1 Do you use the internet to shop at the moment? Do you buy any of the things in the pictures? What other things do you buy?

2))) **2.20** Listen to a conversation and match it to two of the photos. What does the shop sell at the moment? What do two of the speakers want to sell?

3))) Listen again and answer the questions.

1 Where does the first speaker want to sell the products?

2 Do they all agree?

4 Complete the phrases (a–h) in the table. Do you use these phrases to *agree* or *disagree*? Complete the headings 1 and 2.

1 _____	2 _____
a That's t_____.	**e** That's a nice idea, b_____ …
b I a _____.	**f** I d _____.
c That's a _____ idea!	**g** I'm not s_____.
d You're _____.	**h** I don't _____ that's a good idea.

Speaking: Responding to ideas

5 Work in pairs. Take turns to speak and respond to your partner's ideas.

Student A:
Say why it is a good idea to buy products on the internet.

Student B:
1 Respond: say if you agree or disagree.
2 Say something you won't buy on the internet.

Student A:
1 Respond: say if you agree or disagree.
2 Say something you will buy on the internet.

Student B:
1 Respond: say if you agree or disagree.
2 Talk about a company you know on the internet. Is it a good or bad company?

Student A:
Respond: say if you agree or disagree with B's opinion of the company.

6 Take turns to give opinions on these things. Respond to your partner's ideas.

I think …

1 What's the quickest way to become a millionaire?

2 What's the best place to get financial advice?

3 What's the worst thing about travelling on business?

4 Will new technology make life easier or more difficult?

5 What's the best way to celebrate a birthday?

6 How will we travel in the future?

7 Who is your business person of the year?

8 What's the best way to exercise?

Reminder

Grammar reference
pages 151 and 153

We can use *will* to make predictions.
I'll buy my clothes online with a credit card.

We can use the *first conditional* to talk about a situation and result.
If you **bank** on the internet, you**'ll have** a password.

Listening: The best investment

1 Do you think these are good things to invest in? Why?/Why not?

art cars films gold houses

2 ◄)) **2.21** Listen to two companies who want investors. Match the company to the picture.

3 ◄)) Listen again and complete these company information sheets.

TG Electronics

Based in: _____

Number of employees: _____

They make _____.

If profits go up investors will get _____% for a $50,000 investment and _____% for less than $50,000.

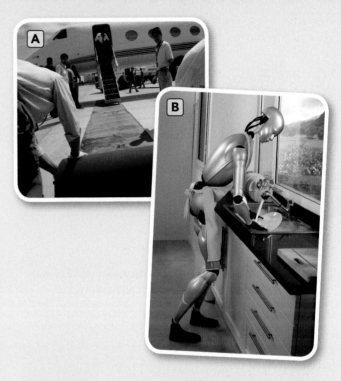

Blanes Travel

Based in: _____

Number of employees: _____

They are an _____.

If profits go up investors will get _____% for a $50,000 investment and _____% for less than $50,000.

Speaking: Saying what will happen

4 Work in pairs. You have $50,000 to invest. Look at more information about the companies.

Student A: Turn to File 26, page 114. Read about TG Electronics and tell your partner about the company.

Student B: Turn to File 54, page 123. Read about Blanes Travel and tell your partner about the company.

5 Discuss the companies and decide how to invest your money. You can invest in both companies or in one company. You need to both agree on the decision.

If we invest in ..., we'll get more/less interest.
If profits go up, we'll get ...
If profits go down, we'll get ...
I think it's a good idea to invest in ...
I'm not sure ...

Writing: Saying what you will do

6 Write an email to a colleague to talk about the company you will invest in. In your email include information about the following.

- the company name
- what it makes
- what interest you will make if the profits go up
- what interest you will make if the profits go down

14

A Future plans: *going to*
B *to* or *-ing*?
C **Communication strategies** Making it better
D **Interaction** Cooperating and competing

Teamwork

future plans: *going to*

Word focus: Working in a team

1 Do you prefer to do the following activities alone or with other people? Tick (✓) one column for each activity.

	Alone	With other people
preparing for an exam writing a report giving a presentation preparing for a birthday party doing the housework cooking dinner for friends or relatives		

2 Work in pairs. Compare and discuss your answers to exercise 1.

3 The sentences below are all about team players*. Complete each sentence with a word from the box.

> communicate cooperate learn relationships reliable

a Team players _____. They talk to other team members about their work, their successes and their problems. They share information with other people. __

b Team players _____. They work with the other team members because they want the team to be successful. __

c Team players are _____. Every team member knows that they will do what they have to do when they have to do it. __

d In a successful team, _____ between team members are good, and every member tries to make them stronger. __

e In a successful team, team members often teach each other and _____ from each other. __

A team player is someone who works well with people as part of a group.

Reading: One for all

4 Read the article about meerkats. Number the qualities in exercise 3 in the order in which they appear in the article.

Meerkats are small, friendly animals that live in the Kalahari desert of South Africa. They live in groups of about 30 members. The desert is a very dangerous place, so how can these small creatures survive?

Meerkats can survive only because they are excellent team players. For example, when they look for food or play outside, they always have a member of the group which just looks around to make sure that no dangerous animals are near. If there is any danger, this meerkat gives a signal* and all the others run back to their underground holes and tunnels. Like in any good team, each member knows that all the others are reliable: it's always 'one for all, and all for one'.

Meerkats are also good team players because they communicate and share information. They teach each other and learn from each other. For example, an adult can teach a young meerkat how to eat a scorpion.

They are also very cooperative: if a female cannot look after her young, another female babysits for her.

Finally, they know that in a group, it is important to work on relationships and make them stronger. To do this, meerkats spend time cleaning each other, and also sunbathing and playing together.

gives a signal: makes a sound or a movement to tell the others what to do

5 Answer these questions.

1 What do you find most interesting about meerkats?
2 How do meerkats show 'team spirit'?
3 What can people learn from them?
4 Which other animals can people also learn from?

Listening: Learning from animals

6 🔊 **2.22** Otylia Janosz is a management consultant from Kraków. She is planning a study trip to South Africa to do some research for her new book on teamwork. Read these statements, then listen to the interview and tick (✓) the ones that are true.

1 Otylia believes only people can learn from animals.

2 She isn't going to make a film about meerkats.

3 She is interested in how meerkats communicate.

4 She isn't going to have a pet meerkat.

Grammar: Future plans: *going to*

7 🔊 Listen to the interview again and complete the examples.

Future plans: *going to*

+ I'¹___ _____ ___ _____ as a volunteer on the Kalahari Meerkat Project.
She's **going to take** a lot of photos.

− I'm ²___ going ___ _____ one back to Europe.
She's **not going to have** a pet meerkat.

? What ³___ you _____ to ___ in South Africa?
Are you **going to shoot** a film? **Yes, I am. / No, I'm not.**

We use *going to* to talk about future plans.
We make the *going to* future with *am / is / are* + *going to* + infinitive.

>> For more information on *going to*, see page 150.

---

8 After the interview, this article about Otylia appeared in a business magazine. Complete it using only these words: *are, going, is, not, to.*

Otylia Janosz, author of the best-selling *Working Together*, is now working on her next book, which is also about teamwork. To find out how people can make better teams, she is ¹_____ to spend some time in South Africa. Why South Africa? What ²_____ she going ³_____ do there? No, she is ⁴_____ going ⁵_____ attend an international seminar or give a presentation at a conference. Believe it or not, Otylia and two other experts ⁶_____ _____ _____ live in the desert and study the life of meerkats, those funny little animals which live in large groups and can survive only because they are all excellent team players.

But her book ⁷_____ _____ _____ _____ be about zoology. Remember that Otylia is a management consultant, and she writes for businesses and organizations.

Speaking: Dream teams?

9 Work in pairs or in small groups. Look at the list of qualities of a team player in exercise 3. What other qualities does a team player have? What else do they or don't they do? Add your own ideas to the list.

10 A company wants to organize a team-building course. First, they ask each member of staff to fill in an online feedback form about each of their colleagues. They do not need to sign the form.

Read the online feedback about Dave Self. What should he do to become a better team player?

'He's always late.'

'When he has interesting information, he never tells us.'

'He talks a lot and he never listens to what others have to say.'

'He doesn't want to be with us when we go out after work.'

'When I ask for help, he says he's very busy.'

'He isn't the boss, but he always tells other people what to do.'

'Sometimes he says "Of course I can help!", but then he just forgets.'

'He has a lot of private meetings with the manager. Nobody knows what they talk about.'

11 After the course, Dave really wants to change. He plans to be an excellent team player. Work in pairs or in small groups. Talk about Dave's plans. Look at the comments above, and say what you think he is/is not going to do.

He's going to be on time every day.
He's not going to be late anymore.

TALKING POINT What team/s are you part of at the moment? What do you like about it/them?

Word focus: *play*, *go* or *do*?

1 Do you play any sports? Do you like to watch sports?

2 Match each sport or activity to the pictures. Which sports do you play in a team? Add two more sports or activities to the list.

 A

 B

 C

 D

 E

 F

 G

H

 I

 J

 K

1 athletics	**5** golf	**9** running	**13** volleyball
2 basketball	**6** hockey	**10** skiing	**14** yoga
3 cricket	**7** jogging	**11** swimming	_____
4 football	**8** martial arts	**12** tennis	_____

3 We use *play*, *go* and *do* with sports and activities. Look at the examples and complete the rules.

> **play, go and do?**
>
> *Do you want to **play** tennis tomorrow?*
> *She **goes** jogging every evening.*
> *They **do** yoga in the morning.*
>
> **1** We use _____ with sports or activities that use a ball. Usually we play these sports with other people or in a team.
> **2** We use _____ with activities that end *-ing*.
> **3** We use _____ for activities that do not use a ball and that we can do alone.

 L

 M

4 Look at the activities in exercise 2. Do you use *play*, *go* or *do*?

5 Work with a partner. Take turns to ask and answer questions about some of the activities. Ask follow up questions.

> *Do you play cricket? Do you go skiing? Do you do yoga?*
> *Yes, and I also … / No, I prefer to …*
> *When/Where do you play golf?*

 N

Listening: Playing and watching sport

6 🔊 **2.23** Listen to two conversations. Which speaker isn't on holiday?

7 🔊 Complete part of the conversations with the words and phrases from the box. Listen again to check.

> book can have here you are holiday
> like lose play playing score Scotland sports
> tennis win winning

Conversation 1	Conversation 2
1 Hi. _____ I have an orange juice, please?	**1** Hello. Are you here on _____?
2 Sure, _____. That's €2. Thanks.	**2** Yes, the _____ facilities are very good here.
3 Who are _____?	**3** Do you _____ sport?
4 Spain and _____.	**4** What sports do you _____?
5 Who's _____?	**5** I enjoy playing _____. Do you play?
6 What's the _____?	
7 Who do you think is going to _____?	**6** Yes, I do. Perhaps we can _____ a game?
8 Spain. Scotland's going to _____.	**7** I can _____ it.

Grammar: *to* or *-ing*?

8 Look at the table and answer these questions.

1 Match these sentences to the verb patterns (a or b).

I need to call the office.
I enjoy playing tennis.

2 Which verb pattern match verbs that follow the words in bold in the table?

to or *-ing*?

a Verb + *-ing*   **b** Verb + *to* + base form

+ **1** She **wants** to go to the gym.
  2 They **suggested** watching the game on TV.
  3 Do you **plan** to get tickets for the game?
  4 I **dislike** playing golf in the rain.

Negative and questions

– *They **don't need to play** sport.*	? *Do they **need to play** sport?*
*He **doesn't enjoy watching** football.*	*Does he **enjoy watching** football?*

>> For more information on **verb patterns**, see page 158.

> ⚠ Some verbs can follow verb + *-ing* or verb + *to* + base verb. The meaning does not change.
> *I **like watching** sport.* OR *I **like to watch** sport.*
> *I **prefer doing** yoga.* OR *I **prefer to do** yoga.*

9 Complete the sentences with the correct verb pattern.

1 Do you need _____ (go) to the gym now?
2 David enjoys _____ (learn) new languages.
3 They don't want _____ (play) golf after the meeting.
4 I suggest _____ (talk) to the manager.
5 She plans _____ (do) martial arts in the summer.
6 We dislike _____ (work) at the weekend.

Speaking: Talking about sport

10 You are away on business. In the lounge in the hotel, the TV is showing one of the games in the photos. Start a conversation about the sport.

Conversation 1

Student A: Choose a photo and start the conversation about the sport. Ask about the game. Find out who is playing and the score.

Student B: Answer Student A's questions and try to keep the conversation going.

Conversation 2

Student B: Use the other photo to start another conversation about sport. Find out who is playing and the score.

Student A: Answer Student B's questions and try to keep the conversation going.

> **TALKING POINT**
>
> Do you think sport is good for team building? Why?/Why not?

Listening: When things go wrong

1 Think of a time when something went wrong at work or home. What did other people say? Did they help you to feel better?

2 You have a problem with your car and are late for work. You phone to tell your boss the problem. When you arrive at the office, do these things make you feel better or worse?

The boss	Better	Worse
shouts at you		
does not want to talk to you		
asks about your car		
offers you a cup of coffee		

3 🔊 **2.24** Listen to three conversations where things go wrong. Tick (✓) two conversations where the person feels better after talking.

Conversation 1

Conversation 2

Conversation 3

4 🔊 Listen to conversations 1 and 2 on Track 2.24 again. <u>Underline</u> a word in italics to complete the sentences.

	Problem	Response
1	There's a *problem / trouble* with my computer.	I'm *sorry / glad* to *hear / see* that.
2	I need to *start / finish* this report for the finance meeting.	It's going to be *fine / OK*. You *can / can't* use my computer.
3	I *found / lost* the address of our new customer.	Oh, *honestly / really*?
4	Now you can't contact her. *Apologies / Sorry*.	Don't *be upset / worry*. We can look *both / together*.

5 🔊 Listen to conversation 3 on Track 2.24 again. What responses can you use to make the situation better?

6 🔊 **2.25** Listen and see if the speaker uses your responses.

Speaking: Responding to a problem

7 Work in pairs. Take turns to read and respond to the problems. Student A reads problem 1 and Student B responds. Then Student B reads problem 2 and Student A responds, etc.

1 We didn't win the tennis yesterday.

2 I lost my bag on the plane.

3 I didn't pass my exam.

4 I can't come to the team meeting. I need to finish my report.

5 I'm ill and I can't come to work today.

6 Steve lost his new mobile phone.

7 I didn't sleep well last night.

8 Paula can't do the presentation. There's a problem with her train.

Reminder

Grammar reference
pages 150 and 158

We use *going to* to talk about future plans.
They're **going to** have a holiday next month.
They're **not going to** do any work.
What are they **going** to do?

Some verbs can only be followed by *to*:
They **want to work** together.
Some verbs can only be followed by *-ing*:
They **enjoy working** together.
Some verbs can be followed by *to* or by *-ing*:
They **like to work / working** together.

Writing: Team dictation

1 Work in pairs. You are going to have one half of a story about teamwork each. Take turns to dictate your half so together you can have the whole story. Student A: Turn to File 27, page 115. Student B: Turn to File 52, page 122.

Here are some sentences you can use if you have a problem. Check together that you understand them before you start.

> Could you speak more slowly, please?
> Could you say that again, please?
> Sorry. What's the word before / after ...?

Board game: Time to team up

2 Work in pairs or in small groups. First read the rules, then play the game.

Rules

1 Toss a coin to move. Heads, move one square, tails move two.

2 Follow the instructions on each square.

3 If you land on a square someone landed on before, move on to the next new square.

3 Which was more interesting, cooperating in exercise 1 or competing in exercise 2? Why?

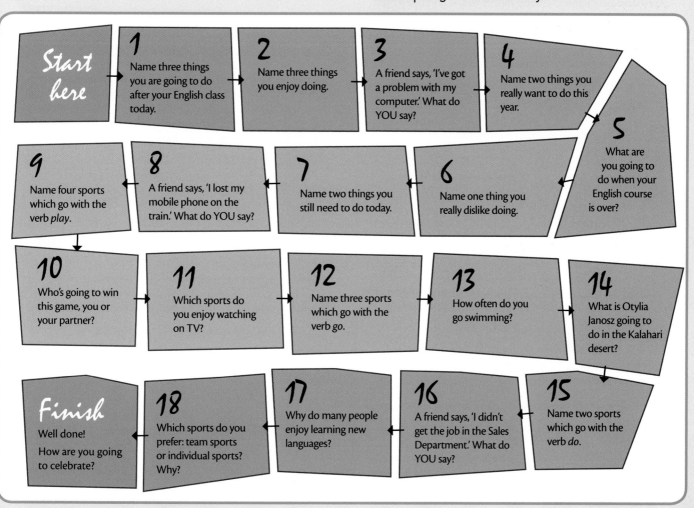

Start here

1 Name three things you are going to do after your English class today.

2 Name three things you enjoy doing.

3 A friend says, 'I've got a problem with my computer.' What do YOU say?

4 Name two things you really want to do this year.

5 What are you going to do when your English course is over?

6 Name one thing you really dislike doing.

7 Name two things you still need to do today.

8 A friend says, 'I lost my mobile phone on the train.' What do YOU say?

9 Name four sports which go with the verb *play*.

10 Who's going to win this game, you or your partner?

11 Which sports do you enjoy watching on TV?

12 Name three sports which go with the verb *go*.

13 How often do you go swimming?

14 What is Otylia Janosz going to do in the Kalahari desert?

15 Name two sports which go with the verb *do*.

16 A friend says, 'I didn't get the job in the Sales Department.' What do YOU say?

17 Why do many people enjoy learning new languages?

18 Which sports do you prefer: team sports or individual sports? Why?

Finish

Well done!

How are you going to celebrate?

15

A Present perfect
B Have you ever ...?
C **Communication strategies** Checking information
D **Interaction** Life experiences

What an experience!

Present perfect

Listening: What's in the news?

1 Look at the photo above. What animal do you think it is? What other animals do you know? Are they wild animals, farm animals or pets?

2 Look at the headline on the right. What do you think the story is about? Read the news report to see if you are right.

3 🔊 **2.26** Listen to the interview and answer the questions.

1 What is the missing animal? What country is it from?

2 How long has Miles Stewart been the director at the zoo?

3 Why is the animal dangerous?

4 🔊 Listen again and complete the interview

> *Have you ¹_____ a problem like this in the past?*
>
> *No, I've ²_____ the director at this zoo for 20 years and this is the first time that an animal ³_____ escaped. We haven't had a problem like this before.*

> *Has anyone ⁴_____ the tiger?*
>
> *Yes, three people have seen him in the park. Our team has ⁵_____ everywhere but we haven't found the tiger.*

> *Why ⁶_____ you caught him?*
>
> *We ⁷_____ done everything possible to find Ronan. Our teams are looking all around the city.*

Big cat on the streets

A big cat has escaped from the city zoo. A member of staff discovered that he was missing yesterday. Listen to our exclusive interview with Miles Stewart, the zoo director.

Grammar: Present perfect

5 Complete the examples with words from the news report.

Present perfect (+ / – / ?)		
+ A tiger ¹____ _____ from the city zoo.		
– We ²_____ ___ a problem like this before.		
? ³___ anyone _____ the tiger?	**Yes, they have. / No, they haven't**.	
We form the present perfect with the verb ⁴_____ + past participle.		
We use the present perfect when past actions are important in the present. We often use the present perfect to give news or to talk about things that happened recently.		
>> For more information on the present perfect, see page 147.		

> ⁸_____ he hurt anyone?
>
> No, he ⁹_____ . But he hasn't ¹⁰_____ for 24 hours so he is dangerous.

6 Look at the audio script on page 139 and find the past participle of these verbs.

1 be _been_   6 catch _____

2 escape _____   7 do _____

3 see _____   8 hurt _____

4 have _____   9 eat _____

5 find _____

7 Here are more verbs. Look at the verb list on page 160 to help you.

1 call _____   4 read _____

2 speak _____   5 visit _____

3 give _____   6 hear _____

8 Complete the sentences with the present perfect.

1 She isn't in the office. She _____ (go) to India on a business trip.

2 _____ you _____ (hear) the news about the CEO?

3 Sorry I'm late, I _____ (have) problems with my car this morning.

4 I _____ (not eat) sushi. Is it good?

5 We need to book the holiday. _____ he _____ (speak) to Jeff about the dates?

6 They _____ (not give) me directions and I don't know how to get to the hotel.

Speaking: An interview

9 Work in pairs and answer the questions.

1 Do you watch news on the internet or on TV?

2 How often do you buy a newspaper?

10 Imagine that you work for a newspaper. Your editor wants you to interview a famous person.

Student A: You are the famous person. Decide who you are and answer questions as that person.

Student B: Turn to File 20, page 112. Ask your partner the questions and make a note of their answers.

11 Now change roles.

Student B: You are the famous person. Decide who you are and answer questions as that person.

Student A: Turn to File 53, page 122. Ask your partner the questions and make a note of their answers.

Writing: A news report

12 Do you think that the information you hear in the news is always true? Look at these headlines. Do you think they are true or false?

A EIFFEL TOWER DISAPPEARS

B Chicken has an accident as it crosses the road

C Pet cat catches the same bus every day for four years.

13 Complete the news report below. The information does not need to be true. Compare your ideas with a partner.

STRANGE LIGHTS IN _____!

Hundreds of people have seen strange lights in _____.
Experts have said that they believe the lights are

_____.

The interesting thing is that the lights have _____.
Students at a local English school said that the lights have made them _____.
The police have asked people who see the lights to

_____.

TALKING POINT Have you heard an interesting news story this week? Tell your partner about it.

Word focus: Positive and negative responses

1 We all have good and bad experiences in life. Do you think a positive or negative person says the statements below?

1 'I've won a competition and the prize is a meal in a restaurant. I'm really disappointed!'

2 'I've won a competition and the prize is a meal in a restaurant. I'm really pleased!'

2 Look at photos A–C. Point to the glass that is full. Point to the glass that is empty. Do you think a positive person sees glass B as half full or half empty?

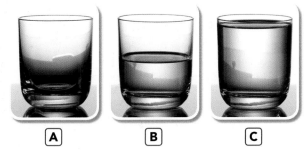

3 Which adjectives describe positive experiences and which describe negative experiences?

> amazing awful exciting horrible fantastic wonderful
> terrible unpleasant

4 What response can you use in these situations?

1 You get tickets to see your favourite band.
That's _____!

2 ... but they cancel the concert! That's _____!

3 You win a short break in a luxury hotel. That's _____!

4 ... but you eat seafood and get ill. That's _____!

Grammar: *Have you ever ...?*

5 Look at the dialogues below, then match the example sentences to the rules in the table below.

> A: *Have you ever learned to play a musical instrument?*
> B: *Yes, I have. I learned to play the piano when I was ten.*
> A: *Have you ever played in a concert?*
> B: *Yes, I have. I played in a school concert and it was awful!*
>
> A: *Have you ever visited the pyramids?*
> B: *No, I haven't.*
> A: *Have you ever been to North Africa?*
> B: *Yes, I've been to Morocco. It was wonderful.*

Have you ever ...?

Have you ever learned to play a musical instrument?
Yes, I have. / No, I haven't.

Has she ever visited the pyramids?
Yes, she has. No, she hasn't.

Have I/you/we/they ever + past participle
Has he/she/it ever + past participle

1	We use *Have you ever*	**a**	to give details about when something happened in the past.
2	We use the past simple	**b**	to ask about the past when the experience is more important than when it happened.

>> **For more information on the present perfect, see page 147.**

6 Complete the chart with verbs. Look at page 149 and the list on page 160 to help you.

	Infinitive	Past simple	Past participle
1	have	had	*had*
2	_____	was/were	been
3	meet	met	_____
4	_____	flew	flown
5	study	studied	_____
6	_____	ate	eaten
7	try	_____	_____
8	_____	lost	lost
9	_____	swam	_____
10	ride	_____	_____

Listening: Interview about experiences

7 🔊 **2.27** Jake Presdale is interviewing people about their life experiences. Listen to the responses and complete the questions.

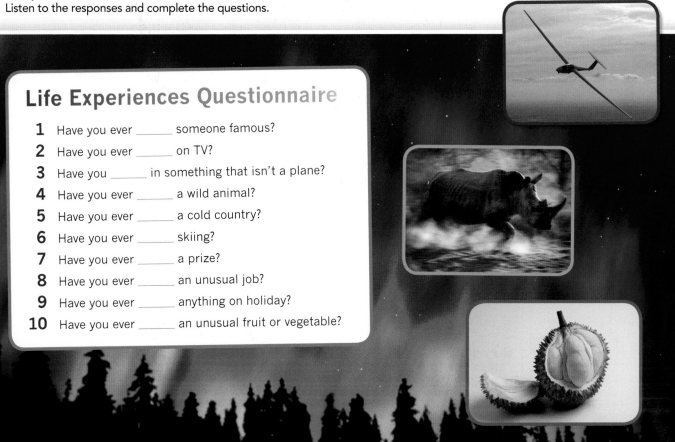

Life Experiences Questionnaire

1 Have you ever _____ someone famous?
2 Have you ever _____ on TV?
3 Have you _____ in something that isn't a plane?
4 Have you ever _____ a wild animal?
5 Have you ever _____ a cold country?
6 Have you ever _____ skiing?
7 Have you ever _____ a prize?
8 Have you ever _____ an unusual job?
9 Have you ever _____ anything on holiday?
10 Have you ever _____ an unusual fruit or vegetable?

8 🔊 **2.28** Listen to the complete conversations. Write 'P' if it was a positive experience or 'N' if it was a negative experience.

Speaking: Talking about experiences

9 Look at the photos and tell your partner about any of the things that you have done.

Have you ever played a card trick?

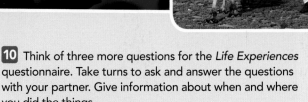

10 Think of three more questions for the *Life Experiences* questionnaire. Take turns to ask and answer the questions with your partner. Give information about when and where you did the things.

A: *Have you ever swum with dolphins?*
B: *No I haven't. / Yes I have. I swam with dolphins last year in Thailand. It was fantastic.*

> **TALKING POINT** Do you think it's a good idea to try new experiences? Why?/Why not?

Listening: An emergency phone call

1 What problems can happen when you give information on the telephone?

Sometimes you don't understand what a person says. You don't hear important information.

2)) **2.29** Listen to the phone conversation. Which photo shows what has happened?

3)) Listen again. What is the telephone number?

4 Complete the phrases from the conversation. Then match the telephone phrases to the situation.

Telephone phrases	Situation
1 Speak a little _____, please.	**a** To explain that the telephone connection isn't good.
2 Sorry, what did you _____?	**b** When the person is speaking fast.
3 _____ you say *presentation*?	**c** You want to say that something is correct.
4 It's a _____ line.	**d** You want to check information you wrote.
5 Can you _____ that?	**e** You want to check a word the person said.
6 Can I read that _____ ?	**f** You want someone to say the information again. (x2)
7 _____ right.	

5 What can you use these phrases to do?

So that's 40249 56617?
Is that 40249 56617?

a Ask for information.

b Check important information.

6)) **2.30** Listen and choose a phrase from exercise 4 in response to these situations on the phone.

Speaking: Checking information

7 Read the information to your partner. Make some of the information difficult to hear. Take turns to read one of the sentences. When you are listening write the information and use phrases to check understanding.

Student A	Student B
1 My account number is 3942kjf9E.	1 Her address is apartment 1388 River Street.
2 He wants you to call him on 423982321.	2 We have an emergency meeting about the CEO.
3 Mr Edwards can't come to the meeting.	3 Their account number is 423fd13C.
4 The garage says your car is ready.	4 Can you call Dean on 2349842?
5 He lives at 35 Walden Street.	5 Have you spoken to Mr Vanja about the new project?

A

B

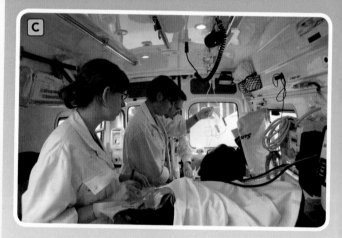

C

D

Reminder

Grammar reference page 147

We use *Have you ever ...?* when we ask questions about experiences. It isn't important when something happened.
Have you ever visited Italy?

We use the present perfect when past actions are important in the present.
I've asked Tom to work in my department.

When past dates or times are important we use the past simple.
*Yes, I **visited** Italy in 2010.*

Rules

1 Choose a colour: blue, green, yellow, purple. This is your subject colour.

2 Flip a coin five times. How many heads did you flip? This is your question number.

3 Your partner reads the question and you answer. Answer more than 'yes' or 'no'.

4 Now it's your partner's turn to choose a colour and flip the coin.

Board game: Life experiences

1 Read the questions. Add one more question to each box.

2 Work in pairs. Read the rules and play the game.

Home

1 How many different places have you lived in your life?

2 Have you ever lived in a different country?

3 What's the most interesting thing you have bought for your home?

4 Have you ever lived in a place that you didn't like?

5 _____

Friends

1 Have you ever contacted an old friend on the internet?

2 Have you ever been on holiday with friends?

3 Have you ever forgotten a friend's birthday?

4 How many times have you texted friends this week?

5 _____

Work

1 How many emails have you written today?

2 Have you ever spoken English on the telephone at work?

3 Have you ever been late for work?

4 What's the most interesting job you have ever had?

5 _____

Travel

1 Have you ever booked a holiday on the internet?

2 How many holidays have you had this year?

3 Have you ever spoken English on holiday?

4 Have you visited another country on business?

5 _____

16

A Future arrangements
B *who* and *which*
C **Communication strategies** Explaining needs
D **Interaction** Planning a trip

Take a break

future arrangements

Reading: A short break

1 Match the pictures to the activities in italics in the blog.

2 Read Lucinda's blog and complete the diary on page 10.

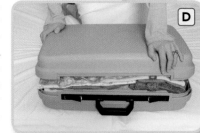

F

Lucinda's travel blog
Travelling to a City of Surprises

E

A

I'm **1** *packing my bag* at the moment. Tomorrow, we're flying to Barcelona for a long weekend and I can't wait. On Saturday morning, we're starting with **2** *a helicopter ride* over the city. After lunch, I'm meeting friends and we're **3** *taking a walking tour* of the city. But this isn't the usual tourist tour. This is with a guy called Geraldo who's showing us all the places that are in movies. I love the music in this city, too. In the evening, I'm meeting some Spanish friends. They're taking me to see a Catalan dance called Sardana at midnight. That's my kind of city, no one goes out until late and there is something to do all the time. On Sunday morning, I'm having a **4** *jet ski lesson*. I'm a bit nervous because I've never been on a jet ski before. But that's why I like travelling – you try lots of new things. I'm visiting my friend Pilar in the evening. She's a chef and she's teaching me to **5** *cook Crema Catalana*, a delicious dessert. On Monday morning I'm **6** *hiring a motorbike* to ride around the city. We're flying back on Monday evening. I'm phoning my friend now to get some advice about jet skiing! Don't forget to read my blog next week to discover where I'm travelling to next.

D

B

C

Grammar: Future arrangements

3 Look at the examples (a and b) in the table and answer the questions. Then complete the rules.

1 Which sentence talks about arrangements in the future?

2 Which sentence talks about now?

Future arrangements

a *I'm packing* my bag at the moment.

b *Tomorrow, I'm flying* to Barcelona.

We can use the _____ _____ to talk about things that are happening now or arrangements in the future.

>> For more information on the present continuous, see pages 146 and 150.

4 Look at the phrases and nouns (1–6) in Lucinda's blog. Which ones use the present continuous. Do they talk about the present or the future?

5 Work in pairs. Lucinda is planning another trip next month. Ask and answer questions to complete the information about her break. Student A: Turn to File 28, page 115. Student B: Turn to File 56, page 123.

A: *What's she doing on Monday morning?*
B: *She's working.*
A: *How do you spell Pilar?*
B: *It's P-I-L-A-R.*

September

10 Saturday a.m.

_____ p.m. ○

○

11 Sunday a.m. ○

_____ p.m.

○

12 Monday a.m. ○

_____ p.m. ○

Word focus: Time expressions for the future

6 Put these time expressions in order closest to now.

___ Now ↓
___ Next year
___ The week after next
___ In two days' time
___ Next week
___ After this lesson
___ Tomorrow

7 Use some of these expressions to tell your partner about some of your arrangements.

I'm meeting friends for a coffee after this lesson.

Speaking: What are they doing next week?

8 Work in pairs. Next week some visitors are arriving at your company for four days. Your manager wants you to entertain them. Read the information about the visitors and think of some entertaining activities for their visit.

9 Look at the information about the visitors and the schedule for their visit. Add more activities. Roleplay a conversation with your manager to explain your arrangements. Student A: Turn to File 29, page 115. Student B: Turn to File 57, page 123.

Conversation 1: Student A is the manager, Student B is the employee.

Conversation 2: Student A is the employee, Student B is the manager.

 Lisa Chung
Hobbies: salsa dancing, restaurants

 Richard Jeffries
Hobbies: walking, cinema

 Jenny Briscoe
Hobbies: the ballet, sport

 Silvio Martel
Hobbies: the opera, shopping

TALKING POINT Is it better to take lots of short breaks or one long holiday? Why?

Word focus: Film and music

1 What books, films or songs do you know about these cities?

Paris   New York   Rome   London

2 Do you use these words to describe films or music? Can you add any more to the list?

action classical comedy country folk historical
horror musical pop rock romance rap thriller

Films	Music
action	*classical*

3 Look at the posters. What sort of book, film or music are they?

4 Work in pairs. Answer the questions in the quiz.

1 Have you seen a film which was made in France or China? What is your favourite film? Who is in it? ▶

2 Can you name three film directors. Where are they from? What sort of films do they make?

3 Name some musicians from these continents: Asia, Europe, North America and South America? What sort of music do they play? What sort of music do you like to listen to? ▼

4 Name an author who writes these sort of books. Talk about a book you enjoyed recently. Who is it by? Is it fiction or non-fiction? ▼

Reading: Making a film

5 Name some of the different jobs that people do when they make a film. Read the article. Circle the jobs it mentions.

When you make a film there are lots of different jobs. The producers organize the money and choose the people to work on the film. The director works with the writers, actors and the camera people. He or she tells everyone what to do. Can you imagine your favourite film without music? John Williams is a composer who writes music for films. His music is in famous films such as *Star Wars*, and *Harry Potter*. The producers, director and actors couldn't make the film without the electricians and builders, cooks and secretaries who are part of the film crew. The builders and electricians help to build the set, the cooks feed the crew and the secretaries are the people who organize all the paperwork. There are many jobs which are important. That's why there are often lots of names on the credits.

6 Match a word from the article and the meaning.

1 the producer   **a** the list of names of everyone that works on the film

2 the director   **b** the person who writes the music

3 film crew   **c** the person who tells everyone what to do

4 credits   **d** the team that works on the film

5 composer   **e** the person who organizes the money

Grammar: *who* and *which*

7 Look at the examples and complete the rules with *who* or *which*.

who and which

We can use *who* and *which* to join two sentences together.

John Williams is a composer. He writes music for films.
*John Williams is a composer **who** writes music for films.*

There are many jobs. They are important.
*There are many jobs **which** are important.*

1 We use _____ to talk about people.
2 We use _____ to talk about animals or things.

>> For more information about *who* and *which*, see page 159.

8 Match the phrases to make sentences.

1 I don't like films   **a** which helps him relax.

2 He likes classical music   **b** who wrote the music for *Avatar*.

3 Do you know the actor   **c** which had a terrible picture.

4 I met the composer   **d** which are very long.

5 She has a bird   **e** who was in *Titanic*?

6 We had a TV   **f** which can talk.

9 Join the sentences together. Use *who* and *which*.

I know a man. He is an actor.
I know a man who is an actor.

1 Next year, I'm travelling down the Oder. It's a river in Poland.

_____

2 I work with a woman. She met Johnny Depp!

_____

3 There is a man in the next flat. He plays rock music all night.

_____

4 I am going to the world film festival. It is in Cape Town.

_____

10 Work in pairs. Think of a person, job, country or company connected to film or business. Describe the person or thing to your partner and use *who* or *which*.

A: *It's a person who organizes all the paperwork.*
B: *A secretary.*
A: *It's the country which makes Bollywood films.*
B: *India.*

Speaking: What is happening?

11 🔊 **2.31** Work in pairs. Listen to music from five films. What sort of film do you think it is?

1 _____
2 _____
3 _____
4 _____

12 🔊 **2.32** Work in pairs. Listen to this film music. What do you think is happening in the film?

Writing: Write about a project

13 You are a producer. You are making a film next year. Write an email to another producer to talk about the film. Include the information below.

- Choose a name for the film.
- Choose a future date when you are starting work on it.
- Choose two actors who are working on the film.

Hi Cameron,
I'm making a film called …

TALKING POINT   Do you think actors get too much money for their job? Why?/Why not?

Reading: It's not what you say

1 Tomorrow you have an important meeting to ask for something that you want. Do you do any of these things? Add more ideas.

- write notes
- practise what you are going to say
- organize your ideas
- wear smart clothes

2 Read the article. Which things does the speaker say not to do? What is the strangest advice?

3 Find words and expressions in *italics* in the article that mean the same as these.

1 strong
2 communicate without words
3 nice
4 move your body
5 advice
6 people you work with

How do you get what you want at home and at work? The person that you are talking to will listen to what you say but your *body language* is also important. Recent research found some interesting things which can help us to get what we want.

Look at these *tips*.

- Make the same *movements* as the person you are talking to. When people make the same movements as us we like them – but we don't know why.

- In an important meeting, wear black and don't smile. People think that *colleagues* who smile less and wear dark colours are *powerful*.

- If you want something from your boss, don't give him a cold drink. Give them a cup of coffee or tea while you talk. The warm drink makes them think that you are a *warm* and kind person.

Listening: I'd like to speak to you

4))) **2.33** Listen to Jason's conversation with his boss. What does he want?

5))) Listen again and answer the questions.

1 Does the meeting go well? Why?/Why not?
2 What does his boss want him to do?
3 What reason does she give?
4 Does she agree with Jason's plan?

6))) **2.34** Listen to another version of the conversation. Does he explain what he wants better or worse this time? Is he more polite or less polite?

7))) Listen again and complete these sentences from the conversation. Write in the missing words.

Explain what you want	Give reasons
1 I ^{1}_____ you to work on the new international team	^{2}_____ you speak Russian.
2 ^{3}_____ to travel to Moscow	in ^{4}_____ to improve my Russian.
3 I want to go to the ^{5}_____ language school in the city	^{6}_____ I can learn business Russian for my work.
4 It's ^{7}_____ to be able to speak Russian in negotiations and meetings,	that's ^{8}_____ this plan is perfect. I can learn business Russian at school and speak Russian all day.

Speaking: Giving reasons

8 Work in pairs. An employee asks to speak to the boss. Look at the information and plan what you are going to say. Start the conversation politely.

Student A: Look at the information below. Student B: Look at the information in File 30, page 116.

Act out the situation in Conversation 1 then change roles and act out Conversation 2.

Student A:

Conversation 1

You start the conversation. You are the employee.
Hi, I'd like to talk to you about something …
You want to plan a trip to a restaurant for the department. You want your boss to pay.

Reason:
Everyone is working very hard on a new project. This is a good way to say 'thank you'.

Conversation 2

Student B starts the conversation. You are the boss.
Listen to what Student B wants and ask for reasons.
Why do you want to …
You can decide to say 'yes' or 'no' to Student B.

Reminder

Grammar reference
pages 146, 150 and 159

We can use the present continuous to talk about the future when we have firm arrangements.
He's **visiting** Russia next April.
We're **flying** to Mexico on Monday.

We use *who* and *which* to join two pieces of information.
*She's the woman **who** presents the travel programme on TV.*
*It is a city **which** is famous for its food.*

Listening: Time away

1 Tell your partner about trips that you have planned. Which was the most interesting / exciting / unusual?

2))) **2.35** Listen to five people talking about taking time away from work. Match the speaker to the photo.

3))) Listen again. How does the person respond to hearing the information?

Speaking: Making plans

4 Here are some things that people do on a break from work. Add more ideas to the list. Which do you think are interesting? Why?

- run a marathon
- climb Mount Everest
- sail the ocean
- write a novel
- take Japanese lessons
- learn to paint
- swim with dolphins
- design a garden
- work with a charity

5 You are taking a six-month break away from work next year. You can do anything that you want to do. Look at the activities on the list and tick (✓) the ones that you want to do. Add five more ideas to the list.

6 Complete the year planner to plan your break. Choose activities from the list and other things that you want to do. Each activity can take one month.

7 Ask your partner questions about what you are doing next year. Respond with comments.

A: What are you doing in January?
B: I'm learning Japanese.
A: That's interesting. Why are you learning Japanese?
B Because I'm visiting friends in Tokyo in February.

A

B

C

D ALFRED HITCHCOCK PSYCO

E

Year planner

| January | February | March |
| April | May | June |

Review 13–16

1 Complete the first conditional sentences with the correct form of the verbs in brackets.

1 If she *saves* (save) her money, she'*ll buy* (buy) a car.

2 It _____ (be) good if Julian _____ (get) the job.

3 If I _____ (work) late tonight, I _____ (leave) early tomorrow.

4 He _____ (travel) by plane if he _____ (go) to Madrid.

5 The manager _____ (not see) you if you _____ (not have) an appointment.

6 If you _____ (look) on my desk, you _____ (find) the report.

7 If we _____ (book) the tickets on the internet, they _____ (not be) expensive.

8 They _____ (call) us if they _____ (have) a problem.

9 If I _____ (talk) to the bank manager, I _____ (ask) her where to invest our money.

10 I _____ (meet) you in the café if you _____ (arrive) by 9.30.

2 Choose the best word to complete the sentences.

1 Is Martina _____ to the training course next week?

a go   **b** goes   **c** going

2 Are you going ___ visit Cape Town when you go to South Africa?

a to   **b** for   **c** in

3 When ___ you going to talk to Giles about his project?

a is   **b** are   **c** do

4 I'm _____ going to Dubai, I'm going to Oman.

a no   **b** don't   **c** not

5 Mark ___ going to talk to you after lunch.

a to   **b** is   **c** are

6 They ___ not going to the trade fair in Shanghai.

a 'll   **b** aren't   **c** 're

3 Look at the schedule about a team meeting next week. Complete the sentences. Use the verbs in brackets and information from the schedule.

Team visit Schedule

Thursday 24th	Jack and Amy arrive by plane 10.30 a.m.
Friday 25th	Kahlani, Max and Edward arrive by car 9 p.m.
Saturday 26th	Team stay at Groves Hotel
Sunday 27th	Edward and Jack play golf with finance director (morning) Max and Amy prepare presentation (evening)
Monday 28th	Jack, Kahlani and Amy visit the factory in Liverpool
Tuesday 29th	Max and Amy give presentation to board of directors (morning) Team meeting with the CEO (afternoon)
Wednesday 30th	Jack and Amy fly to Bahrain 4 p.m. Kahlani, Max and Edward drive to Edinburgh 6 p.m.

1 Amy *is arriving* (arrive) by *plane* with Jack on Thursday.

2 Kahlani and Max _____ (travel) with Edward on _____ 25th.

3 The team _____ (stay) at the Groves _____ on Saturday.

4 Edward and Jack _____ (play) golf with the _____ on Sunday morning.

5 Amy and Max _____ (prepare) their presentation in the _____.

6 On Monday, Jack, Kahlani and Amy _____ (visit) the factory in _____.

7 Max _____ (give) the presentation with Amy to the board of directors on Tuesday _____.

8 In the afternoon the team _____ (meet) the _____.

9 Amy and Jack _____ (fly) to _____ on Wednesday at 4 p.m.

10 Kahlani, Max and Edward _____ (drive) to Edinburgh at _____.

4 Complete the past simple and past participle forms of the verbs.

Infinitive	Past simple	Past participle
1 forget	forgot	forgotten
2 go		
3 have		
4 give		
5 take		
6 do		
7 see		
8 write		

5 Underline the correct word or phrase in *italics* to complete the dialogue.

A: Carlos, ¹*have / did* you ever been to Australia?

B: Yes, I ²*went / been* there last year.

A: What month ³*did you go / have you been*?

B: June. I have ⁴*been / went* to Australia when it was winter.

A: ⁵*Was it / Has it been* cold?

B: No, it ⁶*was / has been* very warm.

A: ⁷*Have you / Did you* visited Sydney?

B: No, but ⁸*I've got / I had* friends in Sydney and I want to visit them.

A: I've ⁹*ever / never* been to Australia. I want to go on my next holiday.

B: ¹⁰*I've got / I got* lots of photographs, do you want to see them?

A: Great, ¹¹*I'm / I've* finished my report, so we can go to lunch and you can tell me about it.

6 Put each word in the box into the correct group according to its stress pattern.

basketball consultant cooperate dangerous emergency
experience holiday motorbike prediction successful
technology tomorrow

Ooo	oOo	oOoo
industry	computer	communicate

7 Complete the verb form of these nouns.

	Verb	Noun
1	*advertise*	advertisement
2		investment
3		product
4		researcher
5		builder
6		payment

8 Underline the word that does not belong on each line.

1 cash cheque *bill* credit card

2 notes coins currency password

3 golf jogging tennis cricket

4 amazing awful exciting wonderful

5 action classical musical thriller

6 producer director teacher actor

9 Match the statement to the correct response.

Statement

1 I was ill last week.

2 I won a trip to Barbados.

3 I can't find my phone.

4 I'm really worried about my presentation.

5 Let's have the meeting at the café.

6 Are you going to the trade fair?

Response

a I'm not sure, I'm very busy.

b I'm sorry to hear that.

c That's a good idea.

d That's wonderful.

e It's OK. It's going to be fine.

f Don't worry, you can use mine.

10 Complete the conversation with one of the words in the box.

account can exciting from help line moment
repeat speaking worry

A: Hello, Renbrook Industries, Paloma ¹_____.

B: Hi, Paloma, It's Douglas Banes ²____ Miller Associates.

A: Sorry, I can't hear you. Can you ³_____ that, please?

B: Sure, it's Douglas Banes. ⁴____ you hear me now?

A: Oh, hi, Douglas. Sorry, it's a bad ⁵____.

B: That's OK. Paloma, I'm in Singapore at the ⁶_____.

A: That's ⁷_____. Are you having a good time?

B: Yes, It's great. But I lost my ⁸_____ number and I want to order some new products.

A: Don't ⁹_____, I can email it to you.

B: That's great. Thanks for your ¹⁰____, Paloma.

Information files

File 1, 1A, page 5

Student A:

1 Read your first line (*We're from Britain.*). Wait for your partner's response (*Oh, so you're British, then.*). Help your partner if necessary. Then read your second line and wait for your partner's response, etc.

You say:	Your partner responds:
• We're from **Britain**.	→ Oh, so you're **British**, then.
• He's from **Mexico**, I think.	→ Yeah, that's right. He's **Mexican**.
• You aren't from **France**?	→ No, we aren't **French**. We're Belgian.
• They aren't from **China**.	→ No, they aren't **Chinese**. They're Vietnamese.
• You mean, Sandra isn't from **Italy**?	→ That's right. Her name is **Italian**, but she's Swiss.

2 Listen to your partner and choose the correct response in the box below.

Responses:

• I know they aren't **Turkish**.
• No, but she works for a **Spanish** company.
• Oh, so they're **American**, then.
• Oh, so you're **Canadian**, then.
• That's right. And his wife is **Japanese**, too.

File 2, 1C, page 8

Student A:

1 Look at the first situation below. What do you say to your partner? Make a request beginning with *Could you ...?* Wait for your partner's response. Then look at the next situation.

• You arrive at a conference. You don't know where to register.

• It's too hot in the room. You want to open the window.

• There's a word you don't understand in the programme. You want your partner to explain it to you.

2 Listen to your partner's requests and respond.

File 3, 2B, page 13

Student A:

1 Look at the table. Complete the sentences to give true information about yourself. Do not write anything in the right-hand column yet.

2 Ask your partner questions to find out about their life. Make a quick note of their answers in the right-hand column.

What time do you come home from work or college?
What do you do when you come home?

3 When you finish, your partner will then ask you a different set of questions.

My life ...	My partner's life ...
I come home from work / college at _____. (*What time?*)	
When I arrive home, I _____. (*What do you do?*)	
I have dinner at _____.	
I go to bed at _____.	
I study English about _____ hours a week. (*How many hours a week?*)	
I watch TV about _____ hours a week.	
On Sunday morning, I _____.	
My favourite day of the week is _____ because I _____.	

File 4 , 2D, page 15

SCORE:

1	a = 2	b = 1	c = 3
2	a = 1	b = 3	c = 2
3	a = 2	b = 3	c = 1
4	a = 3	b = 1	c = 2
5	a = 2	b = 1	c = 3
6	a = 3	b = 1	c = 2
7	a = 1	b = 2	c = 3
8	a = 2	b = 3	c = 1
9	a = 1	b = 3	c = 2
10	a = 3	b = 2	c = 1

Results:

23–30 Your time off is when you get together with friends or meet new people. You know a lot of people already, and you want your relationships to be good. Your social life is busy, but perhaps sometimes you want to be alone.

15–22 It is important to you to be with friends and meet new people, but you also like your private life, and sometimes you really want to be alone. You know what to do if you want a very busy social life, or a very quiet life.

8–14 You do not really try spending time with friends or meeting new people. You like spending time alone. But remember: there are people who would like to spend time with you and get to know you better!

File 5, 3A, page 17

Student A:

1 Look at the table. Ask your partner questions to complete the information about Leila's and Jane and Dan's jobs.

Do Jane and Dan work outside?
Does Leila have regular working hours?

2 Then answer your partner's questions.

3 Discuss these questions with your partner and choose a job from exercise 2, page 16.

- What does Leila do?
- What do Jane and Dan do?

	Leila	Jane and Dan
work outside?	✗	
work with her/their hands?	✗	✓
have regular working hours?		✗
with other people?		✓
use a computer?	✓	
use a company car?	✗	
go to a lot of meetings?		✗
need special qualifications or training?	✓	
wear a uniform?		
earn a lot of money?	✓	
read or write reports, letters or emails?		✓

File 6, 3D, page 21

Student A:

1 Look at the table. Ask your partner questions to complete the information about Yun.

Does Yun have experience in the tourist industry?
Does he have travel experience?

2 Answer your partner's questions about Harish.

	Harish	Yun
	Harish	Yun
experience in tourist industry	2 years	
travel experience	yes, but only in India	
languages	English, Hindi, Urdu; upper-intermediate Spanish	
driving	:-))	
working irregular hours	:-)	
writing emails, faxes, etc.	:-((	
doing business face-to-face	:-))	
doing business over the phone	:-((	

File 7, 4D, page 27

Student B:

You are the marketing director. Try to find a day when you can all meet.

Can we meet on
What about on } *Monday morning?*
Are you free on

Sorry, I usually have a meeting Monday afternoon.

	Morning	Afternoon
Monday		Management team meeting
Tuesday		
Wednesday		
Thursday	Write marketing report	
Friday	Marketing team meeting	

Information files

File 8, 5D, page 35

Student A:

- People born from 1981 to 1991 give $341 a year to charity.

- People born from 1965 to 1980 give $796 a year to charity.

File 9, 5D, page 35

Student B:
Teen Sport
The teenagers in our community have nowhere to meet. Teen Sport is an organization that teaches teenagers exciting sports. We meet every Tuesday and Thursday evening.

Can you help?
Are you good at sport? Do you have two hours a week to spend teaching teenagers? Come and join us. We also want to raise money to buy a minibus. Can you help us raise money?

File 10, 7A, page 43

Student A:

Answer your partner's questions about Karl.

1 Karl eats meat six times a week.

2 He eats oranges every day.

3 He drinks one glass of water a day.

4 He drinks fruit juice three times a week.

Now ask questions about Nina.

1 Nina eats rice _____ times a week.
   How much rice does Nina eat?

2 She eats salad _____ times a week.

3 She drinks a bottle of water _____ day.

4 She eats fish _____ times a week.

File 11, 7B, page 44

Student A:
Describe this chair to your partner.
It's made of ...
It's (small / rectangular / brown).

Which lamp is your partner describing?

File 12, 7D, page 47

Conversation 2:

The buyer	The supplier
You have some questions for the supplier.	
	Offer to help.
You want apple juice from Italy.	
	Choose a response. **a** cartons? **b** bottles?
Choose a response. **a** You prefer cartons. **b** You prefer bottles.	
	Choose a response. **a** I see. **b** That's good.
Ask about the size of each carton / bottle.	
	Choose a response. The apple juice is in **a** small cartons / bottles. **b** large carton / bottles.
Choose a response. **a** You want this size. **b** You don't want this size.	
	Offer a list of prices.
Say you'll think about it and thank the supplier.	
	Say thank you and goodbye.

2

File 13, 8C, page 52

Student A:

You have steps 1 – 3 – 5 – 7 – 9, but in the wrong order. Your partner has steps 2 – 4 – 6 – 8. Together you need to put all the steps in the correct order. Use some of the phrases below.

First, you have to ...
Next, you have to ...
The next thing you have to do is ...
After that, you ...
Finally, ...

- When your message is ready, press 'Send'.
- To type a space between words, press '0'.
- To type a letter, press the key with the letter that you need.
- Press 'OK' ... and that's it!
- Go to your phone's menu and select 'Messages'.

File 14, 8D, page 53

Student B:

1 Read the information about Shanghai. Then answer your partner's questions.

Shanghai: information for the business traveller

If you go to China on business, you have to apply for an 'F' visa. It lasts three months.

From Pudong International Airport, you can take a train, a bus or a taxi to the city centre. If you don't know Shanghai well, you shouldn't hire a car because driving can be very difficult. There is a very fast train, but if it's your first trip, you should take a taxi.

There is no tipping in China, so you don't have to worry about that. But in international restaurants and hotels, service staff usually expect a tip.

Spring and autumn are very good times to be in Shanghai. In winter, it can be very cold. So make sure to take enough warm clothes.

Shanghai is a safe city, but you always have to be very careful when crossing streets: not all car drivers stop for you. Also, the air is often very bad, so you should wear something on your nose and mouth.

2 You have to go to Mexico City in September. Ask your partner for some information. Here are some ideas.

- get a visa?
- worry about health problems?
- take warm clothes?
- use public transport or taxis?

Do I have to get a visa?
Should I worry about health problems?

File 15, 9D, page 61

Student A:

1 Read the information about Barbridge (Site #2).

Barbridge is a lively commercial area of Redhill. It has got lots of shops, cinemas and theatres. From Barbridge, you can walk to the city centre, it takes about ten minutes. Public transport is good: there are a lot of buses to all the suburbs, but there aren't any trains. The school can have 30 to 40 rooms in a beautiful historic building. The rooms can be on two or three different floors. Parking is difficult in Barbridge, but there are some paying car parks not far away from the building. There aren't many houses in the area, but it is not difficult to find flats in Oldfield, a suburb near Barbridge.

2 Ask your partner questions about Peakside (Site #3) and make notes to complete your card below. Then answer your partner's questions about Barbridge.

How far is Peakside from the city centre?
Are there any trains or buses?

Peakside (Site #3)

Distance from city centre: _____ km
Transport: Trains: _____ Buses: _____
Number of rooms: _____
Number of parking places: _____
Flats and houses: _____
Other useful information: _____

File 16, 10A, page 63

Student A:

Use the information about the Sun Hotel to answer your partner's questions.

THE SUN HOTEL
- You were on holiday at the Sun Hotel in England last year.
- The taxi driver needed 35 minutes to take you there!
- One of the receptionists was nice, but his English was difficult to understand.
- The room was just OK. There was a view of a car park on the left and a big wall on the right. But the bed was uncomfortable.
- Breakfast wasn't bad. A lot of fruit and cheese but no yoghurt! Great coffee.
- You weren't very happy about the facilities. The advertisement said there was a swimming pool. But the pool wasn't in or near the hotel: it was a 15-minute walk from the hotel.

Information files

File 17, 10C, page 66

Student A: Call 1

You are on the phone. You speak first.

- Say the first sentence to your partner. (*Good afternoon. Home Stores,* etc.)
- Wait for your partner's response. (*Hello. Kim Stevens here,* etc.)
- If it is correct, say the next sentence. (*Yes. Is there …*)
- If it is not correct, say 'Wrong' and let your partner try again.

You say:	Correct response:
Good afternoon. Home Stores. Aki Nagata speaking.	
	Hello. Kim Stevens here. It's about my new digital camera.
Yes. Is there a problem?	
	Yes. It doesn't work.
Can you give me some more information, please?	
	Sure. It's the Zoomex Deluxe.
And what's the order number?	
	It's JG405.
I'm sorry about this problem. We can ask our specialist to look at it.	
	Fine. Thanks for your help.
You're welcome. Thank you for your call. Goodbye.	
	Bye.

Student A: Call 2

Now it's your turn to answer the phone.

- When you hear your partner, choose the best response from the list below.
- If your response is correct, your partner will continue the conversation.

Responses:
• My pleasure. And thank you for calling, Mr Rosier. Goodbye.
• Oh, I'm very sorry to hear that. Can you give me some more information, please?
• OK. I've got that now. Right. We can send our engineer to look at it. Is 2.30 this afternoon a good time?
• So it stops after two or three copies? Mm. Which model is it?
• Speaking. How can I help you?
• Sorry. Was that BS14?

File 18, 10D, page 67

Student A:

You are Sam Bagley, the centre manager. Prepare for your meeting with Alex Cruse, your general manager.

1 When Alex asks you, give information about your customers' complaints.

2 Suggest solutions to the different problems BUT:

- you don't want to buy more machines
- you think it's OK to have 12 or 15 people in a class
- you don't like Joe Reno – you think it's a good idea to have a new instructor
- you don't want to change the membership system – so, one month = $100 for everyone

File 19, 11D, page 73

Curriculum Vitae

- A CV (Curriculum Vitae) is a document that has information about your education, qualifications and work experience.
- Keep it short! Most employers prefer CVs to be two pages or less.
- Only include information that is important for the job you are applying for.
- Check your CV regularly and update information about new qualifications, training or work experience.
- It's usually a good idea to send a letter with your CV to explain why you want to work for the company and what skills you have for the job.

File 20, 15A, page 95

Student B:

Ask your partner questions in the interview. Find out about these things.

Has he/she ever …?
When?

won a prize?
been in film?
driven a Rolls Royce?
met the president?
been on the news on TV?
married someone famous?

3

File 21, 11D, page 73

Student A:

Curriculum Vitae

Personal details

Jo Foyle

Telephone number: 55283912731

Email: _____

Jo

Education

2008   MBA _____

_____   _____ in garden design, Cardiff college, UK

Career

Date	Company name
_____	**SF Designs** I started my own company and designed gardens for companies in Europe, the USA and Dubai.
2009	_____, Sydney, Australia I was a manager in the _____ department of the top garden design company in the country.

Skills

I can speak _____, _____ and _____.

Interests

Painting and _____.

File 22, 12A, page 75

Student A:
Do not speak or write – only mime! Do not use any objects.

1 You are checking in at the airport. There is a problem: where is your passport?

2 Someone is giving you directions to your hotel. You are just listening. Now you are 'repeating' the directions to make sure you understand.

3 You are making yourself a nice cup of tea / coffee.

4 You are having a shower. Oh no! There is no more water!

File 23, 12B, page 77

Student A:

1 Look at the graphs below. Describe graphs 1–4 to your partner. Then listen to your partner and label the graphs A–D in the order in which you hear them (5–8).

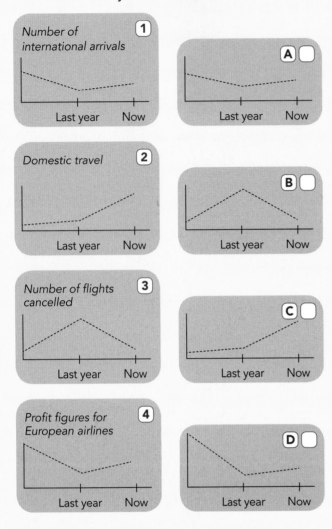

2 When you both finish, check your answers together.

File 24, 12D, page 79

Student A:

You are CEO of Aquila Tours. Read the information about your company. Then answer all the interviewer's questions.

Aquila Tours

Aquila Tours is a multinational travel company which began in Brazil in 1998. Its headquarters are in Manaus (Brazil), and it has branch offices in Venezuela, Colombia and Peru. It employs over 40 people. It specializes in short adventure holidays in the rainforest and on the Amazon. Its main clients are US and European business people. This year, the company is introducing team-building adventures for business executives: the clients do a three-day survival course and then spend three days in the jungle with their colleagues without food or water.

Aquila Tours had about 800 customers last year. This number is now going down slightly, but sales are rising because business visitors spend a lot of money on extra services and options.

File 25, 12D, page 79

Student A:

1 You work for a business magazine. Prepare your interview questions. You want to get all the information for the table below plus two other facts.

2 Interview your partner and complete the table with a few notes.

Pegasus Travel Fact File

Started in:	
Headquarters:	
Offices:	
Products and services:	
New product:	
Present trends in sales and number of customers:	
_____ :	
_____ :	

File 26, 13D, page 87

Student A:

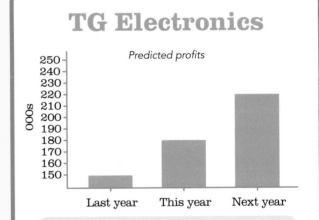

TG Electronics

Predicted profits

The product

• Some large companies are using the cleaning robots at the moment.
• A Science TV programme will show the robots next month.
• The CEO wants to produce small cleaning robots for the house.

Advantages

• People who invest $50,000 or more get a robot.

Possible problems

• Their best designer is 59.
• Will he retire?

4

File 27, 14D, page 93

Student A:

1 Look at the illustration. What do you think the story is going to be about?

2 You speak first. Dictate the beginning of the text to your partner. Then it is your partner's turn to dictate and you write the missing words in your text. Then you dictate the next part of the text, and so on. You can help each other, but you can't look at your partner's text!

He's digging

Two men are working along the roadside. One of them digs a hole, and the other one _ _ _ _ _ _ _ _ _ _ _ _ _ _ _ _ _ _ . Then they do the same a few metres away, and then the same again, and so they spend _ _ _ _ _ _ _ _ _ _ _ . A woman is watching them from the other side of the road, and she doesn't understand. She walks up to the two men and asks: '_ _ _ _ _ _ _ _ . What exactly are you doing?'

'Well, we're working,' one of the men says. 'But _ _ _ _ _ _ _ _ _ _ there's nothing wrong with what you're doing?'

'If there's something wrong, it's not because of us. _ _ '_ _ _ _ _ _ _ _ _ _ _ _ _ _ . He didn't come to work today.'

'And who's Jack?' _ _ _ _ _ _ _ _ _ _ _ _ .

'He's the guy _ _ _ _ _ _ _ _ put trees _ _ _ _ _ _ _ _ _ _ .'

File 28, 16A, page 101

Student A:

Monday

9 a.m

2:20 p.m — Fly to Mumbai, India

Tuesday

11:30 a.m — Visit Water Kingdom, Water Park

8 p.m.

Wednesday

10:30 a.m. — Meet Pilar at the Science Centre.

9 p.m.

Thursday

8.30 a.m. — Walk in National park

7 p.m.

File 29, 16A, page 101

Student A: Conversation 1
You are the manager. Ask about the arrangements for the visit.
• find out what they are doing morning and afternoon each day.

• think of more questions about the arrangements.
   Where are they staying?
   How are they travelling?
   When are they returning to Turin?

Student A: Conversation 2

1 You are the employee. Look at the schedule and add more activities in the morning and afternoon. Decide these things about the visitors

   where / stay? how / travel? when / return / Turin

2 Answer your manager's questions.

	Morning	Afternoon
Monday	Visit the offices	
Tuesday		Meet CEO and director
Wednesday	Have a presentation about New project	
Thursday		Fly back to Turin

Information files

File 30, 16C, page 104
Student B:

Conversation 1

Student A starts the conversation. You are the boss. Listen to what Student A wants and ask for reasons.

Why do you want to …

You can decide to say 'yes' or 'no' to Student A.

Conversation 2

You start the conversation. You are the employee.

I'd like to talk to you about something …

You want to work in the office four days a week and work at home every Friday.

Reasons:

- On Friday you write reports all day.

- You travel two hours to work. You can do more work at home.

File 31, 1A, page 5
Student B:

1 Listen to your partner and choose the correct response from the box below.

Responses:

- No, they aren't **Chinese**. They're Vietnamese.
- No, we aren't **French**. We're Belgian.
- Oh, so you're **British**, then.
- That's right. Her name is **Italian**, but she's Swiss.
- Yeah, that's right. He's **Mexican**.

2 Now read your first line (*We're from Canada.*). Wait for your partner's response (*Oh, so you're Canadian, then.*). Help your partner if necessary. Then read your second line and wait for your partner's response, etc.

You say:	Your partner responds:
• We're from **Canada**. →	Oh, so you're **Canadian**, then.
• They aren't from **Turkey**. →	I know they aren't **Turkish**.
• She isn't from **Spain**. →	No, but she works for a **Spanish** company.
• He's from **Japan**, I think. →	That's right. And his wife is **Japanese**, too.
• They're from **the USA**. →	Oh, so they're **American**, then.

File 32, 1C, page 8
Student B:

1 Listen to your partner's requests and respond.

2 Look at the first situation below. What do you say to your partner? Make a request beginning with *Could you …?* Wait for your partner's response. Then look at the next situation.

- You lose your registration badge. You don't know how to get another one.
- You get one conference programme. You want another copy for a colleague.
- You have a camera and you want a photo of yourself.

File 33, 2B, page 13
Student B:

1 Look at the table. Complete the sentences to give true information about yourself. Do not write anything in the right-hand column yet.

2 Answer your partner's questions. They are different from yours.

3 Ask your partner your questions to find out about their life. Make a quick note of their answers in the right-hand column.

What time do you get up when you go to work or college?
Do you do exercises to keep fit?

My life …	My partner's life …
When I go to work / college, I get up at _____ . (*What time?*)	
I do/don't do exercises to keep fit.	
I have a small / big breakfast and a cup / glass of _____ .	
I leave home at _____ .	
I go to work / college by bus/on foot/by car. (*How?*)	
I work _____ hours a week. (*How many hours a week?*)	
My favourite time of the day is _____ because I _____ .	
At the weekend, I _____ . (*What do you do?*)	

5

File 34, 3A, page 17

Student B:

1 Look at the table. Answer your partner's questions about Leila's and Jane and Dan's jobs.

2 Then ask your partner questions to complete the information about Leila's and Jane and Dan's jobs.

> *Does Leila work outside?*
> *Do Jane and Dan work with their hands?*

3 Discuss these questions with your partner and choose a job from exercise 2, page 16.

- What does Leila do?
- What do Jane and Dan do?

	Leila	Jane and Dan
earn a lot of money?		✓
go to a lot of meetings?	✓	
have regular working hours?	✓	
need special qualifications or training?		✓
read or write reports, letters or emails?	✓	
use a company car?		✗
use a computer?		✓
wear a uniform?	✗	✓
work with other people?	✓	
work outside?		✗
work with her/their hands?		

File 35, 3D, page 21

Student B:

1 Look at the table. Answer your partner's questions about Yun.

2 Ask your partner questions to complete the information about Harish.

> *Does Harish have experience in the tourist industry?*
> *Does he have travel experience?*

	Harish	Yun
	Harish	**Yun**
experience in tourist industry		8 years
travel experience		yes (Asia, South America)
languages		Chinese, English, French, intermediate Spanish
driving		:-)
working irregular hours		:-(
writing emails, faxes, etc.		:-)
doing business face-to-face		:-))
doing business over the phone		:-)

File 36, 4D, page 27

Student C:

You are the production manager. Try to find a day when you can all meet.

> *Can we meet on* ⎤
> *What about on* ⎬ *Monday afternoon?*
> *Are you free on* ⎦
> *Sorry, I usually have a meeting on Monday morning.*

	Morning	Afternoon
Monday	Production team meeting	
Tuesday	Meeting about new IT system	
Wednesday		New products presentation
Thursday		
Friday		

File 37, 5D, page 35

Student B:

- People born from 1946 to 1964 give $901 a year to charity.
- People born earlier than 1945 give $1,066 a year to charity.

File 38, 5D, page 35

Student C:

Be a friend

Be a friend is an organization that helps elderly people. We work with people in their homes and help with cooking, gardening and shopping.

Can you help?

We want donations of cooking and gardening equipment. We also want to raise money to help elderly people go on holiday. Can you cook, garden, help shop? Do you have an hour a week when you can help someone in their home?

File 39, 7B, page 44

Student B:

Which chair is your partner describing?

Describe this lamp to your partner.

> It's made of ...
> It's (small / rectangular / brown).

File 40, 8C, page 52

Student B:

You have steps 2 – 4 – 6 – 8, but in the wrong order. Your partner has steps 1 – 3 – 5 – 7 – 9. Together you need to put all the steps in the correct order. Use some of the phrases below.

> First, you have to ...
> Next, you have to ...
> The next thing you have to do is ...
> After that, you ...
> Finally, ...

- Press 'Search' to find the phone number that you need. Move up or down the list with the arrow key (↑ or ↓).
- Press once for the first letter, twice for the second and three times for the third.
- Select 'Write message' and start writing.
- To type a special character, press the star key ('*') and select the symbol that you need.

File 41, 8D, page 53

Student A:

Read the information about Mexico City. Then answer your partner's questions.

Mexico City: information for the business traveller

To enter Mexico, you have to get a tourist card, for example from your airline. You also have to keep the copy of the card that they give you at the airport, because you have to show it when you leave the country. Mexico City is a very big city. Getting around can be difficult, but the metro system is very good: it is fast, safe and very cheap. If you take a taxi, make sure that the licence plate starts with an 'L' or an 'S'. To be safe, you should phone for a taxi. Be careful with the water. You should only drink bottled water, and when you get ice cubes, ask if they are made with clean water. Mexican food is fantastic, but you should not eat anything that people sell in the street. Go to restaurants or 'fondas'.

The weather is always nice, but from June to September, it often rains in the afternoon. Also, it usually gets a bit cold in the evenings, so you should take a warm jacket.

File 42, 9D, page 61

Student B:

1 Read the information about Peakside (Site #3).

Peakside is an exciting part of Redhill, only ten kilometres from the city centre. It has got a sports centre, a park and a big shopping centre. Public transport is excellent: there are three metro stations and there are some buses as well. The school can have a building with 28 rooms, and it is possible to make six new rooms on the top floor. There are ten parking places in front of the building and a free car park on the other side of the street. Peakside is not a very expensive place, and it has got lots of nice houses and flats.

2 Answer your partner's questions about Peakside. Then, ask questions about Barbridge and make notes to complete your card below.

> How far is Barbridge from the city centre?
> Are there any trains or buses?

Barbridge (Site #2)

Distance from city centre:	_____ km
Transport:	Trains: _____ Buses: _____
Number of rooms:	_____
Number of parking places:	_____
Flats and houses:	_____
Other useful information:	_____ _____

6

File 43, 10A, page 63
Student B:

Use the information about the Flying Boot Hotel to answer your partner's questions.

> **THE FLYING BOOT HOTEL**
> You were at the Flying Boot Hotel in 2009, when you were on business in Cork, Ireland.
> It was easy to find. It was only a ten-minute walk from the airport. There was a view of the airport from your room on the sixth floor. Sometimes, there was a problem with the lift, so you had to walk.
> The staff were always very polite, and always very busy. It was difficult to get information because there were always a lot of guests waiting at the reception desk.
> Your room was big, but it wasn't very clean. There were pieces of paper and plastic under your bed. And the bed wasn't very comfortable!
> Breakfast was nothing special, just 'hotel food'.
> The facilities? Well, the 'Business Centre' had only two computers! There was an internet connection ... but only from 7 a.m. to 11 a.m.

File 44, 10D, page 67

> **Student B:**
> You are Alex Cruse, the general manager. Prepare for your meeting with Sam Bagley, the manager of your new fitness centre.
>
> **1** Ask Sam for information about your customers' complaints.
>
> **2** Suggest solutions to the different problems BUT:
> - you don't want to buy more machines
> - you want only 10 people in a class (not 12 or 15!) because the advertisement says '10 people maximum'
> - Joe Reno is your friend – you think it's a good idea to talk to him (why is he late? what are his problems?, etc.); you don't want a new instructor
> - you think it's a good idea to change the membership system – one month = £80 OR 10 classes = £90.

File 45, 10C, page 66

> **Student B: Call 1**
>
> **1** You are on the phone. Your partner speaks first.
> - When you hear your partner, look for the best response from the list below.
> - If your response is correct, your partner will continue the conversation.
>
> | **Responses:** |
> | --- |
> | • Bye. |
> | • Fine. Thanks for your help. |
> | • Hello. Kim Stevens here. It's about my new digital camera. |
> | • It's JG405. |
> | • Sure. It's the Zoomex Deluxe. |
> | • Yes. It doesn't work. |

> **Student B: Call 2**
>
> **Now it's your turn to start a phone conversation.**
> - Say the first sentence to your partner. (*Good morning. This is ...*, etc)
> - Wait for your partner's response. (*Speaking. How can I ...*, etc)
> - If it is correct, say the next sentence. (*I've got a problem ...*, etc)
> - If it is not correct, say 'Wrong' and let your partner try again.

You say:	Correct response:
Good morning. This is Marc Rosier. Can I speak to Mr White, please?	
	Speaking. How can I help you?
I've got a problem with our new photocopier.	
	Oh, I'm very sorry to hear that. Can you give me some more information, please?
Yes. Well, it makes two or three copies, then it stops.	
	So it stops after two or three copies? Mm. Which model is it?
It's the Lansung PS40.	
	Sorry. Was that BS14?
Sorry, no. It's P-S-four-zero.	
	OK. I've got that now. Right. We can send our engineer to look at it. Is 2.30 this afternoon a good time?
Yes, 2.30 is fine. Thank you for your help.	
	My pleasure. And thank you for calling, Mr Rosier. Goodbye.
Goodbye.	

File 46, 11D, page 73
Student B:

Curriculum Vitae

Jo

Personal details

Jo Foyle

Telephone number: _____

Email: j2foyle@wfgmail.com

Education

_____ _____ Milan University

2006 Diploma in garden design, Cardiff college, UK

Career

Date	Company name
2007	_____
	I started my own company and designed gardens for companies in _____ , _____ and _____ .
_____	**Aztec Design,** _____
	I was a _____ in the Marketing department of the top garden design company in the country.

Skills

I can speak English, Polish and Italian.

Interests

_____ and golf.

7

File 47, 4D, page 27

Student D:

You are the Finance director. Try to find a day when you can all meet.

Can we meet on
What about on } *Monday morning?*
Are you free on

Sorry, I usually have a meeting on Monday afternoon.

	Morning	**Afternoon**
Monday		Management team meeting
Tuesday		Finance team meeting
Wednesday	Present finance report to CEO	
Thursday		
Friday		

File 50, 12A page 75

Student B:

Do not speak or write – only mime! Do not use any objects.

1 You are getting on the plane. You are looking for your seat. Oh no! Someone is sitting in your seat!

2 You are giving a presentation. Your mobile phone starts ringing. You can't find it!

3 You are making yourself a cheese and tomato sandwich.

4 You are on a plane. You are giving the pre-flight safety demonstration.

File 48, 12D, page 79

Student B:

1 You work for a business magazine. Prepare your interview questions. You want to get all the information for the table below <u>plus</u> two other facts.

2 Interview your partner and complete the table with notes.

Aquila Tours Fact File

Started in:	
Headquarters:	
Offices:	
Products and services:	
New product:	
Present trends in sales and number of customers:	
_____:	
_____:	

File 49, 12B, page 77

Student B:

1 Look at the graphs below. Listen to your partner and number the graphs E–H in the order in which you hear them. Then describe graphs 5–8 to your partner.

2 When you both finish, check your answers together.

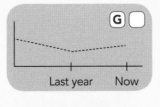
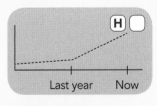

E ⬜   F ⬜   G ⬜   H ⬜

Last year — Now

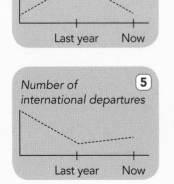
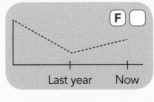
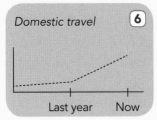

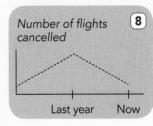

5 Number of international departures

6 Domestic travel

7 Profit figures for European airlines

8 Number of flights cancelled

Last year — Now

Information files

File 51, 12D, page 79

Student B:

You are the CEO of Pegasus Holidays. Read the information about your company. Then answer all the interviewer's questions.

> **Pegasus Holidays**
> Pegasus Holidays is a Czech company with its headquarters in Prague. It started in 2008 but it is quickly becoming a true Central European company with offices in Vienna and in Budapest. Its CEO, Petra Kryl, believes that people want 'less travel, more discovery'. So Pegasus wants to offer not just a holiday, but a complete experience. For example, it provides holidays where customers can take part in ecological projects. So visitors not only discover the countryside, they also do something good for the environment and the local community. At the moment, Petra is working on a new project: holidays for food lovers. Visitors don't go to expensive restaurants; they spend a few days in small towns and villages in different regions and learn to cook traditional dishes with the local people in their homes. How is business at the moment? It's a difficult year, so sales are not going up. The number of customers isn't changing either, but a lot of people are already enquiring about the foodie holidays.
> Pegasus is opening a new office in Slovakia, so it now has 24 employees in four different countries.

File 52, 14D, page 93

Student B:

1 Look at the illustrations. What do you think the story is about?

2 Your partner speaks first. Write the missing words in your text. Then it is your turn to dictate. You can help each other, but you can't look at your partner's text!

Two men are working along the roadside. One of them _ _ _ _ _ _ _ _ _ _ , and the other one puts the earth back in. Then they do the same a few metres away, and then _ _ _ _ _ _ _ _ _ _ _ _ , and so they spend the whole day. A woman is watching them from the other side of the road, and she doesn't understand. _ _ _ _ _ _ _ _ _ _ _ _ _ _ _ _ _ _ _ _ _ and asks:

'Excuse me. What exactly are you doing?'

'_ _ _ _ , _ _ ' _ _ _ _ _ _ _ _ _ ,' one of the men says.

File 53, 15A, page 95

Student A:

Ask your partner questions in the interview. Find out about these things.

> Has he/she ever ...?
> When?
> been to the Oscars?
> had dinner in the Ritz?
> written a book?
> had tea with the queen?
> won a sports competition?
> bought something very expensive?

He's digging.

'But are you sure there's nothing wrong with what you're doing?'

'If there's something wrong, _ _ ' _ _ _ _ _ _ _ _ _ _ _ _ _ _ _. It's because of Jack. He didn't come to work today.'

'_ _ _ _ _ _ ' _ _ _ _ _ ?' the woman asks.

'_ _ ' _ _ _ _ _ _ _ who has to _ _ _ _ _ _ _ _ in the holes.'

8

File 54, 13D, page 87
Student B:

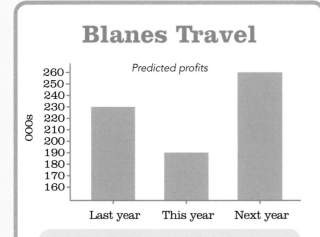

Blanes Travel

Predicted profits

000s

Last year — 230
This year — 190
Next year — 260

The planes
• Small luxury planes with chef, waiters and excellent food. Passengers are usually rich.
• People who don't have their own private plane. Tickets are very expensive at the moment.
• The CEO wants to increase ticket prices in the future.

Advantages
• People who invest $50,000 or more get five free flights a year.

Possible problems
• Oil prices in the future?

File 55, 11B, page 71

Mostly A: You learn best by doing things. When you learn something new, you like to try it yourself.

Mostly B: You learn best when someone tells you information. You prefer to listen to instructions.

Mostly C: You learn best when you can see things. You prefer information to be in writing or with diagrams and pictures.

File 56, 16A, page 101
Student B:

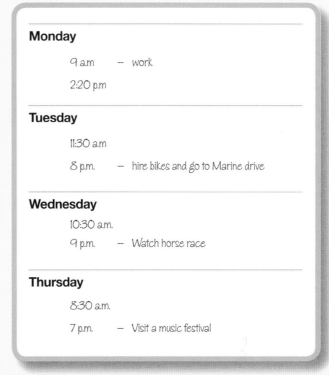

Monday
9 a.m — work
2:20 p.m

Tuesday
11:30 a.m
8 p.m. — hire bikes and go to Marine drive

Wednesday
10:30 a.m.
9 p.m. — Watch horse race

Thursday
8:30 a.m.
7 p.m. — Visit a music festival

File 57, 16A, page 101

Student B: Conversation 1

1 You are the employee. Look at the schedule and add more activities in the morning and afternoon. Decide these things about the visitors:

where / stay?   how / travel?   when / return / Turin

2 Answer your manager's questions.

	Morning	Afternoon
Monday	Visit the offices	
Tuesday		Meet CEO and director
Wednesday	Have a presentation about New project	
Thursday		Fly back to Turin

Student B: Conversation 2
You are the manager. Ask about the arrangements for the visit.

• find out what they are doing morning and afternoon each day.

• think of more questions about the arrangements.

Where are they staying?
How are they travelling?
When are they returning Turin?

Audio scripts

1A, Page 4, Exercise 2

M = Matt, **P** = Paul

M: Hi, I'm Matt Heyns.

P: Pleased to meet you, Matt. I'm Paul Alexander.

M: Pleased to meet you, too. So what are you here for, Paul? Are you a journalist?

P: No, I'm not. I'm a creative designer for the City Star label.

* * * *

P = Pamela, **T** = Tom

P: Excuse me. I can't find my pen. Could I use yours for a minute?

T: Sure. Here you are.

P: Thanks a lot. By the way, my name's Pamela. Pamela Elson.

T: You mean Pamela Elson, the Australian model?

P: Yeah, that's right.

T: Oh ... Really? ... Erm ... Nice to meet you, Pamela. I'm Tom.

* * * *

J = Jackie, **C** = Chorus

J: Good evening, everyone. I'm Jackie Yang. I'm a photographer for the Hong Kong *Trendsetter Magazine*. Can I take a photo of all four of you together?

C: Yes, OK. / Sure.

* * * *

R = Reporter, **V** = Victor

R: Hi! You must be Antonio Felipe Rivero, the Mexican supermodel.

V: No, I'm not. My name's Victor Serrano. I'm Mr Rivero's bodyguard, actually.

R: Oh, sorry! I'm a reporter for Catwalk TV. Erm ... Could I speak to Mr Rivero?

V: Sure. He is right here behind me.

1A, Page 4, Exercise 3

M = Matt, **P** = Paul

M: Hi, I'm Matt Heyns.

P: Pleased to meet you, Matt. I'm Paul Alexander.

M: Pleased to meet you, too. So what are you here for, Paul? Are you a journalist?

P: No, I'm not. I'm a creative designer for the City Star label.

M: Mm, that's interesting. City Star is a Canadian brand, is that right?

P: Yeah. Our headquarters are in Vancouver, but I'm from Toronto originally, like Ana, my wife.

M: Is she in the fashion business as well?

P: Well, yes, she's a make-up artist. She works for two fashion houses, and also for the Stanley Theatre. That's where she is this evening, by the way!

1A, Page 5, Exercise 7

Good afternoon ... This is Catwalk TV live from the Urban Horizon international trade show. With over 60,000 visitors this year, Urban Horizon is probably the Number 1 event in our city. Designers and business people from Brazil, Germany and Turkey are here, and also for the first time from Japan and the USA. Of course people come to a show like this not just for the clothes, but also for the people who wear them on the catwalk. This year, the supermodels from Mexico and Australia are everybody's favourite topic of conversation. Two young designers from Russia are also the focus of a lot of attention. So many different people from the fashion industry are here today ... you can feel a buzz of creativity everywhere ... it's just incredible. Urban Horizon is absolutely unique!

1A, Page 5, Exercise 8

1 Brazil
2 Germany
3 Turkey
4 Japan
5 the USA
6 Mexico
7 Australia
8 Russia

1B, Page 6, Exercise 3

Every year, about 30 million visitors come to Britain. About 50 per cent of them are from France, Ireland, Germany, Spain, Italy and the USA.

Over 60 per cent of all visitors to the UK come for a holiday or to visit friends and relatives, and 25 per cent travel on business.

Visitors from outside Europe sometimes find it strange that they need to fill in a 'landing card' before entering the UK. But they just need to give basic personal details: family name, forenames, sex, date and place of birth, occupation, nationality, address in the UK, and a signature.

And what about British tourists, by the way? Where do they go? The top destinations for British tourists are usually ... Spain, France, the USA, Ireland, Italy and Germany!

1B, Page 6, Exercise 6

349 8175

0495 122566

00 44 607 948 7843

ahmed@yahoo.com

laurie.brown@ntlworld.com

bressangf@tiscali.it

1B, Page 6, Exercise 9

W = Woman, **J** = Jeff Lloyd

W: What's your name, please?

J: Jeff Lloyd.

W: How do you spell 'Jeff'?

J: J-E-F-F.

W: J-E-F-F. Fine. Great. Could you also spell your surname for me, please?

J: Sure. That's L-L-O-Y-D.

W: L-L-O-Y-D ... Thanks. And what's your phone number?

J: 305 6697.

W: Sorry, could you say that again?

J: Yeah. 305 6697.

W: Just one more thing. What's your email address?

J: It's jlloyd@gmail.com.

W: Great! Thank you.

1C, Page 8, Exercises 2 and 3

N = Nicola, **K** = Karol

N: Hi! Are you from G.W. Electronics?

K: Yes, I am.

N: Great! Phew! This suitcase is so heavy ... Could you help me?

K: But ... erm ... excuse me. What's your name?

N: Sorry?

K: Could I have your name, please?

N: My name? My name's here, on your board: first name, Nicola; surname, Berry.

K: But, er ... but, er ... that's impossible!

N: Impossible? What do you mean?

K: Mr Nicola Berry is a gentleman.

N: Well, I'm a woman and my name's Nicola Berry. Look, here's my passport. See?

K: Ms Ni-co-la Ber-ry ... So Nicola is your first name?

N: Yes, that's right.

K: How interesting! In my country, Nikola is a man's name. My brother's name is Nikola. I'm sorry, Ms Berry, very sorry.

N: That's alright. Now I understand.

K: Here, let me help you with your luggage. Please come this way, Nicola, erm, I mean, Ms Berry. The car park is over there. Oh, and my name is Lenner, by the way. Karol Lenner.

N: Carol? How do you spell your name? Carol is a woman's name in my country. We spell it with a C.

K: I spell my name with a K!

2A, Page 11, Exercises 8 and 9

I = Interviewer, **R** = Rob, **M** = Mother-in-law, **J** = Jill

I: So, Rob, the holiday season is not far from us, but you don't feel very happy about it, is that right?

R: Yeah, that's right. You see, my wife and I ... erm ... we kind of like our relatives, but we don't like those big dinners where you just sit, eat and drink all day long. It's so boring! Imagine 15 people in a room who talk, talk, talk all the time and don't listen to each other ... Terrible! I just can't relax! And then, there's something else, you know. I'm a taxi driver and my wife is a telephone operator for the same taxi company. A lot of our colleagues don't want to work when there's a holiday, but we're OK with that. You know what? We like to work during the holiday season because we get more money. And my customers feel happy because they're on holiday, so they often give me very big tips.

M: Rob! Dinner's ready! ... Robert!

R: Yeah! Coming!

I: Your wife?

R: Nah. The mother-in-law ...

* * * *

I: Jill ... You say you don't feel very happy when there's a special occasion. Why's that?

J: Well, I don't feel very happy when I'm not together with all my children and grandchildren. My children don't live in England anymore, they're thousands of miles away, one in New Zealand and one in Canada. We don't celebrate special occasions together, we don't spend our holidays together. So these days what we do, my husband and I, when there's a special celebration, we ... we just get everyone together via the web. We're all on Skype, you see, and we've got this fantastic computer with a webcam. ... Of course, we all know the time differences. ... We leave the computer on all day long. We chat, or we just smile or just say 'hello'. That way we don't miss each other so much!

2B, Page 12, Exercise 3

I = Interviewer, **L** = Laura

I: Hello. This is Radio 5, and it is now time for our special edition of 'Life After Work'. In this programme, we want to find out what people do after work. Do they go straight back home? Do they go shopping? Or do they get together with colleagues to have a bit of fun?

Let's find out ... Erm ... Excuse me ... Hello ... Could I just ask you two or three questions for our radio programme?

L: Erm ... Yeah ... Alright.

I: So ... what's your name, please?

L: I'm Laura.

I: Now then, Laura, do you go to work, or are you a student?

L: I work. I'm a software designer for Grapple, the electronics manufacturer.

I: Wow, that's interesting. Tell me, do you sometimes meet your colleagues after work?

L: Yes, of course. We meet two or three times a month, at the end of the week.

I: And ... where do you get together?

L: Well, it depends. We go to a club or a restaurant, or to someone's home.

I: On those occasions, what sort of clothes do you wear? Do you wear formal or informal clothes?

L: Well, again, it depends. If we meet straight after work, then I'm dressed informally, because I wear informal clothes at work. If we meet later, then I like to wear more formal clothes.

I: When you are together with your colleagues, do you discuss problems you have at work?

L: No, we don't do that! Never. We have meetings at work to discuss those problems ... And another thing I don't do, for example, is make phone calls on my mobile phone. I answer the phone if it rings, of course, but I don't make calls when I'm with a group of people. After work, I just want to relax and have fun.

I: There's just one more question, Laura, but I think I already know the answer to that one. Do you enjoy yourself when you go out with your colleagues?

L: Yes, I do. I always have a good time. Some of my colleagues are really good friends. All of us have fun, we are easy-going ...

2B, Page 12, Exercise 4

1
Of course we do! Men and women, juniors and seniors, we don't make any differences. We're all in the same business. I'm not one for the all gals' night out.

2
Well, all I can say is that I don't look at my watch and time goes by really fast. So yes, sometimes it's past midnight by the time I get home.

3
Well, if walking is a sport, then, yes, we do. We've got some lovely hills just outside the city, and it's great to go hill walking together in the summer.

4

No, not usually. We don't go to expensive places. But if it's someone's birthday, then I don't mind getting a really nice present. So then, of course, I spend a bit more.

5

Only with very good friends. And as I said some of my colleagues are really great friends, so with them it's OK to talk about my family ... or about my partner ... things like that.

2C, Page 14, Exercises 1 and 2

H = Helen, **D** = David
Conversation 1
H: Hi! Is this seat free?
D: Yes.
H: Do you work in Accounts, too?
D: No.
H: Do you have lunch here every day?
D: No.

Conversation 2
H: Hi! Is this seat free?
D: Sure. Go ahead.
H: Do you work in Accounts, too?
D: No, I don't. I'm in IT.
H: Really?
D: Yes, I'm the new graphic designer.
H: Oh, that's interesting. ... Do you have lunch here every day?
D: Well, not every day. Sometimes I just have a sandwich at my desk.

2C, Page 14, Exercise 5

a
Well, this year I have three weeks. I'm very happy about that.

b
Yes, I do. But I often go to work by train.

c
Yeah, I'm online all day long, at work and at home.

d
Well, I speak French, and I want to speak English.

e
No, never. My weekend is for family and friends.

f
Well, never before eleven.

3A, Page 17, Exercise 8

Photojournalists, air traffic controllers, librarians, surgeons, ... Who has the most stress at work? Psychologist Saqib Saddiq says that librarians have the most stressful job. Why? How is that possible? A photojournalist often travels to dangerous places, but a librarian spends every day in a quiet room. A surgeon looks inside people's bodies, but a librarian only opens books. An air traffic controller manages new situations every day, but a librarian sees the same old books all the time. What, then, is so stressful about a librarian's job? To find out, Mr Saddiq interviewed a lot of librarians. Here are the things that librarians say about their job: 'Libraries are boring places.' 'A librarian doesn't do a lot of different things: every day at work is the same, week after week.' 'Other people always tell us what to do.' People in dangerous jobs, for example police

officers, get a lot of help and training, but librarians are all alone with their stress because we think they have an easy job.

3B, Page 18, Exercises 2, 3 and 4

1
I = Interviewer, **E** = Enrica

I: Good morning, Enrica. I know the Marketing Department is very busy this week, and you're the manager ... So, just two or three questions about the things you like or don't like at the office.

E: Oh, I like that! It's good to talk about those things, sometimes. Well, first, look at this photocopier. I think it's 20 years old. It takes my assistant five minutes to make five photocopies. It's terrible, really. We need a new machine as soon as possible. Another thing I don't like is queuing in the cafeteria. Our cafeteria is beautiful, but the people there are slow, and our lunch break is short, so that's a problem.

I: Any other pet hate?

E: Well ... look at that desk over there, for example. Can you see?

I: Erm ... Yes ... Well, it's not very tidy ...

E: You're very polite. That desk is so untidy, it's terrible. How can anyone sit there and work?

I: Erm ... Is that your assistant's desk?

E: No – it's mine!

2
I = Interviewer, **S** = Sergei

I: Sergei ... You work in a bank in the city centre, is that right?

S: Yeah.

I: We know that in all jobs, there are always things we like, and things we don't like. So ... please tell me: what do you like and what don't you like at your workplace?

S: That's an easy question, thank you. I'm pleased it's not about the global economic crisis! So ... things I like or don't like ... Well, ... we all have a mobile phone, that's OK, but some people have very loud ringtones. That's terrible! I hate those loud ringtones! ... Then, I don't like being late for work. We start at nine, but I'm always there 20 minutes earlier or more. Now, on the positive side ... well ... I like my boss, she's great ... And the colleagues in my department are great, too. I love helping them.

3C, Page 20, Exercises 2 and 4

D = Davide, **S** = Sarah
D: Two weeks already! So, how are you, Sarah?
S: Very well, thanks. And you?
D: I'm alright. I think the salespeople are really nice.
S: Me too. And I like talking to customers on the phone ...
D: Really? I don't. In fact, I hate doing business on the phone. I want to be face-to-face with my customers. That's the best thing in our job.
S: Yeah, I know what you mean, but that's not always possible. For me the best thing in our job is teamwork. I just love working in a team.
D: Me too. You know, I really hate working alone.
S: And what do you think of the hours?
D: Well, I'm not too happy about the flexible working hours ...
S: Me neither. Four hours last Tuesday, and then twelve hours the next day!

D: Yeah, I know. I think it's stressful. I don't like staying at the office after six. I want to go out with my friends.

S: Really? I never go out on weekdays. Only on Saturdays. And sometimes … That's your phone, Davide. Not a business call, I hope …

3D, Page 21, Exercises 3 and 4

I = Interviewer, **R** = Rita

I: Good morning, Ms Oliveira. Thank you for coming to the interview. At Rihla, we don't do formal interviews, so just relax. Alright?

R: Yes. Thank you.

I: Right. So I see from your CV here that you have some experience in the tourist industry.

R: That's right, yes. Sometimes I work as a hotel receptionist in the summer holidays.

I: Mm. I see … Summer jobs, then … And do you travel a lot?

R: Well, not a lot, but I go back to Brazil every year to see my parents. And then we often go to Argentina and Chile together.

I: So, mostly South America … Now then, what foreign languages do you speak?

R: Portuguese is my mother tongue. I speak English and Spanish. And then, I also have upper-intermediate level Arabic.

I: So … Portuguese, English, Spanish and Arabic. Excellent. Do you drive?

R: I have a driving licence, but I don't drive much because I don't like driving. I think it's better to use public transport.

I: Maybe, but we can't ask our customers who arrive at Juan Santamaría airport to wait for a local bus! Our tour manager meets them there and drives them into the jungle three times a week.

R: I understand. That's why the advertisement asks about irregular hours …

I: Exactly. How do you feel about working irregular hours?

R: Well, I do a lot of sport, so it's good to have the weekend free.

I: I see. You're not very happy about irregular hours, then. Erm … How about writing? Do you like writing?

R: Yes. I love writing, and I have a lot of experience of writing business letters …

I: That's great. Finally, what type of communication do you like?

R: Well, I think in business face-to-face communication is best, but of course it's not always possible. We also do business with customers over the phone. In fact, I love all types of communication. And as you can see from my CV, I have experience of working as a personal assistant in a global company …

I: Yes, that's interesting. Could you tell me more about that …

3D, Page 21, Exercise 7

Well, all three candidates are interesting. Rita is very energetic and she is a very good communicator. But she doesn't know the tourist industry very well. Besides, she doesn't like driving or working at weekends, so we don't think she can be happy in this job. Yun has a lot of experience and he is also a good communicator. But he also has a problem with working

irregular hours. We think Harish is the best person for this job. He is OK with irregular hours and he loves driving. Of course, he has only two years' of experience and he says he hates writing and phoning. But we don't believe experience is everything. We believe people can learn, and at Rihla we help our staff learn what they need for the job.

4A, Page 23, Exercise 9

1
True. People use both hands to show respect. In everyday life, don't use your left hand when you give somebody something. Use your right hand.

2
False. Business lunches in Italy are often quite long. But in the company I work for, they are usually short. Too bad!

3
True. It's the same as in my family in England!

4
True. Never use your left hand when you eat!

5
True. It sometimes happens. But my Brazilian colleagues never ask me such questions.

6
True. 'You are my guest,' they say.

7
True. It happens to me not just sometimes, but very often. Maybe because I don't like singing!

8
False. But I know two or three German managers who always keep their office doors open.

9
True. People in India often start a meeting with an informal conversation. But not everybody does that.

10
False. In Japan, people usually use surnames in business meetings.

4B, Page 24, Exercise 5

Conversation 1
O = Owen Lewis, **W** = woman

O: Hi, I'm Owen Lewis. I'm calling about the gardening club.

W: Sorry, can you repeat that, please? I'm in the garden on my mobile.

O: Can you tell me about the gardening club?

W: The gardening club? Certainly. How can I help?

O: When does it start?

W: It starts in April and we have another club that starts in May.

O: It starts in April?

W: Yes, that's right. And another club starts in May. It's lovely to work in the garden in spring … and in the summer, of course. … Yes, it's lovely to be outside.

O: OK, thanks for your help.

Conversation 2

A: Hi, my friend and I are interested in your skiing course.

B: Great.

A: Do you have big or small groups?

B: Small. There are eight people in each group.

A: What day is the beginners' class?

B: There's a class every morning.

A: What time does it start?

B: Well, the beginners' class starts at 10 a.m. There's an advanced class in the evening.

A: Oh no, the beginners' course is fine, thank you.

Conversation 3

A: Hi, I'd like to buy tickets for Khaled's concert on Saturday.

B: One moment, please. The concert's on Saturday 22nd October?

A: That's right.

B: Oh, sorry. It's sold out on Saturday.

A: What about Friday 21st October?

B: I can check. Yes, I have a couple of tickets for Friday.

A: What time does the concert start?

B: Let's see. At eight o'clock.

A: That's fine. Can I have two tickets, please?

Conversation 4

P = Philip Clifton, T = Teresa Gonzalez

P: Is that the Spanish dance school?

T: Si, Olá. Teresa Gonzalez, speaking. How can I help?

P: Hi, my name's Philip Clifton. I'm calling about your dance class.

T: Wonderful. How can I help? … OK, everyone please continue dancing. One, two, three … one, two, three…

P: Is there a class on Monday evening? I want a class after work.

T: No, sorry. All the dance classes are at the weekend. And one, two, three and turn.

P: So, what time does the class start?

T: One, two, three … one two, three … now turn again.

P: Sorry?

T: Not you, my students. The class is on Saturday evening at seven o'clock.

P: And is there an evening class on Sunday?

T: No, on Sunday the class is in the afternoon at two o'clock. Oh, be careful Señor Drake! …

P: Thank you for your help.

T: Bye, I hope we see you at the class.

4C, Page 26, Exercise 1

Conversation 1

A: Right. That's it. Now, I'm sure you want to see our new company magazine.

B: No. There is no time for that.

A: Oh, OK. Fine then. Before we finish, are there any questions?

B: No.

A: Great. Now, let's agree a date for our next meeting. Is 9:30 next Thursday convenient?

B: No.

Conversation 2

C: OK. That's it. Now, I'm sure you want to see our new company magazine.

D: Great. Could we look at it during the break?

C: Of course! Now, before we finish, are there any questions?

D: Well, I think we have all the information we need. Thank you.

C: Great. Now, let's agree a date for our next meeting. Is 9:30 next Thursday convenient?

D: I'm afraid Thursday is a bit difficult. But we are free on Wednesday morning.

4C, Page 26, Exercise 2

1

C: I'm sure you want to see our new company magazine.

D: Great. Could we look at it during the break?

2

C: Now, before we finish, are there any questions?

D: Well, I think we have all the information we need. Thank you.

3

C: Is 9:30 next Thursday convenient?

D: I'm afraid Thursday is a bit difficult. But we are free on Wednesday morning.

4D, Page 27, Exercise 4

F = Fernando, A = Aisha

F: Hi, Aisha. It's Fernando. Would you like to meet to see the new designs for your office?

A: Hello, Fernando. That's great. When are you free?

F: Can we meet on Tuesday at 2 p.m.?

A: Sorry, I always have a team meeting on Tuesday afternoon. What about Wednesday?

F: I'm afraid I'm busy. I usually have my meeting with the design department on Wednesday. Are you free on Friday?

A: Yes, Friday is fine. Morning or afternoon?

F: What about 10:30 at the Carlton hotel?

A: Great. See you on Friday at 10:30.

4D, Page 27, Exercise 6

F = Fernando, A = Aisha

A: Hi, Fernando. Sorry I'm late. The traffic was terrible.

F: No problem, Aisha.

A: I'm not usually late for meetings.

F: I know. It's OK. It's always busy on Friday mornings, and it's also a public holiday today and there are lots of visitors in town. Now, would you like a coffee?

A: Oh, yes, please. Oh, are these your designs? They're wonderful.

F: Great, I'm really glad you like them.

5A, Page 30, Exercises 1, 2 and 4

Miles

I work in an office and my manager is younger than me. It isn't a problem for me but I think it is for him. I'm 63 but I don't want to stop work. I want to retire when I'm 70. I like my job and I think I'm a better employee now. Experience is more important than age. I enjoy my life. I'm happier now than at 21 and I'm probably a nicer colleague, too.

Chris

I'm younger than the other managers in this company. I'm 21. Sometimes it's a problem because all of my employees are older than me. Miles is in my sales team and he's over 60. He's a great guy. But it's easier for younger people to learn new things. And it's more difficult to manage older people. Miles does things his way and not my way. Sometimes I think it's worse to be a young manager than to have a young manager!

5B, Page 32, Exercises 3 and 4

A

I know I put it in my pocket but it isn't here now. Oh no, this is the worst time to lose something like this. Jessie is wonderful. She's the loveliest girl in the world. And she's the nicest girl in the world. Well, she is usually. Oh dear. This isn't the best way to start married life.

B

I'm 64 and I have my own business but I don't go into the office every day. I have a list of things I want to do before I'm 70. The first thing on the list is 'learn to fly'. I have lessons every week. It's the greatest feeling in the world. Life's an adventure now.

C

I go to university and I'm in a club that does dangerous sports. The youngest person is 18 and the oldest person is 73. This is the most exciting time of my life. Wheee!

5C, Page 34, Exercises 2 and 3

1

A: Hello, I'd like to donate these to your charity.

B: That's very kind of you. What's in the box?

A: There are some children's clothes and adult clothes. They're nearly new.

B: Thank you very much.

2

A: Would you like me to give you marketing advice for your new company?

B: That's really useful. Thank you.

3

A: Hi, I heard that you want someone to help in your garden. I'm a gardener and I work for a local charity for elderly people. I could help you every week.

B: Thanks for the offer, but I'm fine, dear. I like doing the gardening.

4

A: Do you need volunteers to visit people in hospital? I have time on a Monday or Tuesday afternoon.

B: That's really helpful, thanks.

5

A: Can I help your organization deliver food? I have two hours free every Thursday.

B: Thursdays are perfect. Thanks.

6B, Page 38, Exercises 5 and 6

Conversation 1

A: Excuse me. Can you tell me the way to the conference centre, please?

B: Sure, no problem. Go past the library and turn right. The conference centre is opposite the Sun Hotel.

A: Thanks for your help.

B: You're welcome.

Conversation 2

A: Excuse me, is there a bank near here?

B: Yeah, turn left and go straight on. Turn right and there is a bank on the corner of the street.

A: Thank you.

B: No problem.

Conversation 3

A: Where's the Garden Hotel, please?

B: Give me your map for a moment. OK, take the first right and go to the end of the road. Turn left and the Garden Hotel is next to Zen's Restaurant.

A: Great. Thanks for your help.

Conversation 4

A: Excuse me, how do you get to the hospital from the station? Do I turn left?

B: No, don't turn left, turn right. Then go past the supermarket and take the first left. The hospital is opposite the park.

A: Thanks.

B: You're welcome.

6C, Page 40, Exercises 2 and 4

Speaker 1

A: Can you help me? How do I register for the conference?

B: Sure, no problem. Go to reception and the conference registration is next to the café.

A: And can I get a conference badge there?

B: Yeah, they give you the badge after you register.

A: Cheers. Thanks for your help.

B: You're welcome.

Speaker 2

A: Where are the toilets, please?

B: Sorry?

A: Can you tell me where the toilets are, please.

B: Yes, certainly. Right. Erm, let me think. There's an internet café next to the canteen and I think there are toilets opposite the internet café.

A: Many thanks!

B: My pleasure.

Speaker 3

A: Tell me where the meeting point is.

B: Pardon me?

A: Where's the meeting point? I want to meet my friends.

B: I don't know.

A: Give me your conference programme. I want a map.

B: No!

A: Hey, you, give me your programme!

Speaker 4

A: Excuse me, can you tell me who the speaker is at the next seminar?

B: Oh yes. It's Malcolm Gladwell. He's really good.

A: Wow, I have all his books. Where's his seminar?

B: He's speaking in the main hall after the lunch break.

A: Great, thanks.

B: Glad to help.

7A, Page 42, Exercises 1 and 2

M = Market researcher, **W** = Woman

M: Excuse me, I work for Café Starbean. I have a survey, can I ask you some questions?

W: Erm, what's the survey about?

M: It's about what our customers drink.

W: I don't have much time. It's my lunch break. How many questions are there?

M: There're six. It's a very quick survey.

W: Oh, OK. What do you want to ask?

M: Great. Well, the first question is do you prefer hot or cold drinks?

W: Er, I usually prefer hot drinks.

M: And how much tea do you drink every day?

W: Hm, about six cups.

M: And question three is: What type of tea do you usually choose? Black or green?

W: Oh, I like green tea. It's a healthy drink so it's good for me.

M: And how many cups of coffee do you drink?

W: Hm, maybe two a day. I usually get one from the drinks machine at work in the mornings and I sometimes have a cup of decaffeinated coffee in the afternoon.

M: OK, this is question number five. What other hot drinks do you buy? Not tea or coffee.

W: Erm, other hot drinks? Oh, I like hot chocolate. It's a good drink on a cold day.

M: And the final question is about cold drinks. What cold drinks do you buy?

W: Well, I buy milk and water. Oh, and orange juice.

M: That's great. Thank you for your help. Here is a voucher for a cup of tea or coffee next time you come to Café Starbean.

W: Oh, thanks. Bye.

7B, Page 44, Exercise 1

I don't usually tell people that I work as a mystery shopper. I go into shops and talk to the shop assistants and ask about products. The shop assistants don't know that I'm a mystery shopper. They think I'm a customer. Then I go home and write a report about customer service in the shop and send it to my company and they give the information to the shop manager. My report answers questions like 'are the assistants helpful and polite?', 'Can they give me information about the products?' That sort of thing. I like the job because I'm always doing something new and it's interesting. So, next time you are in a shop look at the customer next to you. It could be me. Shhh! It's our secret.

7B, Page 44, Exercises 3 and 4

M = Mystery shopper, **S1** = Shop assistant 1, **S2** = Shop assistant 2

M: OK. I'm in a shop called Fabio Furniture to look at desks and report on customer service. Look, I can see some shop assistants. I'll see if they can help me. Hi, I'd like some information about one of your desks, please.

S1: Here! Look at this text.

S2: That's funny.

M: Excuse me, I'd like some information about one of your desks, please.

S1: What? Oh, right. How can I help?

M: Well, the desk is still in the box. What size is it?

S1: Erm, It's desk size.

S2: [laughs]

M: I want to know is it a big desk or a small desk. I have a small office.

S1: Oh, right. Erm, It's small. I think.

M: And what shape is it?

S1: It's square.

S2: No, it's not, it's rectangular.

S1: Oh, yeah.

M: What's it made of?

S1: Erm, plastic, I think.

M: Does it come in any other colours?

S1: It comes in brown and black.

M: How much is it?

S1: It's £145. Look, do you want it?

M: OK, I'll think about it. Thanks for your, erm, help.

S1: You're welcome. Ha!, Look here's another text.

S2: Ooh, let me see.

7B, Page 44, Exercise 6

M = Mystery shopper, **S1** = Shop assistant 1, **S2** = Shop assistant 2

M: Hi, I want to buy some furniture for my new home office.

S1: How can I help?

M: Do you have any desks for a small office? Wood, maybe?

S1: Certainly. What about this one? I have the same at home.

M: Yes, it's nice. Does it come in any other colours?

S1: It comes in brown and white.

M: I like white. That's the colour of my office.

S1: James, do we have any desks in white at the moment?

S2: I'm afraid not.

S1: I'm sorry, we don't have any in white. But I can order one for you.

M: OK, I'll think about it. Thanks for your help.

S1: You're welcome, Madam.

7C, Page 46, Exercises 3 and 4

S = Shop assistant, **C** = Customer

1

S: Hi, do you want any help?

C: This is a nice jacket but I don't like the colour. I hate brown.

S: How about green?

C: Hm, I'm not sure about green.

S: We have it in blue.

C: Oh, OK, I like blue. That's fine. Can I try it on?

2

S: Can I help, sir?

C: I like this shirt but it's too big.

S: You could try a smaller size.

C: Hm. That's a good idea.

S: Oh, sorry, we don't have it in stock.

C: Ah. That's OK. Thanks for your help.

3

B = Buyer, **S** = Supplier

B: Hello, I'm the buyer for Kings Designs. I like your black shoes.

S: Yes, they are really popular. We supply these shoes to shops in New York and Paris.

B: Really? Do they come in any other colours?

S: We have red in stock.

B: Hm. I'm not sure about red. How about green or brown?

S: I'm afraid we don't have them in brown but we have green.

B: Yes, that's great.

7D, Page 47, Exercise 3

A: Hi, I have some questions about your products.

B: Certainly, how can I help?

A: I want to buy some olives from Spain.

B: Sorry, we don't have any Spanish olives in stock at the moment. How about some from Turkey. They're great. Here you are.

A: Mm, They're good. Are the olives in tins or jars?

B: They're in glass jars.

A: Hmm, I'm not sure. I prefer tins. They're easier to transport.

B: Oh, I see.

A: What size are the jars?

B: We sell small and large sizes. Here is a list of our prices.

A: OK, I'll think about it, thanks.

8A, Page 49, Exercises 7 and 8

Conversation 1
S = Steve, **G** = Goran

S: Goran! What's the matter?

G: I've got a headache. It always happens when the air conditioning is on.

S: I know what you mean. The air conditioning gives me headaches, too.

G: A lot of people say that. But nobody switches it off.

S: Mm. Interesting, isn't it?

Conversation 2
J = Joan, **P** = Pete

J: So, how are you today, Pete?

P: Not very well, I'm afraid. I have a pain in my shoulder. It really hurts. I can't move my arm. I think I should stay at home tomorrow.

J: I'm sorry to hear that. You work on one of the new cutting machines, is that right?

P: Yes, I do. Why?

J: Well, you can't work on those machines all day. You should take a ten-minute break every two hours or so. Everybody does that.

P: And what do I do during the breaks?

J: Do what you like, but just don't move your shoulders!

Conversation 3
C = Connie, **J** = Jeff

C: Hello, Jeff! Why are you crying?

J: I'm not crying. My eyes hurt. And I can't see very well.

C: It's because you look at your computer monitor all day long.

J: I know. Well, that's my job. What can I do?

Conversation 4
J = Julia, **R** = Richard

J: Hello Richard. Have you got a problem? You look terrible today!

R: Oh, thank you very much. Very kind of you. I've got backache. I can't sleep at night, and I can't carry anything.

J: Poor you, that's terrible! Is there something I can do?

R: Thanks for asking. Well, you see that box over there?

J: You mean the big brown box behind the desk?

R: Yeah, that's right. If you could just take it to Room 507 for me. Ow, with my bad back, I can't carry 30 kilos up to the fifth floor.

J: Um.

Conversation 5
K = Ken, **R** = Rosa

K: Hi Rosa! Are you alright?

R: Not too bad, not too bad. But I have a pain in my wrists.

K: Um. Too much tennis?

R: No, unfortunately. Too much typing on the computer.

K: Why don't you have a personal assistant?

R: I am a personal assistant!

Conversation 6
K = Kate, **L** = Lucy

K: A pain in the neck!

L: Who?

K: Me. I mean, my neck hurts. I feel ill.

L: Sorry to hear that, Kate. What does the doctor say?

K: He says I need a new desk. Or a new desk chair. Or both.

L: Mm. The office manager will be very pleased to hear that.

8B, Page 51, Exercises 7 and 8

H = Human resources manager, **R** = Rajit, **B** = Bob

H: ... Right. So now you know about salaries and travel expenses. Any other questions? I'm here to help and inform, so just ask anything you like.

R: Well, I've got some more questions about safety. Do I have to buy safety clothes myself?

H: No, you don't. You don't have to buy any safety clothes. You get everything from the company – hard hat, boots – everything.

B: How much luggage can we take, by the way?

H: Just one middle-sized bag. Remember, you travel by helicopter with the whole team, so you can't take a large bag.

R: Can we smoke on board?

H: Yes. You can bring your cigarettes, but leave your matches and lighters at home. There is a special room for smokers. You can't smoke outside. And you can only use the special safety matches that are in the smoking room.

R: I see. Now, what about phoning? Should I leave my mobile phone at home, too?

H: No. You can take your cellphone of course, but everybody says you shouldn't use it offshore. Calls are very, very expensive. You should use a payphone. A lot of rigs have a payphone onboard, and on some of them you can also make calls via the internet.

B: Should we take our own computer?

H: You can, but I'm not sure it's a good idea. Some rigs have computers for their staff. Just ask before you leave.

R: How much money do we have to take with us?

H: Where do you think you can spend it? There's just a small shop where you can buy sweets and soft drinks and things like soap and toothpaste. And you can pay by credit card anyway. ... OK, Gentlemen. Any other questions?

B: Well ... erm ... not really.

R: No, I think that's all.

H: You mean you don't have any questions about the work itself?

8C, Page 52, Exercises 4 and 5

F = Frieda, **S1** = Service technician 1,
S2 = Service technician 2

Conversation 1

F: Excuse me. I have a problem with my new burglar alarm. What do I have to do when I leave the house? Could you show me how to set it?

S1: Yeah, no problem. First, make sure all windows and doors are closed. Then, this green light here has to be on.

F: Right.

S1: Then, you have to enter your user code.

F: OK. That's easy. But what happens if I make a mistake? Do I just put my hands over my ears and run away?

S1: No. You just have to press 'clear' and enter your user code again.

F: I see. Is that all?

S1: So you enter the correct code. After that, the red light flashes and the keypad beeps.

F: Oh, dear!

S1: You then have 20 seconds to leave the house and lock the door. And that's it! You want to try?

F: Oh, yes, please. I think it's better if I try when you are here with me.

Conversation 2

F: Excuse me. I have a problem with my new burglar alarm. What do I have to do when I leave my house? Could you show me how to set it?

S2: Sure. It's very easy. Enter your user code and then quickly get out of the house. Of course, a lot of people make a mistake when they enter the code. You should really remember your code. If you make a mistake, enter your code again. Any questions?

F: Erm ... Well ... is that all?

S2: Yeah, that's all. Well, you know, before you enter your code, the green light has to be on. Then after you enter your code, the red light flashes. And the keypad beeps.

F: I see. Right. Thanks very much.

S2: You're welcome. Oh, I forgot. Make sure you close all doors and windows. That's the first thing you have to do.

F: Right. Thanks.

8D, Page 53, Exercises 5 and 6

This is Radio 5. Today in our edition of 'Making business travel easy', we look at Cairo.

Visitors to Egypt don't usually have to have a visa. But if you need one, you can usually get it at the airport when you arrive. You can take a bus or a taxi, but you should know that many people prefer to hire a limousine from one of the companies in the arrivals hall. The journey to the centre of the city can take between 20 minutes to two hours – it depends on the time of day.

To travel around Cairo, you can use the metro. The metro system is very good. If you want to hire a car, you have to have an international driving licence, of course. And you also need a lot of patience because there is a lot of traffic. Cairo is a very busy city. Remember that you have to tip restaurant and hotel staff, and all other services, so you should always have a lot of small banknotes on you.

For business meetings, you should wear smart clothes. It doesn't rain very often in Cairo, so you don't have to take a raincoat or an umbrella. And remember that in summer, the temperature is often above 35 degrees, so you don't have to take any warm clothes.

If you have some free time during your visit, there is a rich cultural life for you to enjoy. But you should also take a sunset trip on the Nile. It's a very good way to relax. And this brings us to the end of today's programme.

Next week in 'Making business travel easy', we take our listeners to Tokyo ...

9B, Page 59, Exercises 4, 5, 6 and 7

Conversation 1
M = Martin, **R** = Renata

M: So, Renata, this is your favourite room?

R: That's right, yes. This is where I can relax in the evening before going to bed. I watch TV or listen to music when no one is at home.

M: I can see you've got lots of CDs.

R: Yeah. Over one thousand.

M: Wow! ... And you've got an interesting sofa ... I really like it!

R: Do you? Well, you can have it if you want. It's very old. I need to buy a new one.

Conversation 2
J = John, **N** = Nedim

J: This is a nice room, Nedim. And it's got a terrace!

N: Yes, it's my favourite room in the house. It's the only room in which I spend six hours or more every day. My job is very stressful, but in this room I've got all the peace and quiet I need at the end of the day.

J: You've got a lot of pictures. They're all very beautiful.

N: Thank you.

J: Tell me, why aren't there any curtains?

N: I don't need curtains. I don't like them. The first thing I do when I get up in the morning is to look out of the window. I love the view from this room.

Conversation 3

B = Becky, **J** = Jack

B: Hi Jack! Your mum says you're always down here!

J: Well, we've got two cars. Someone needs to look after them. Dad doesn't know anything about engines, but I love them!

B: So, you don't spend much time in the living room, then?

J: That's right. It's much better down here. I've got all the things I need.

B: Erm ... Do you need some help?

J: No, I'm alright. Thanks.

Conversation 4

F = Freya, **M** = Meiying

F: Tell me, Meiying, what do you like most about this room?

M: You know, this room is the heart of the house. We're all together in the morning and in the evening. This is where we cook, eat and talk. I love it. We need to be together sometimes!

F: The fridge is really big!

M: We need a very big fridge because we are a big family.

F: Mm, I understand. But ... erm ... you haven't got a dishwasher.

M: Well, I've got my husband!

9C, Page 60, Exercises 2, 3 and 4

Conversation 1

B = Ben, **L** = Liz

B: Hi Liz! How are you?

L: Fine, thanks. And you?

B: I'm alright. You know what? My wife wants to go to Paris this weekend.

L: Wow! A weekend in Paris! That's wonderful. You're a lucky man.

B: The bad news is, I can't go.

L: What? Why not?

B: I have to be at a trade show in Frankfurt from Friday afternoon till Monday morning.

L: That's a shame. Can't you go next weekend?

B: I'm afraid not. It's my mother's birthday next weekend.

Conversation 2

A = Alexey, **B** = Becky

A: You look happy!

B: Yes. I work in the new building now. My office is very big and it's got a beautiful view.

A: That's nice. Can you see the river and the old town?

B: Yes, I can. And another thing: there are only two other people in this large office.

A: That's great. Are they nice?

B: Yeah, very nice. I think you know one of them. Nikola. Nikola Kos.

A: Nikola? ... Yes, of course! ... He's an old friend from Slovenia.

Conversation 3

S = Sally, **J** = John

S: I've got a lot of books about Turkey, as you can see.

J: Mm. That's interesting. Do you want to go on holiday there?

S: I often go there on holiday. But now I can go on an exchange visit. I'm so happy!

J: Erm ... Sorry, I don't understand. What's an 'exchange visit'?

S: Well, I can go and teach at the University of Antalya, and a lecturer from Antalya comes here to work at our university.

J: Ah! I see. ...

S: And I know Antalya. I've got some friends there.

J: That's cool. Do they know about your plans?

Conversation 4

C = Colin, **E** = Elvira

C: Elvira! What's the matter?

E: It's my boss. He's always so rude to me!

C: That's terrible! What do you want to do?

E: I don't know. Maybe I should look for another job.

C: Yes. Maybe you should.

E: Why is everything so difficult sometimes?

Conversation 5

L = Linda, **R** = Roger

L: I don't like our new cafeteria.

R: Really? That's too bad. What's the problem with it?

L: They haven't got any salads or health foods. Just sandwiches, and they all have meat in them.

R: Um. That's a problem if you're a vegetarian.

L: It sure is. But the good news is, starting next month we have 45 minutes for lunch, not just 30.

R: That's great!

L: Yeah. So I think that's enough time to go to that Italian salad bar down the road.

9D, Page 61, Exercise 4

S = Simon Campbell, **M** = Mina Nasir

S: So, where exactly is this building?

M: Let's have a look at the map. You see ... Long Park is 20 kilometres away from the centre of Redhill. There's a fast train to the city centre every 15 minutes and lots of buses all day ...

S: Mm. That's very good.

M: Yes. And the building in Long Park is very modern. We can have 25 rooms there. Ten on the second floor and 15 on the fourth floor.

S: What about parking places?

M: There's a very large parking lot next to the building. Eighty places, maybe one hundred.

S: Are there a lot of houses and flats for our new staff?

M: There aren't many flats in that area, but there are lots of big houses, a lot of them with their own swimming pool.

S: Well, that's not really what our teachers want ...

M: No, but it could be interesting for our international students in summer. They usually want to stay with a family.

9D, Page 61, Exercise 7

It was difficult to choose, because all three sites have got good things to offer. In Long Park public transport is very good, and there are lots of parking places. In Barbridge, the building is beautiful, and it's very near the city centre. But we think that Peakside is best. Of course, it's a bit far from the centre, and there are only 24 rooms in the building now. But we can have more rooms next year if we need them. And the metro can take you anywhere in just a few minutes. If you drive, parking is not a problem, and if teachers want to move near the school, it's easy to find a house or a flat.

10A, Page 63, Exercise 8

1

A: Excuse me. I need to talk to the manager. Where is he?

B: I don't know, but he was here at ten o'clock.

2

Last year, we were at the Imperial. Our room was OK, but the food wasn't very good.

3

Don't stay at the Astoria! The reviews say it is cheap, but the people are very rude.

4

I phoned you yesterday, but you weren't at work. Where were you?

5

A: You are in room 115. Here is your key.

B: Thank you.

10B, Page 65, Exercises 10 and 11

Call 1

C = Customer, **CS** = Customer Service rep

C: Hello. It's about my order for orange juice.

CS: Yeah?

C: I wanted it on Monday. That was the day before yesterday. Where is it?

CS: All orders are delayed. Sorry about that. I'm afraid there's nothing we can do.

C: Well, that's not good enough. I want to talk to the manager.

Call 2

C = Customer, **CS** = Customer Service rep

C: Good morning. Is that customer service?

CS: Yes. What can I do for you?

C: It's about the jeans I ordered. I got two pairs but I only ordered one pair.

CS: Can I have your order number, please?

C: Yes. It's JO413. And there's something else. They are the wrong colour.

CS: Oh, I'm terribly sorry about that. We can send you the right jeans this afternoon.

Call 3

C = Customer, **CS** = Customer Service rep

C: Hello. Anne Jones here. Could I speak to Sarah Dennis, please?

CS: Speaking.

C: Good afternoon. I'm calling about my digital camera. It's the wrong model.

CS: You ordered a Weiss X1 Deluxe, is that right?

C: Yeah, that's right. But I got the X1 Powershot.

CS: I'm very sorry about that. Please return it. We can send you the Deluxe early next week.

C: Thanks for your help.

Call 4

C = Customer, **CS** = Customer Service rep

C: Elektrocentre. Good morning. How can I help you?

CS: Hello. I've got a problem with my new radio. It doesn't work.

CS: I'm sorry to hear that. Our specialist can look at it for you. Is ten o'clock tomorrow morning a good time?

C: Yes, it is. Thank you.

CS: Thank you for your call. Goodbye.

C: Goodbye.

Call 5

T = Tariq Mirza, **J** = Julie Leval

T: Hello. This is Tariq Mirza. Can I speak to Julie Leval, please?

J: Speaking. How can I help you, Mr Mirza?

T: I've got a problem with our new air conditioning unit. The instructions are not in the box.

J: I'm sorry to hear that. Was anything else missing?

T: No, just the instructions.

J: Could you give me the model number, please?

J: Sure. It's the AC82.

CS: Thank you. I can send you the instructions right away.

J: Thanks for your help.

10C, Page 66, Exercises 2 and 4

A = Anna Baranowska, **C** = Customer Service rep

Conversation 1

A: Hello. Anna Baranowska here. I'm ...

C: Yes?

A: I have a problem with my new DVD player.

C: Yes?

A: Yes. It doesn't work.

C: Are you sure? What's your order number?

A: I can't believe this is happening again ...

Conversation 2

C: CBA Customer Service. Good morning.

A: Hello. Anna Baranowska here. It's about my new DVD player. I have a problem with it.

C: Oh, I'm very sorry to hear that. We can give you your money back, or we can send a specialist to look at the DVD player.

A: OK. Please send a specialist. Thanks for your help.

C: You're welcome. Once again, sorry about this problem, and thank you for calling. Goodbye.

A: Goodbye.

10C, Page 66, Exercise 5

1

a Hi. Are you from Hong Kong?

b Thank you for phoning.

c Hello. How can I help you, Mr Luk?

2

a It's about my new desk. There's a part missing.

b No, you can't. Sorry.

c We all need help.

3

a Speaking.

b Yes, you can.

c Why not?

4

a That's a big problem.

b Oh, I'm very sorry to hear that.

c And I have a problem with my DVD player.

5

a Yes, I can.

b That information was useful.

c Yes. One side is broken and the top is missing.

6

a Sure. That was G-T-S-one-hundred.

b Again, please.

c No. I think it's very good.

7

a It was a great help.

b My pleasure.

c And thank you for complaining.

10D, Page 67, Exercise 3

CM = Centre manager, **C** = Customer

Conversation 1

CM: Good afternoon. What can I do for you?

C1: Well, there are some problems.

CM: Sorry to hear that. What sort of problems?

C1: I come here after work with two colleagues. Very often we wait for 10 or 15 minutes. You see, there aren't enough exercise machines for everybody. We pay for one hour, but we can only exercise for 30 or 40 minutes.

Conversation 2

C2: Excuse me, are you the manager?

CM: That's right, yes. How can I help you?

C2: I want to complain about the showers. Can't you get somebody to clean them? I need a bath after I have a shower here!

Conversation 3

CM: James! Hi! How are things?

C3: Not so good, I'm afraid.

CM: Oh dear! What's wrong?

C3: You know, the problem is the size of the group. In the advertisement, you say maximum ten people per group. But very often there are 12 or even 15 people here. That's no good. You know the room is not big enough for so many people.

CM: Right. Thanks for telling me this. I need to talk to the general manager about this. I think we need to deal with this problem.

Conversation 4

C4: Excuse me. I'd like a word with you. Is this a good time?

CM: Sure. Take a seat. How can I help you?

C4: Well, it's about Mr Reno, our trainer. He knows his job, of course, but the problem is, he's often late for our classes. Last Thursday, for example, he was 15 minutes late.

CM: Oh, I'm sorry to hear that. That's no good.

C4: No, it's bad. Very bad. Your advertisement says 'personal instructor', but I don't get enough attention when I exercise. He hasn't got enough time for everyone.

Conversation 5

CM: Oh, no! What now? If this is another complaint, I go home. Yes! Come in! Sit down! What can I do for you?

C5: Hello. I just need some information about …

CM: Information? Great! I can give you a lot of information!

C5: My problem is, I'm too busy to come here three times a week. I can only come once, sometimes twice a week. Membership is £80 per month, that's for three classes every week. Why is there only one kind of membership? At other fitness clubs, you can pay each time you take a class. I think that's a very good system for busy people.

CM: Mm. Interesting idea. I need to talk to our general manager about this. Oh, by the way. Do you know where those other fitness clubs are?

11A, Page 69, Exercise 8

After school I studied Economics. Ten years ago I started work in a bank in Tokyo. It was great, I learned Japanese and made lots of friends. The turning point was when I started a rock group with some colleagues at the bank. We played concerts at the weekend. I realized that I wanted a career in music. So I moved back to England and trained as a music teacher. It was a good decision. I love my job and I'm very happy with my life.

* * * *

I decided to go to college in Australia. The turning point in my life happened when I worked in a restaurant to help pay for my studies. I realized that I enjoyed my work more than I enjoyed college. So when I finished my studies, I opened my own restaurant in Sydney. It was very successful. Last month I opened another restaurant in Melbourne. This isn't what I expected to do for a job but I'm my own boss and I love it!

11B, Page 70, Exercises 3 and 5

Speaker 1

Did you lose anything today? Don't worry, you're not alone. We all lose things. These are some of the things that I lost last month: keys, my phone, a bag, my wallet, an important document and my passport. I found them all again. The document was in my office and the rest were at home. I read a report that said that people spent an hour a day looking for things. Imagine what you could do with an extra seven hours a week!

Speaker 2

I went to a party last week and I met a scientist. He was really interesting. He told me that some animals have a very good memory. He said scientists in Japan did a test with people and chimpanzees. And they found that some chimpanzees have a better memory than people! I didn't believe him at first, I thought it was some sort of scientist joke. But he gave me the name of the scientist and I checked the information. I got a surprise when I discovered it was true.

11C, Page 72, Exercises 2, 3 and 4

Interview 1

I = Interviewer, **R** = Robert

I: Good morning, Robert. Sit down, please. Did you have a good journey here?

R: Yes.

I: Good. Do you want a drink? Tea or coffee perhaps?

R: No.

I: Oh, OK. Well, let's start. You sent in a very interesting CV. You studied business at college. Did you study for a degree?

R: No.

I: Oh, um … Oh, I see you studied for an MBA, is that correct?

R: Yes.

I: That's good. Do you know what Langford Industries does?

R: No.

I: OK, I'll tell you a bit about the company. We train staff who work in Finance companies. Did you train staff in your last job?

R: No.

I: Ah, I see. And did you work in finance?

R: No.

I: OK. Um, some companies want us to train their staff to use computers. Can you use a computer?

R: Yes.

I: Good. Good. Are you interested in training people to use computers?

R: No, not really.

I: Right. Well thank you for coming to the interview, Robert.

R: OK. Bye.

Interview 2

I = Interviewer, **D** = Duncan

I: Good morning, Duncan. Sit down, please. Did you have a good journey here?

D: Yes, thank you. Your instructions were very easy to follow.

I: Oh, good. Do you want a drink? Tea or coffee perhaps?

D: No, thank you. I had a coffee on my way here.

I: Great, let's begin then. You included some interesting information about your qualifications in your CV. So, let's start with some questions about your education and training. I see from your CV that you studied computing at college. Did you study for a degree?

D: Yes, I did.

I: What did you do after that?

D: I worked in Saudi Arabia for a year and after that I studied for an MBA.

I: Excellent. Do you know what Langford Industries does?

D: Yes, I looked at your website.

I: Excellent. What do you know about our company?

D: Well, I know that you train staff who work in Finance companies and your teams train people all over the world.

I: Good. Did you train staff in your last job?

D: Yes, I did.

I: What training did you do?

D: Um, I worked on a course helping new employees to use new technology. It was a great success and my manager was very pleased with the results.

I: Good. What department did you work in?

D: In Human Resources.

I: Ah. What other qualifications do you have?

D: Er, well, I studied for a diploma in Finance Management. I worked during the day and studied in the evening.

I: Um. That's interesting. Why did you study Finance Management?

D: Well, I'm very interested in the subject. And I wanted to learn about financial planning. I knew that I wanted to work for a company where my interest in training people and finance could work together.

I: Excellent. Finally, tell me why do you want to work for Langford Industries?

D: Certainly. I want to work for you because you're the best in the world at financial training and I'd love to be part of your team.

12A, Page 74, Exercise 3

S = Sarita, **A** = Alan

S: Hi, Alan! Where are you?

A: Hi, Sarita. I'm at the airport. I'm waiting for my flight. I think there's a delay.

S: Sorry to hear that. What about the report?

A: Well, I'm working on it right now. But I need some more information from Shin for the graphs. What is she doing? Could you phone her?

S: Yes, of course. But I think she's sleeping. It's 2:30 a.m. in Seoul!

12A, Page 75, Exercises 6 and 7

A = Alan, **D** = Debra

A: Hi, darling. How's it going?

D: Fine. I'm not working today. You?

A: Still waiting for my flight. I'm just having a walk around the lounge. There are a lot of people here. We're expecting a long delay because of the volcano and the ash cloud.

D: What's everyone doing, then? Sleeping?

A: Well, no. Only one man is sleeping … Then some kids are playing computer games, and some are eating hamburgers non-stop …

D: … What fun! …

A: … Yeah. I think they're having a good time. Then there's a guy who's reading the papers and phoning all the time … He's very loud … The woman next to him is texting … I think she's angry … She's standing up … She's looking for another seat … Oh no!

D: What's happening?

A: I can't believe it … She's taking my seat!

12C, Page 78, Exercises 2 and 3

Conversation 1

A: This suitcase is too heavy. I need one of those little cars ... erm ... what do you call them?

B: Do you mean a baggage trolley? Hold on, I'll get you one.

A: Oh, thanks!

Conversation 2

A: How was your flight?

B: The flight was OK, thanks. But then I had to wait a long time for my luggage.

A: Why was that?

B: Well, there were a lot of delays. So there were dozens of people around ... erm ... you know, the thing that goes round and round with all the luggage.

A: Oh, I know. You mean the carousel.

B: Yeah. So there were dozens of people around the carousel, pushing and shouting, and then this big guy came along ...

Conversation 3

A: What a terrible airport!

B: Yeah. Just like ours back home.

A: No information anywhere. Where's that thing where you can read all the times and flight numbers and destinations?

B: Do you mean the departures board? Well, there's one over there. Let's go and have a look.

A: Oh no! It's not working!

Conversation 4

A: Excuse me.

B: Yes?

A: I'm afraid I can't find my ... erm ... you know, that piece of paper I need to get on the plane. What do you call it?

B: You mean your boarding pass.

A: That's right, yes. I can't find my boarding pass. What should I do?

B: Well, I'm afraid you have to go back to the check-in desk.

12D, Page 79, Exercise 5

I = Interviewer, **L** = Layla

I: Good morning, Ms Ajram, and thank you for being with us in our Travel Weekly programme. So, you are the Chief Executive Officer of Heritage Travel, an extremely successful travel company that is now attracting customers from all over the world. When did the company start?

L: Heritage Travel began in 2004. We had some difficult years, but things are better now.

I: And where is your main office?

L: Our headquarters are in Cyprus. And we have offices all over the Middle East: in Cairo, Damascus, Amman, and in Beirut of course.

I: How many people do you employ?

L: At the moment we have 47 staff, but we are getting bigger.

I: What products and services does Heritage Travel provide?

L: Well, we provide all the traditional family and cultural tours and holidays, as well as cruises. But this year we're also introducing à la carte holidays for students and teachers of History and Architecture.

I: Mm. That's very interesting. And what are the trends in sales and in the number of customers?

L: It's all looking really good. Both are increasing. Slowly maybe, but definitely increasing.

13A, Page 82, Exercise 2

M = Market researcher, **A** = Alec

M: Excuse me, I'm from Voxcom, it's a market research company. Do you have time to answer a few questions about money?

A: Erm, will it take long?

M: No, there are only five questions. I'll be really quick.

A: OK, then.

M: Great. Thanks. Right, the first question is: how do you usually pay for things at the moment? a) cash, b) credit card or c) cheque?

A: I usually pay cash.

M: OK, And how do you think we'll pay for things in ten years' time? Will we a) use cash and credit cards, b) use internet banking, or c) we won't use money?

A: Hmm. c). I don't think we'll use money in ten years' time. There'll be some new technology by then and we won't use cash.

M: Hm. Interesting. OK, question 3. What do you think you'll spend most money on next year? a) holidays and travel, b) house and car or c) food and clothes?

A: I want to move to a bigger house, so it'll be b).

M: And question 4. Do you think the cost of living will a) go up, or b) go down or c) stay the same?

A: By cost of living, you mean what I spend on food shopping, electricity bills and petrol, that sort of thing?

M: Yes, that's it. Just the normal things you spend money on every week.

A: I think it'll stay the same so c).

M: Right. Question 5. This is about salary. Do you think most people's salary will a) increase, b) decrease, or c) stay the same?

A: In what, the next year?

M: The next two years.

A: Well, salaries won't go down. Hmm. Stay the same? No, a). I think they'll go up.

M: That's a very positive answer. I hope you're right. Thanks very much for answering the questions.

A: No problem.

13A, Page 83, Exercise 7

1
I think I'll buy a house in the next five years.

2
I'll buy my clothes online with a credit card.

3
I listen to the financial news on the radio.

4
We'll spend all our money on restaurants.

Audio scripts

13B, Page 85, Exercises 6 and 7

If you open an internet bank account with KDW bank today, we'll give you a free MP4 player. And if you save £2,000 a month, you'll get three per cent interest. Not only that, we'll arrange foreign currency if you go on holiday. Go online or go into one of our banks and open an account with KDW today!

13C, Page 86, Exercises 2 and 3

D = Don, **M** = Marina, **J** = Joanna

D: Thanks for coming today. I want to talk about an idea that I have about the store. I think in the future people will use e-readers, so why don't we sell them?

M: That's a nice idea but I don't think people will buy an electronic reader from a bookshop. They'll buy it online or they'll go to the same place they buy their laptops or cameras. You know, electronic stuff.

D: I disagree. If we sell electronic readers, people will buy them. People who come into our stores like to read.

M: A lot of our customers are older. They won't want to read books on a machine. And electronic readers are expensive.

D: That's true. But they'll be cheaper in a year or two. And it's not true that older people won't use them. Anyway, we want older and younger customers to buy from us.

J: Yeah, I agree. And if we sell e-readers, we can sell e-books online on our website.

D: That's a good idea. We could change the name of the shop as well, something like 'Future Books'.

M: Wait a minute. Our customers want to look at books and talk to us. They ask us for tips about what to read.

J: Yeah, I agree. And they'll continue to do that. We won't stop selling books, we'll sell e-readers, e-books and our usual books. It's a great idea. And if we sell online, we'll have customers all around the world.

M: Hmm. But at the moment customers don't use the website.

D: Well, yes. But if we design a better website, customers will want to use it. We need to think about what customers will want in the future. Internet shopping is popular now, and in a few years people will buy everything online from food and clothes to furniture. They won't want shops like this one.

J: You're right. We'll spend some money on our website to make it more exciting.

M: Hmm. I'm not sure. E-readers and a new website. This is all very expensive.

J: No, it'll be fine. All bookshops will be like this in the future. We need a shop, a good website and new technology.

D: Great, I'll order some e-readers and Marina, you talk to the web designer. Joanna, you talk to the bank manager and see if he will give us more money to spend on the shop.

M: Listen, I don't think that's a good idea. We don't want to borrow more money from the bank.

D: Good, I'm glad we're all agreed. Thanks for coming to the meeting.

13D, Page 87, Exercises 2 and 3

Speaker 1
Hello, we are TG Electronics. TG Electronics is a small company based in Japan and we have 40 employees. We make robots for industry. We believe that in the future more companies will use robots to do jobs such as cleaning, and they will be used in the home, too. If profits go up, our investors will get 20 per cent interest for a $50,000 investment. Investments less than $50,000 will get 12 per cent interest. If profits go down, investors will get 0 per cent interest. We hope you will invest in our company.

Speaker 2
Hi, we're Blanes Travel and we are based in Sydney, Australia. We have 150 people who work for the company. We are a small airline and we fly to Europe, Asia and Africa. Our small planes are perfect for people who like luxury and spend a lot of money on business travel and holidays. If profits go up, our investors will get 15 per cent interest for an investment of $50,000. Investment less than $50,000 will get 10 per cent. If profits go down, all our investors will get four per cent interest. We'd really like you to invest in our company!

14A, Page 89, Exercises 6 and 7

I = Interviewer, **O** = Otylia

I: So, Ms Janosz, what are you going to do in South Africa?

O: Well, as you know, I'm interested in how some animals work in teams. I believe people can learn a lot from animals – not only people, but organizations, too. So I'm going to work as a volunteer on the Kalahari Meerkat Project.

I: Does that mean meerkats make good teams?

O: Exactly. I think they are the best team players in the animal world! I'm going to take a lot of photos, shoot a film, and study how they communicate.

I: That's very interesting. Are meerkats friendly animals?

O: Yes, they are very friendly. But I'm not going to bring one back to Europe!

I: Why not?

O: They are friendly, but they are not pets. They are only happy when they are together in a large group in their natural environment.

14B, Page 91, Exercises 6 and 7

Conversation 1
C = Customer, **W** = Waiter, **FC** = Football commentator

C: Hi. Can I have an orange juice, please.

W: Sure, here you are. That's €2. Thanks.

C: Who are playing?

W: Spain and Scotland.

C: Oh. Who's winning?

W: Spain.

C: Ah. What's the score?

W: 3–2 to Spain at the moment.

C: Uhuh. So, who do you think is going to win?

W: Spain. Scotland's going to lose.

FC: And it's a draw! Spain 3–Scotland 3. …

W: Oh, no! So are you here on holiday?

8

C: No, on business. I'm going home tomorrow. By the way, do you have a phone in here? My mobile isn't working and I need to phone the office.

W: Sure. Go out the door and turn right and there's a public phone opposite reception.

C: Great, thanks.

Conversation 2

A: Hello. Are you here on holiday?

B: Yes, the sports facilities are very good here.

A: Do you like sport?

B: Oh, yes.

A: What sports do you play?

B: I enjoy playing tennis. Do you play?

A: Yes, I do. Perhaps we can have a game?

B: That's a good idea. Actually, I want to arrange a game tomorrow morning. Would you like to play?

A: Yeah, that's fine for me. I'm going to the reception now and I can book it.

14C, Page 92, Exercises 3, 4 and 5

Conversation 1

A: There's a problem with my computer.

B: Oh, I'm sorry to hear that.

A: I need to finish this report for the finance meeting. What am I going to do?

B: It's going to be OK. You can use my computer.

A: Can I? Thanks very much.

Conversation 2

A: I lost the address of our new customer. I can't find it anywhere.

B: Oh, really?

A: Yeah. Now you can't contact her. Sorry.

B: Don't worry. We can look together.

A: Oh, thank you.

Conversation 3

A: I didn't get the job in the Marketing department.

B: Oh, really?

A: Yeah, and I really wanted that job.

B: I know.

14C, Page 92, Exercise 6

Conversation 3

A: I didn't get the job in the Marketing department.

B: Oh, really? I'm sorry to hear that.

A: Yeah, and I really wanted that job.

B: I know. It's going to be OK.

A: Yeah, I know.

15A, Page 94, Exercises 3 and 4

L = Lucinda, **M** = Miles Stewart

L: This is Lucinda Miles reporting from the city zoo. Ronan, a three-year-old Indian tiger has escaped and several people have phoned to say that they have seen the tiger. I'm talking to Miles Stewart, the director at the zoo.

Mr Stewart, have you had a problem like this in the past?

M: No, I've been the director at this zoo for 20 years and this is the first time that an animal has escaped. We haven't had a problem like this before.

L: Has anyone seen the tiger?

M: Yes, three people have seen him in the park. Our team has looked everywhere but we haven't found the tiger.

L: Why haven't you caught him?

M: We have done everything possible to find Ronan. Our teams are looking all around the city.

L: Has he hurt anyone?

M: No, he hasn't. But he hasn't eaten for 24 hours, so he is dangerous.

L: What advice do you have for people in the city?

M: Don't panic. Stay inside. If you see the tiger, call the zoo or the police immediately.

L: Mr Stewart, thank you for speaking to us. Keep listening for more news on the tiger later in the programme.

15B, Page 97, Exercise 7

1 Yes, I have. I met a footballer last year.

2 Yeah, I was on *Who wants to be a Billionaire*?

3 No, I haven't. I've only flown in planes.

4 Yes, I have. I saw elephants in Africa.

5 Yes. I visited the Arctic two years ago on a cruise.

6 I went skiing a few years ago.

7 Yeah, I won a prize at work. I was salesperson of the year.

8 Yes, I had a job cleaning an elephant in a circus.

9 Yes, I lost my passport on holiday last year.

10 Yes, I tried Durian fruit in Malaysia three years ago.

15B, Page 97, Exercise 8

Conversation 1

M = Market researcher, **W1** = Woman 1

A: Hi. I'm from a website called Life Experiences and I'm interviewing people for my website. Can I ask you a few questions?

W1: Um, OK, sure.

M: Have you ever met someone famous?

W1: Yes, I have. I met a footballer last year. Um, you know. Thingy. He's always in the newspapers. He's got long hair. Oh, I can't remember his name but he was really friendly.

M: Have you ever been on TV?

W1: Yeah, I was on *Who wants to be a Billionaire*?

M: Did you win?

W1: No, I didn't. I lost £30,000. It was terrible.

Conversation 2

M = Market researcher, **M1** = Man 1

M: Have you flown in something that isn't a plane?

M1: No, I haven't. I've only flown in planes. Oh, wait! Yes, I have. I flew in a glider about ten years ago.

M: Did you enjoy it?

M1: Yes, it was wonderful. I flew over a forest. It was amazing.

M: Have you ever seen a wild animal?

M1: What, in a zoo?

M: No, not in the zoo.

M1: Yes, I have. I saw elephants in Africa.

M: Was it exciting?

M1: No, it was frightening. They ran after our coach.

Conversation 3

M = Market researcher, **W2** = Woman 2

M: Hi, have you ever visited a cold country?

W2: Yes. I visited the Arctic two years ago on a cruise.

M: Did you enjoy it?

W2: Yes, it was fantastic. We saw the Northern lights.

M: And have you ever been skiing?

W2: I went skiing a few years ago and I broke my leg. It was awful.

Conversation 4

M = Market researcher, **M2** = Man 2

M: Hi, have you ever won a prize?

M2: Yeah, I won a prize at work. I was salesperson of the year. The prize was a holiday in the Caribbean. It was amazing.

M: Have you ever had an unusual job?

M2: Yes, I had a job cleaning an elephant in a circus when I was a student. It was horrible. Animals are happier in the wild.

Conversation 5

M = Market researcher, **W3** = Woman 3

M: Have you ever lost anything on holiday?

W3: Yes, I lost my passport on holiday last year. It was great – I stayed at my hotel for three extra days until I got a new one. My family went home so it was lovely and quiet.

M: Have you ever tried an unusual fruit or vegetable?

W3: Yes, I tried a Durian fruit in Malaysia three years ago. It smells terrible but it tastes wonderful.

15C, Page 98, Exercises 2 and 3

A = Antoni, **S** = Sue

A: Hi Sue, It's Antoni. I have a problem.

S: What's happened?

A: Yeah, I'm fine but I've had an accident in my car.

S: Speak a little slower, please, Antoni. Now what's happened?

A: I've had an accident in my car.

S: Oh no! Are you OK?

A: Yeah, I'm fine but my car isn't.

S: Can I help?

A: Yes, I haven't called XXXX to say that I can't do the XXXXX.

S: Sorry, what did you say?

A: I haven't called David to say that I can't do the XXXXX.

S: Did you say *presentation*?

A: Yes, I can't do the presentation. Can you call David and tell him?

S: Sure. Can I have his phone number?

A: Yes, it's 40249 XXXXX.

S: Sorry, Antoni. It's a bad line. Can you repeat that?

A: Sure, it's 40249 56617.

S: OK. Can I read that back? It's 40249 56617.

A: That's right.

S: Are you sure you're OK?

A: I'm fine. Ah, good. The police have arrived. Speak to you later.

S: OK. See you later. Take care.

15C, Page 98, Exercise 6

1 Hello? Hello?

2 I haven't had a delivery since last Monday.

3 This is important. I want you to change the colour of the design to black.

4 The account number is 232JG5.

5 This is important. I can't meet XXXX at XXXX. … Can you phone her?

16B, Page 103, Exercise 11

[Soundtracks of film genres]

16B, Page 103, Exercise 12

[Soundtrack of thriller film]

16C, Page 104, Exercises 4 and 5

J = Jason, **M** = Martina

J: I want to talk to you, Martina.

M: Sure. What do you want to talk about?

J: I want to take two months off work.

M: This is a surprise. Two months? Why?

J: I want to travel.

M: Jason, I want you to work on the new international team because you speak Russian.

J: But I want to travel.

M: Sorry, it's not possible.

9

16C, Page 104, Exercises 6 and 7

J = Jason, M = Martina

J: Hi, Martina. I'd like to talk to you about something.

M: Sure. What do you want to talk about?

J: I'd like to take some time off work – without pay, of course.

M: This is a surprise. How long do you want to take off?

J: I'm thinking of two months.

M: Two months? Why?

J: Well, I'd like to travel.

M: Jason, I want you to work on the new international team because you speak Russian.

J: That's great. I'd like to travel to Moscow in order to improve my Russian.

M: But for two months?

J: Yes. I want to go to the best language school in the city so that I can learn business Russian for my work.

M: Hmm. I'm not sure.

J: It's important to be able to speak Russian in negotiations and meetings, that's why this plan is perfect. I can learn business Russian at school and speak Russian all day. It's great for the international team.

M: OK, I'll think about it.

16D, Page 105, Exercises 2 and 3

Speaker 1

A: Is it true that you're leaving work?

B: Yeah, I'm travelling with my sister to South America for six months.

A: Wow! That's amazing. Why are you going to South America?

B: Because we're meeting our friends in Brazil and then we're flying to Peru.

A: Brilliant!

Speaker 2

A: Jack is retiring next month. I suppose he's spending more time in his garden.

B: No, he isn't. He's learning to fly. He's buying his own plane.

A: That's exciting! Does he like flying?

B: I don't know. He's never been in a plane. He's having his first lesson next week.

Speaker 3

A: Lola says that you're taking time off work.

B: Yes, I'm doing a course at university.

A: What are you studying?

B: I'm learning about films.

A: Really! What sort of films do you like?

B: I'm interested in horror films.

A: Hmm! That's unusual.

Speaker 4

S = Shona, G = Greta

S: Hello Greta, how are you?

G: Fine thanks. Are you enjoying your time away from work?

S: Yes, it's wonderful. I'm spending lots of time in my garden. It looks beautiful.

G: That's nice and relaxing. Much better than being in an office.

S: Yes, but I'm coming back to work next week.

Speaker 5

M = Megan, C = Charles

M: Hi, Charles, what are you doing in May? We're having a big party. Everyone from work is coming.

C: In May? I'm flying to Italy. I'm doing research in Rome.

M: What research are you doing?

C: I'm writing a detective novel.

M: Oh, that sounds interesting!

Grammar reference

Present tenses

Present simple: *be* (+)

Use

We use contractions in conversation and in informal written English.

Form

Contraction	Full form
I**'m** Chinese.	I **am** Chinese.
You**'re** a designer.	You **are** a designer.
He**'s** Paul.	He **is** Paul.
She**'s** Sandra.	She **is** Sandra.
It**'s** a trade fair.	It **is** a trade fair.
We**'re** photographers.	We **are** photographers.
You**'re** journalists.	You **are** journalists.
They**'re** hairdressers.	They **are** hairdressers.

Present simple: *be* (–)

Use

We often use *'re not* and *'s not* instead of *aren't* and *isn't*:

> They**'re not** Swiss.(= They aren't Swiss.)
> It**'s not** Italian.   (= It isn't Italian.)

Form

Contraction	Full form	
I**'m** not	I **am not**	
You **aren't**	You **are not**	Japanese.
He **isn't**	He **is not**	Egyptian.
She **isn't**	She **is not**	Brazilian.
It **isn't**	It **is not**	Russian.
We **aren't**	We **are not**	
You **aren't**	You **are not**	
They **aren't**	They **are not**	

Present simple: *be* (?)

Use

We use full forms for short answers with *yes*:

Is Tom an events manager? – Yes, he **is**. ~~Yes, he's.~~

We use contractions for short answers with *no*:

Are Federico and Enrica designers? – No, they **aren't**.

Form

(?)			Short answer (+)		Short answer (–)
Am I **Are** you **Is** he/she/it **Are** we **Are** you **Are** they	German? Mexican? Syrian? Vietnamese?	Yes,	I **am**. you **are**. he/she/it **is**. we **are**. you **are**. they **are**.	No,	I'**m not**. you **aren't**. he/she/it **isn't**. we **aren't**. you **aren't**. they **aren't**.

> **!** In questions, put *be* before *you, he, she*, etc:
> **Are you** French? ~~You are French?~~
> Where **is she** from? ~~Where she is from?~~

Present simple

Use

We use the present simple to talk about regular activities, long-term situations and things that are always true.

I **watch** TV every evening.

Leila and Selim **live** in Tunis.

Winter **begins** on 21 December.

Form

(+)	
Use the base form of the verb. Add -s to third person forms.	I/You/We/They **work**. He/She/It **works**.
(–) Use *don't (do not)*. Use *doesn't (does not)* with third person forms.	You **don't work**. He **doesn't work**.
(?) Use *do* or *does*.	**Do** I/you/we/they **work**? **Does** he/she/it **work**? Where **do** you **work**?
Short answers Use *do* or *does*.	Do you play tennis? Yes, I **do**. Does she travel a lot? No, she **doesn't**.

> **!** Word order in questions:
>
> | | **Auxiliary** | **Subject** | **Infinitive** |
> |---|---|---|---|
> | | *Do* | *you* | *travel a lot?* |
> | | *Does* | *he* | *like his job?* |
> | **Question word** | **Auxiliary** | **Subject** | **Infinitive** |
> | *Where* | *do* | *you* | *work?* |
> | *How often* | *does* | *she* | *travel?* |

Spelling rules for the *he / she / it* forms

1	General rule	+ -s	speak → speaks play → plays
2	do go have		does /dʌz/ goes has
3	Verbs ending in *ch, sh, s, x, z*	+ -es	watch → watches push → pushes kiss → kisses box → boxes
4	Verbs ending in consonant + *y*	→ ies	fly → flies try → tries

Pronunciation

1 Verbs ending in /f/, /k/, /p/, /t/, we pronounce the -s ending as /s/.	laughs, books, stops, puts, etc.
2 Verbs ending in /tʃ/, /ʃ/, /s/, /ks/, we pronounce the -es ending as /ɪz/. Make sure you pronounce the extra syllable as /ɪz/!	catches, washes, misses, fixes, etc.
3 Verbs ending in other sounds: /l/, /n/, /v/, /m/, /eɪ/, we pronounce the -s ending as /z/.	calls, learns, loves, comes, plays, etc.

Frequency adverbs

Use

We use adverbs of frequency to say *how often* we do something.

always usually often sometimes hardly ever never

100%--●-------●-------●--------●----------●-------------●--0%

1 We usually put the frequency adverb **before** the main verb.

*They **often** spend their summer holiday in Greece.*

*We don't **usually** work on Saturday.*

2 We usually put the frequency adverb **after** the verb *be*.

*Jim is **never** late for meetings.*

*Buses aren't **always** on time.*

Imperatives

Use

We use the imperative to give orders or instructions. It is also useful when you want to communicate information urgently.

***Don't open** the window! (urgent information)*

***Finish** the report today. (order)*

***Go** to reception and get a name badge. (instruction)*

We often use imperatives when writing instructions.

***Take** the second left and go straight on. **Go** past the station and **turn** right.*

Form

(+) The sentence starts with the base form of the verb without *to*.	***Close** the door, please.*
(–) We use *don't* + the base form of the verb without *to*.	***Don't start** the machine.*

> ⚠ When a verb follows the infinitive it uses the base form + *to*:
> ***Ask** Jill **to** call me today.*
> NOT *Ask Jill call me today.*

have got

Use

In British English, we often use *have got* instead of *have* when we talk about possession, relationships, illness, etc. This is particularly the case in conversation and informal writing:

> I**'ve got** a new laptop.
>
> They **haven't got** a reservation.
>
> **Have** you **got** any brothers or sisters?
>
> Tina**'s got** a headache.

Form

(+) Contraction	Full form	
I**'ve got**	I **have got**	
You**'ve got**	You **have got**	
He's/She's/It**'s got**	He/She/It **has got**	*a large kitchen.*
We**'ve got**	We **have got**	
You**'ve got**	You **have got**	
They**'ve got**	They **have got**	

(–) Contraction	Full form	
I **haven't got**	I **have not got**	
You **haven't got**	You **have not got**	
He/She/It **hasn't got**	He/She/It **has not got**	*a large kitchen.*
We **haven't got**	We **have not got**	
You **haven't got**	You **have not got**	
They **haven't got**	They **have not got**	

(?)		Short answer (+)		Short answer (–)	
Have I **got**			I **have**.		I **haven't**.
Have you **got**			you **have**.		you **haven't**.
Has he/she/it **got**	*a large kitchen?*	**Yes,**	he/she/it **has**.	**No,**	he/she/it **hasn't**.
Have we **got**			we **have**.		we **haven't**.
Have you **got**			you **have**.		you **haven't**.
Have they **got**			they **have**.		they **haven't**.

> ⚠ I**'ve got** an iPad. = I **have** an iPad.
>
> He **hasn't got** a job. = He **doesn't have** a job.
>
> **Have** you **got** a dictionary? = **Do** you **have** a dictionary?
>
> The forms without *got* are more common in American English and in 'global English'.

Present continuous

Use

We use the present continuous to talk about actions happening now or around now.

> I'**m waiting** for my flight.
>
> We'**re working** here in Denver for a week.

We also use it to talk about present trends.

> The number of passengers **is rising**.

Form

(+)		
Contraction	**Full form**	
I'm You're He/She/It's We're You're They're	I **am** You **are** He/She/It **is** We **are** You **are** They **are**	waiting for a train. playing. having lunch.

(–)		
Contraction	**Full form**	
I'm **not** You **aren't** He/She/It **isn't** We **aren't** You **aren't** They **aren't**	I **am not** You **are not** He/She/It **is not** We **are not** You **are not** They **are not**	waiting for a train. playing. having lunch.

(?)		Short answer (+)		Short answer (–)	
Am I **Are** you **Is** he/she/it **Are** we **Are** you **Are** they	waiting for a train? playing? having lunch?	Yes,	I **am**. you **are**. he/she/it **is**. we **are**. you **are**. they **are**.	No,	I'm **not**. you **aren't**. he/she/it **isn't**. we **aren't**. you **aren't**. they **aren't**.

Present continuous or present simple?

Use

We use the present continuous to talk about something that is happening now or around now.

We use the present simple to talk about something that is always true or to talk about habits and routines.

Present continuous	Present simple
Please be quiet. I'**m working**.	I **work** from 9 to 5 every day.
We **aren't watching** TV this evening.	We **don't** often **watch** TV.
What **are** you **writing** now?	How often **do** you **write** reports?

> ⚠ There are some verbs that we do not usually use in their continuous form: *believe, depend, forget, hate, know, like, love, mean, need, prefer, remember, understand, want.*
>
> I **need** to go to the office now.   ~~I'm needing to go to the office now.~~
>
> **Do** you **want** it now?   ~~Are you wanting it now?~~

3

Present perfect

Use

We use the present perfect to talk about the past and the present together.

1 Present results – we use the present perfect for past actions with results that are important in the present.

> *The oil companies **have increased** the price of petrol. (it's more expensive now)*
>
> *We **have chosen** a new CEO. (we made the choice in the recent past and the result is now)*
>
> *They **haven't finished** the new designs. (they didn't finish the designs and we don't have them now)*

2 Experience – we use the present perfect to talk about finished actions that happened in the past.

> *I**'ve worked** in sales and marketing. (in one of my past jobs)*
>
> *She**'s been** to Bali. (at some time in the past)*

We often use *ever* in questions when the exact time isn't important.

> ***Have** you **ever been** to Cairo? (at any time in your life?)*
>
> ***Has** he **ever given** a presentation? (at a past time in his work life?)*

3 We often use time expressions like *never, recently, already, before* with the present perfect.

> *I**'ve never visited** Nepal.*
>
> *They**'ve recently started** a new computer project.*
>
> *He**'s already finished** the report.*
>
> *We **haven't eaten** sushi **before**.*

4 Sometimes we follow a present perfect question with a past simple question to find out when the event occurred.

> ***Have** you **been** to Australia? Yes, **I have**.*
>
> ***When did** you **go** there?*
>
> *I **went** to Sydney last year.*

Form

(+)	
I/You/We/They + *have* + past participle. *He/She/It* + *has* + past participle. We often use contractions (*I've/you've/he's*, etc.) Irregular verbs sometimes have a special past participle form. For a list of irregular verbs, see page 160.	*I **have done** the accounts.* *She **has done** the accounts.* *You**'ve met** the new Sales director. / You **have met** the new Sales director.* *She**'s met** the new Sales director. / She **has met** the new Sales director.*
(–)	
I/You/We/They + *haven't* (*have not*) + past participle. *He/She/It* + *hasn't* (*has not*) + past participle.	*We **haven't seen** Alice this week. / We **have not seen** Alice this week.* *The company **hasn't opened** a new factory. / The company **has not opened** a new factory.*
(?)	
Change the word order.	***Have** you **listened** to the news report?* ***Has** he **talked** to the manager?*
Short answers	
I/You/We/They + *have/haven't* *He/She/It* + *has/hasn't*	*Have you ever played rugby?* *Yes, I **have**. / No, I **haven't**.* *Has she been on holiday?* *Yes, she **has**. / No, she **hasn't**.*

> We don't use contractions with affirmative short forms.
> *Have you been to Turkey?*
> *Yes, **I have**.* NOT ~~*Yes, I've.*~~   *Has he sent the letter?*   *Yes, **he has**.* NOT ~~*Yes, he's.*~~

Past tenses

Past simple

Use

We use the past simple to talk about finished actions and situations in the past. One common use is to tell stories.

*Yesterday I **waited** 35 minutes for a bus.*

*Then I **went** to work on foot.*

*I **was** one hour late.*

Past simple: *be*

(+)			(–)		
I	was		I	wasn't	
You	were		You	weren't	
He/She/It	was	at the office.	He/She/It	wasn't	at the office.
We	were		We	weren't	
You	were		You	weren't	
They	were		They	weren't	

(?)				Short answer (+)		Short answer (–)	
Was	I			I was.		I wasn't.	
Were	you			you were.		you weren't.	
Was	he/she/it	at the office?	Yes,	he/she/it was.	No,	he/she/it wasn't.	
Were	we			we were.		we weren't.	
Were	you			you were.		you weren't.	
Were	they			they were.		they weren't.	

Past simple: regular and irregular verbs

(+) Add *-ed* to the base form of the verb. There is no special third person form. Irregular verbs have a special past form. See page 160 for a list of irregular verbs.	I/You/We/They **worked**. He/She/It **worked**. The train **left** at ten. We **drove** to the station.
(–) Use *didn't* (*did not*) + the base form of the verb.	I/You/We/They **didn't work**. The train **didn't leave** on time.
(?) Use *did* + the base form of the verb.	**Did** I/you/we/they **work**? **Did** he/she/it **drive** to the office? When **did** you **leave**?
Short answers Use *did*/*didn't*.	Did you play tennis? **Yes**, I **did**. Did she travel a lot? **No**, she **didn't**.

Spelling rules for regular verbs

1 General rule	add -ed	work → worked play → played watch → watched
2 Verbs ending in *e*	add -d	live → lived dance → danced like → liked
3 Verbs ending in one vowel + one consonant	double consonant + -ed*	stop → stopped prefer → preferred rob → robbed
4 Verbs ending in a consonant + *y*	change *y* to *ied*	try → tried study → studied carry → carried

* Do not double the consonant if the syllable is not stressed: *happen → happened*

Pronunciation of regular verbs

1 Verbs ending in /f/, /k/, /p/, /tʃ/, /ʃ/, /s/: we pronounce the -ed ending as /t/.	*laughed, booked, stopped, watched, washed, missed, etc.*
2 Verbs ending in /d/ or /t/: we pronounce the -ed ending as /ɪd/. Make sure you pronounce the extra syllable as /ɪd/!	*decided, invited, wanted, needed, shouted, etc.*
3 Verbs ending in other sounds: we pronounce the -ed ending as /d/.	*called, learned, loved, changed, played, earned, discovered, etc.*

Future forms and modal verbs

There are many different ways to talk about the future in English. We can use it to make predictions, talk about plans and to make arrangements.

going to

Use

1 We use *going to* to talk about intentions and future plans:

*We**'re going to** meet Carlos in Madrid at the weekend.*

*The company **is going to** increase salaries next year.*

2 We don't usually use *going to* with the verb *go*.

I'm going to Singapore is better than *I'm going to go to Singapore.*

Form

(+) Use *be going to* + the base form of the verb (without *to*).	*You**'re going to work** in a new team next month.* *The CEO **is going to give** a presentation this afternoon.*
(–) Use the negative form of the verb *be* + *going to* + the base form of the verb.	*We**'re not going to move** office next week.* *Kate **isn't going to fly** to Brazil on Monday.*
(?) Change the word order of the verb *be*.	***Are** you **going to finish** the project today?* ***Is** Dominic **going to write** the report tomorrow?*
Short answers Use the verb *be*.	***Are** they **going to travel** by car?* ***Yes**, they **are**. / **No**, they**'re not/aren't**.* ***Is** she **coming** to the meeting?* ***Yes**, she **is**. / **No**, she**'s not/isn't**.*

Present continuous

Use

We can use the present continuous to talk about future plans and arrangements.

*I**'m flying** to Rio tomorrow. (I have the tickets)*

*She**'s meeting** the CEO on Friday at 11a.m. (it's in her diary)*

*What **are you doing** at the weekend? (what are your plans?)*

Form

For information on the form of the present continuous, see page 146.

5

The modal verb *will*

Use

1 We use *will* to make predictions.

*In the future, we **will work** longer hours.*

2 We also use *will* in sentences with *if* (see notes on the first conditional, page 153.)

*If the product is in stock, I'**ll phone** you.*

3 We often use contractions in conversation and informal written English.

*He'**ll be** president of this company in ten years.*

Form

(+) Use *will* (or '*ll*) + the base form of the verb. There is no special *he/she/it* form.	*I'**ll pass** my exams next year.* *Our products **will be** more expensive next week.*
(−) Use *won't* (*will* + *not*).	*They **won't move** office next year.* *She **won't leave** her job.*
(?) Change the word order.	***Will** you **buy** a new car next year?* *When **will** you **finish** your project?*

Grammar reference

Modal verbs: *can / can't* and *should / shouldn't*

Use

1 We use *can* to talk about things that are possible.
You **can** *finish work in an hour.*

We use *can't* to talk about things that are not possible.
I **can't** *come to your presentation.*

We also use *can* and *can't* to talk about ability.
He **can** *speak Spanish.*

She **can't** *play the piano.*

2 We use *should* to give advice or to say that something is a good idea.
You look ill, you **should** *go to the doctor.*

There is a concert tonight, we **should** *buy tickets.*

We use *shouldn't* to give advice not to do something or to say that something isn't a good idea.
They **shouldn't** *drive to the station, the traffic is terrible.*

He **shouldn't** *sit at the computer all day.*

Form

(+) Use *can* or *should* + the base form of the verb (without *to*). The third person form does not change. It is the same as all other forms.	*You* **should speak** *to the manager.* *She* **can park** *at the station.* *He* **can start** *the machine.* *The company* **can send** *you a price list.*
(–) Add *not*. We often use contractions when we speak or write informally.	*Employees* **cannot use** *the café in the evening.* *You* **should not swim** *after lunch.* *He* **can't work** *at the weekend.* *We* **shouldn't be late** *for the meeting.*
(?) Change the word order.	**Can** *we* **smoke** *in the restaurant?* **Should** *she* **wear** *safety clothes?*

> ⚠ Do not use *to* after full modal verbs, e.g *can* and *should*.
> *We* **can meet** *on Friday.*
> NOT ~~We can to meet~~ *on Friday.*

Modal verbs: *have to / don't have to*

Use

We use *have to* to talk about things that are necessary.
You **have to** *report to reception when you arrive.*

We use **don't have to** talk about things that are not necessary.
You **don't have to** *report to reception when you arrive.*

Form

(+) Use *have to* + the base form of the verb (without *to*). *Have to* changes in the third person form.	*I* **have to work** *late tonight.* *He* **has to work** *late tonight.* *She* **has to wear** *a name badge.* *The company* **has to give** *you safety equipment.*
(–) Use *don't* (*do not*). Use *doesn't* (*does not*) in the third person form.	*They* **don't have to finish** *the designs today.* *They* **do not have to finish** *the designs today.* *You* **don't have to wear** *special clothes to work.* *You* **do not have to wear** *special clothes to work.* *He* **doesn't have to go** *on a training course.* *He* **does not have to go** *on a training course.*
(?) Change word order.	**Do** *I* **have to go** *to the hospital?* **Does** *she* **have to take** *a test after the course?*

6

Conditional sentences

First conditional

Use

1 We use the first conditional to talk about positive or negative possibility. The *if* clause contains the situation and the *will* clause contains the result.

> **If** you **work** late, you**'ll miss** your train.
>
> They**'ll miss** their train **if** they **work** late.
>
> **If** you **don't study**, you **won't pass** your test.
>
> She **won't pass** her test **if** she **doesn't study**.

2 We don't usually use *will* in the *if* clause.

> **If** you **give** me your email address, **I'll send** you a price list.
>
> **NOT** ~~If you will give me your email address, I'll send you a price list.~~

Form

Use *if* + present simple, will/won't.	**If** we **change** bank accounts, we**'ll get** more interest. **If** he **buys** a computer, he **won't pay** by credit card.

Punctuation

The *if* clause can be the first or second part of the sentence. When a sentence begins with *if*, we put a comma (,) between the two clauses.

> **If** Carla **saves** her money, she**'ll buy** a new car.
>
> **If** we **go** to the USA, we**'ll** take $1,000 dollars.

We don't use a comma when the sentences begin with the *will* clause.

> Jared **will call** you later **if** you **leave** your telephone number.
>
> The sales team **will be** angry **if** we **are late** for the meeting.

Nouns and adjectives

there is / there are

Use

1 We can use *there is / there are* to describe what we see and to talk about things that are present or not present.

2 We can use *there is / there are* with:

Singular nouns:
> **There is** a café in the park.

Plural nouns:
> **There are** two banks in the centre of town.

Uncountable nouns:
> **There is** information about prices in the catalogue.

3 We often use contractions when we speak or write informally.
> **There's** a café in the park. / **There're** two banks in the centre of town.

Form

Affirmative sentences	**There's / There is** a hotel in town. **There're / There are** three spas.
Negative sentences	**There isn't / There is not** a hotel in town. **There aren't / There are not** three spas.
Questions	**Is there** a hotel in town? **Are there** three spas?
Short answers	Yes, **there is**. / No, **there isn't**. Yes, **there are**. / No, **there aren't**.

Countable and uncountable nouns

Use

A noun is a word or group of words that we use to name people, places and objects.
A countable noun can be singular: *He has a* **car**, or plural: *He has two* **cars**.
An uncountable noun cannot be plural: *Do you* **sell bread**? (not *Do you sell breads*).
Sometimes we can use *a/an* or a number with an uncountable noun. This happens when we talk about what it is in or describe part of it:

> She has **two cups** of tea.

> He wants **six bottles** of water.

> Do they want **a slice** of bread / meat / cake?

> You can have **a piece** of fruit / cheese.

How many

We use *How many* in questions with countable nouns when we want to know the amount. The noun is usually plural.

> **How many** drinks do you have every day?

> **How many** restaurants are in your city?

How much

We use *How much* in questions with uncountable nouns.

> **How much** money is in the bank?

> **How much** fruit is in the kitchen?

7

Form

Countable nouns ...	Uncountable nouns ...
can be singular or plural. *a bottle* → *five bottles* *an orange* → *two oranges*	cannot be plural. *milk* → ~~*milks*~~ *rice* → ~~*rices*~~
use singular or plural verb forms. **An apple is** *a healthy snack.* **Apples are** *healthy snacks.* **An orange isn't** *a vegetable.* **Oranges aren't** *vegetables.*	use singular verb forms. **Tea is** *a hot drink.* **Coffee isn't** *a cold drink.*

It is a good idea to use a dictionary to check whether a noun is countable or uncountable. Here are some common uncountable nouns:

accommodation	*luggage*
advice	*money*
bread	*news*
equipment	*pasta*
information	*work*

some and *any*

Use

We can use *some* in questions when we are offering or asking for things.

> **Do you want some** *information about our company?*
>
> **Can I have some** *water, please?*

Form

some ...	
is used in positive sentences. can be used with countable or uncountable nouns.	I **have some** *sandwiches for lunch.* There**'s some** *coffee in the kitchen.*
any ...	
is used in questions and negative sentences. can be used with countable or uncountable nouns.	**Are** *there* **any** *sandwiches for lunch?* / *There* **aren't any** *sandwiches for lunch.* **Is** *there* **any** *coffee in the kitchen?* / *There* **isn't any** *coffee in the kitchen.*

much / many / a lot of / lots of

Use

We use *many / a lot of / lots of* with countable nouns:

> Coimbra has **many** interesting buildings.
>
> There aren't **lots of** students in summer.
>
> Are there **a lot of** people in winter?

We use *much / a lot of / lots of* with uncountable nouns:

> Our country has **a lot of** sunshine.
>
> Our town hasn't got **much** public transport.

Form

(+)

Use *many / a lot of / lots of*:

We meet **a lot of (lots of / many*)** interesting people.

Do NOT use *much*:

~~There is much noise in the streets.~~

There is **a lot of (lots of)** noise in the streets.

*many is more formal than a lot of / lots of.

(–) and (?)

Use **much / many / a lot of / lots of**:

There isn't **much (a lot of / lots of)** noise at night.

There aren't **many (a lot of / lots of)** good hotels in our town.

Have you **got much (a lot of / lots of)** work to do?

Are there **a lot of (lots of / many)** tourists?

Are there any restaurants?	Yes, there **are a lot**.	~~Yes, there are a lot of.~~
It rains **a lot** in winter.	~~It rains a lot of in winter.~~	
Dave speaks **a lot**.	~~Dave speaks a lot of.~~	

8

Comparative and superlative adjectives

Use

1 We can use comparative adjectives to compare two things.

Jacques is **older than** Martina.

Is marketing **more interesting than** accountancy?

2 We use superlative adjectives to compare one thing with a group of things.

The Amazon, the Nile and the Volga are long rivers but the Amazon is **the longest**.

London, Tokyo and Rome are expensive cities but Tokyo is **the most expensive**.

Form

Comparative adjectives	
Short adjectives	
Most short adjectives e.g. rich, fast, small	Add -er: I work short**er** hours in my new job than in my old job.
Adjectives ending in e, e.g. nice, simple, wise	Add -r: Your office is large**r** than my office.
Adjectives ending in y, e.g. friendly, funny, noisy	Change -y to -ier: Is it eas**ier** to learn Russian than English?
Adjectives ending in one vowel + consonant, e.g. thin, hot, fat	Double the consonant + -er: A Mercedes is big**ger** than a Mini.
Long adjectives	
All long adjectives, e.g. exciting, interesting, difficult	Use more: My new office is **more comfortable** than my old office.

Superlative adjectives	
Short adjectives	
Most short adjectives	Add -est: Karl is the young**est** person in the department.
Adjectives ending in e	Add -st: This is the simpl**est** way to print a letter.
Adjectives ending in y	Change y to -iest: This is the friendl**iest** team in the company.
Adjectives ending in one vowel + consonant	Double the consonant + -est: The hot**test** place in the world is El Azizia in Libya.
Long adjectives	
All long adjectives	He has **the most interesting** job in the company.

Irregular adjectives		
adjective	**comparative**	**superlative**
good	better	best
bad	worse	worst
far	further / farther	furthest / farthest

Grammar reference

to + base form or -ing form

Use

1 Some verbs are followed by *to* and some are followed by *-ing*.

Leo **wants to play** tennis.

Leo **enjoys playing** tennis.

2 Some verbs can be followed by *to* or by *-ing*. The meaning usually stays the same.

They **prefer to travel** by train. / They **prefer travelling** by train.

We **like to meet** customers. / We **like meeting** customers.

I **started to learn** the piano last year. / I **started learning** the piano last year.

3 It is a good idea to check in a dictionary to see if a verb takes *to* or *-ing*.

Form

verb + to	
choose decide forget need plan promise try want	We **decided to change** the design. He **forgot to bring** his luggage. They **want to start** the meeting.

verb + -ing	
dislike enjoy finish hate like love stop suggest	Please **finish writing** the essay now. You **hate watching** sport. They **stopped sending** me catalogues.

like, love and hate + -ing

After *like / love / hate*, we use a noun or the *-ing* form of a verb:

I **like**	Thai food.
She **likes**	gangster films.
He **doesn't like**	work**ing** in the evening.
We **don't like**	play**ing** tennis.
I **love**	shop**ping**.
They **hate**	driving at night.

9

Spelling rules for the *-ing* form

1 General rule	add *-ing*	speak → speaking play → playing study → studying
2 Verbs ending in *e*	Change *-e* to *-ing*	drive → driving dance → dancing write → writing
3 Verbs ending in one vowel + one consonant	double consonant + *-ing**	shop → shopping get → getting sit → sitting

* Do not double the consonant if the syllable is not stressed:
happen → happening

Relative pronouns: *who* and *which*

Uses

We can use *who* and *which* to join two sentences or clauses together.

1 We use *who* to talk about people.
> He's the director **who** made Slumdog Millionaire.

2 We use *which* to talk about groups, things or animals.
> It's a fruit **which** is long and yellow.

Form

who	
She's a manager. She is good at her job.	She's a manager **who** is good at her job.
He's a director. He makes action films.	He's a director **who** makes action films.

which	
It's a modern car. It's very fast.	It's a modern car **which** is very fast.

Irregular verb list

Verb	Past simple	Past participle	Verb	Past simple	Past participle
be	was / were	been	know /nəʊ/	knew /njuː/	known /nəʊn/
beat	beat	beaten	learn	learnt / learned	learnt / learned
become	became	become	leave	left	left
begin	began	begun	lose	lost	lost
break	broke	broken	make	made	made
bring	brought /brɔːt/	brought /brɔːt/	mean	meant /ment/	meant /ment/
build	built /bɪlt/	built /bɪlt/	meet	met	met
buy	bought /bɔːt/	bought /bɔːt/	pay	paid	paid
catch	caught /kɔːt/	caught /kɔːt/	put	put	put
choose	chose	chosen	read	read /red/	read /red/
come	came	come	ring	rang	rung
cost	cost	cost	run	ran	run
cut	cut	cut	say	said /sed/	said /sed/
dig	dug	dug	see	saw /sɔː/	seen
do	did	done /dʌn/	sell	sold	sold
draw	drew /druː/	drawn /drɔːn/	send	sent	sent
dream	dreamt / dreamed	dreamt / dreamed	show	showed	shown
drink	drank	drunk	shut	shut	shut
drive	drove	driven /drɪvən/	sing	sang	sung
eat	ate	eaten	sit	sat	sat
fall	fell	fallen	sleep	slept	slept
feel	felt	felt	speak	spoke	spoken
fight	fought /fɔːt/	fought /fɔːt/	spend	spent	spent
find	found	found	stand	stood	stood
fly	flew /fluː/	flown /fləʊn/	swim	swam	swum
forget	forgot	forgotten	take	took	taken
get	got	got	teach	taught /tɔːt/	taught /tɔːt/
give	gave	given	tell	told	told
go	went	gone	think	thought /θɔːt/	thought /θɔːt/
grow	grew /gruː/	grown /grəʊn/	throw	threw /θruː/	thrown /θrəʊn/
have	had	had	understand	understood	understood
hear /hɪər/	heard /hɜːd/	heard /hɜːd/	wake	woke	woken
hide	hid	hidden	wear	wore	worn
hit	hit	hit	win	won	won
hurt	hurt	hurt	write	wrote	written
keep	kept	kept			